The Upset
That Wasn't

The Upset That Wasn't

HARRY S TRUMAN AND
THE CRUCIAL ELECTION OF 1948

Harold I. Gullan

IVAN R. DEE   CHICAGO

1998

THE UPSET THAT WASN'T. Copyright © 1998 by Harold I. Gullan. All rights reserved, including the right to reproduce this book or portions thereof in any form. For information, address: Ivan R. Dee, Publisher, 1332 North Halsted Street, Chicago 60622. Manufactured in the United States of America and printed on acid-free paper.

Library of Congress Cataloging-in-Publication Data:
Gullan, Harold I., 1931–
The upset that wasn't : Harry S. Truman and the crucial election
of 1948 / Harold I. Gullan.
p.   cm.
Includes bibliographical references and index.
ISBN 1-56663-206-4 (alk. paper)
1. Presidents—United States—Election—1948.   2. Truman, Harry
S., 1884–1972.   I. Title.
E815.G85   1998
324.973'0918—dc21   98-26167

Dedicated to the memory of Dr. Philip H. Edwards.

Sorry it took so long.

PREFACE

STANDING on the rear platform of the train he used for his celebrated "whistle-stop" campaign, a triumphant Harry Truman
beams out at us from the St. Louis Union Station. He holds aloft
the *Chicago Tribune* of November 3, 1948, bearing its perpetually premature headline, DEWEY DEFEATS TRUMAN. Having van-
quished not only his overconfident Republican opponent,
Thomas E. Dewey, but also defectors from both wings of his own
Democratic party, Truman is on his way back to an incredulous
Washington. Our collective memory of the 1948 presidential
campaign as well as of Harry Truman himself is captured by that
photograph. To present-day Americans, few of whom can remember Truman in office, their most vivid image of him is as the
courageous, tireless campaigner of 1948. This plain-talking,
straight-shooting everyman from the nation's heartland, who had
proven he could make the most momentous decisions, won the
presidency in his own right in what is still viewed as "the greatest
upset in American political history."

Many observers then and since have concluded that Truman's
triumph was more dramatic than decisive. Writing the day after
the election, Walter Lippmann, the most prominent pundit of his
time, titled his column "The Triumph of Roosevelt's Party."
"The coalition which Franklin Roosevelt formed held together,"
Lippmann wrote, "and has prevailed once again. It can be
said . . . without detracting from Mr. Truman's remarkable personal performance that of all Roosevelt's electoral triumphs, this
one in 1948 is the most impressive."

Building on the theories of "critical elections" pioneered by
V. O. Key, Jr., and Walter Dean Burnham, a group of political scientists at the University of Michigan Survey Research Center in
the 1960s separated American presidential elections into three
categories: maintaining, deviating, and realigning. A *maintaining*
election such as Truman's in 1948, they wrote, in the language of
political scientists, is one in which "a pattern of positive attachment prevailing in the preceding period persists and is the primary influence on forces governing the vote." *Deviating*
elections were defined as those in which widely esteemed personalities or significant events for a time reverse the prevailing division of partisan loyalties. Examples cited were the elections of
Woodrow Wilson in 1912 and 1916 in the midst of a period of
Republican dominance lasting from 1896 to 1932, and the elections of Dwight Eisenhower in 1952 and 1956, when Democrats
were the majority party. *Realigning* elections represent more than
short-term divergence from established patterns of partisan loyalty; they lead to new political configurations. According to the
"experts," Truman brought out just enough of the Democratic
"core" vote in 1948 to squeak through, "maintaining" the New
Deal electoral coalition.

In the past fifty years much has been written about the Truman administration and, especially in the 1990s, about Truman
himself. There has been little reevaluation, however, of the 1948
presidential election and the interpretations that have so long defined it. A fresh appraisal reveals that it was not an upset at all. It
would have been had Dewey won, as he nearly managed to do.
Given all the factors in his favor, Truman should have done better. The true surprise was the low turnout, reflecting the campaign
weaknesses of all four presidential candidates. Moreover, the
contest in 1948 was a maintaining election in only the narrowest
sense. Its enduring impact on politics and policy make it, along

with 1932 and 1968, one of the three most significant American elections of the twentieth century.

In *Paul Revere's Ride,* the historian David Hackett Fischer writes, "The image of the solitary rider . . . is etched indelibly upon the national memory, but it is not what actually happened that night." The dual mythology of "Trumania" and "upset" have merged in American minds as the reality of the 1948 election. Truman was rarely alone, however. The actions of many others, not all of them favorably disposed to his candidacy, helped seal his narrow victory. Alben Barkley, James Rowe, Elliott Bell, Robert Taft, even Joseph Stalin—each forms an important part of the story. But one always comes back to Truman. As the historian Herbert S. Parmet observes, "His reelection *should* have been obvious all along."

ACKNOWLEDGMENTS

I OWE a debt of gratitude to many people at Temple University, particularly Jim Hilty and Herb Bass, and graduate secretary Joanne Follmer. Many of those who played important roles in the 1948 campaign were good enough to correspond with me or endure brief interviews, notably John M. Burton, Donald S. Dawson, George M. Elsey, Leon Shull, Harold E. Stassen, J. Strom Thurmond, and the late Herbert Brownell, Jr. My thanks also to Barbara Myers Forde, daughter of the late Senator Francis J. Myers of Pennsylvania, who provided a great deal of material, particularly on the 1948 Democratic National Convention.

My research was conducted in felicitous surroundings, especially the Harry S Truman Library in Independence, Missouri, where the incomparable Liz Safly, Pauline Testerman, Dennis Bilger, and Sam Rushay (who has since gone on to greater responsibilities) were so helpful. I was aided as well by Karl Kabelac, whose province at the University of Rochester included the Thomas E. Dewey Papers; Larry Bland at the George C. Marshall Foundation in Lexington, Virginia; Leslie McAneny at the Gallup Organization in Princeton; Grace Hill of the *Congressional Quarterly;* Jannie Cobb of the George Meany Memorial Archives Library; Butch Foutz of the AFL-CIO Committee on Political Education; Sarah Culp of the University of Pennsylvania; and many others at the University of Kentucky, the Roper Center in Connecticut, the Library of Congress, and other locations. I've enjoyed the generous use of the libraries at Temple (especially its

Urban Archives), St. Joseph's University, the University of Pennsylvania, and Davidson, Bryn Mawr, and Haverford colleges.

Among those deserving of special thanks are Randall Miller of St. Joseph's University for his unceasing encouragement; James N. Giglio of Southwest Missouri State University for his helpful counsel; Robert H. Ferrell, who probably knows more about Truman than any living American, for his informative correspondence; and my editor and friend, Elsa Efran.

Finally my thoughts turn, as always, to my perpetually supportive wife, Betsy, a prime candidate for canonization, and to our son Bill, who has won a few elections of his own.

H. I. G.

Philadelphia
August 1998

CONTENTS

The Upset
That Wasn't

INTRODUCTION

BY ANY measure, the state of the union was sound. Harry Truman had ample justification to point with pride on January 7, 1948, in his annual report to the Congress. The nation enjoyed virtually full employment. Fourteen million more people held jobs than in 1938. During a single decade, which encompassed four years of world war, the output of goods and services had increased by two-thirds, the average income of Americans by more than 50 percent. Despite forebodings, there had been no severe recession following World War II. The gross national product had risen 10 percent in 1947 alone. The United States was more prosperous and powerful than at any time in its history. Even such residual problems as inflation had declined to 3 percent in 1948, and the housing shortage appeared on the way to eventual solution. Millions of veterans enjoyed the benefits of the GI Bill, especially its educational component and the opportunity for low-cost loans. As measured by public opinion polls, fear of international communism had gradually replaced domestic problems as the primary concern of most Americans. Polls also indicated that the administration's firm foreign policy enjoyed general approval. Indeed, Truman's Gallup poll ratings had been consistently positive since his proposal of aid to Greece and Turkey in the spring of 1947.

As he delivered his third State of the Union address, Truman had been president for all but three months of what was to have been Franklin Roosevelt's fourth term. Should Truman choose to run for the presidency in his own right in 1948, he was favored by at least nine percentage points over any potential challenger.

Yet in addressing the packed House chamber and a national radio audience, Truman chose not to recite his achievements but to focus on the nation's unfinished business. Prosperity was not yet shared equitably; farm families lagged behind; schools and hospitals were inadequate; racial discrimination persisted. While most Americans still suffered from high prices and artificial scarcity, Truman noted that "profits of corporations reached an all-time high in 1947." After all the reforms of the New Deal and successful postwar reconversion, a truly just society was still more a goal than a reality.

Truman invested most of his five thousand words in laying out an ambitious agenda for the future. He announced that he would shortly send a detailed message to Congress "to secure fully the essential human rights of our citizens." He went on to recommend an extensive list of programs, including broader Social Security coverage, a national health-care system, federal aid for housing and education, preservation *and* development of natural resources, expanded price supports for farmers, rural electrification and other agricultural improvements, passage of the ten-point anti-inflation program already in Congress, an increase in the minimum wage from forty to seventy-five cents an hour, statehood for Alaska and Hawaii, and the overall goal of stamping out poverty "in our generation." All this was to be accomplished within a balanced budget—even Truman's final proposal, which astonished many of his listeners. In order to allow Americans, especially low-income Americans, to buy more of "the necessities of life," Truman recommended an immediate forty-dollar cost-of-living credit to each individual taxpayer and an additional forty-dollar credit for each dependent, to be financed by increased taxes on corporate profits. (He had twice vetoed Republican proposals for tax reductions, insisting that such relief had to be deferred until inflation was under control.)

Surprisingly, foreign and defense policies, areas in which the president most often enjoyed bipartisan support, were left to the latter part of his address. After reviewing programs already in force, Truman endorsed universal military training, tariff reduction, and legislation that would allow greater numbers of displaced persons to enter the United States. He particularly urged the passage of the European Recovery Program, which was to become known as the Marshall Plan. The nation's objective remained "to achieve world peace based on principles of freedom and justice and the equality of all nations," a goal of suitable universality.

The response in the House chamber to this comprehensive manifesto was restrained. In his domestic program, Truman had made similar if less specific proposals each year since 1945. Most of them stood little chance of passage in the parsimonious, conservative Congress the president faced in 1948, controlled by Republicans since the off-year elections of 1946. What this latest version—especially the forty-dollar surprise—told partisans on both sides of the aisle was something more immediate. Truman had decided to run for the presidency in 1948, for what amounted to a second term. His laundry list of improbable proposals previewed his platform, seized the initiative, and threw down the gauntlet. Even the largely Republican press gave the president his due. An editorial in the *Denver Post* declared, "As a sendoff for the 1948 presidential election . . . it was a political masterstroke."

CHAPTER I

The Making
of a Politician

In 1948 Harry Truman had been a professional politician for twenty-six years. As promising as his prospects appeared to be at the beginning of that year, Truman well understood the vagaries of public opinion. His nearly three years in the White House had been a jarring roller-coaster ride. The president's decision to run in 1948 could not have been easy. He was nearing sixty-five, his wife, Bess, longed to return to a life of relative normalcy, and Truman had often voiced his own frustration with the demands of "the Great White Jail." In his memoirs he stresses "unfinished business" but dwells more on continuity—his responsibility to preserve the gains of the New Deal and continue to "lead from strength" with the Soviet Union. But to a career politician who had reached the pinnacle of his profession, the recognition that he was still viewed as an "accidental president" must have helped shape Truman's determination in 1948 to win on his own.

Perhaps he had also been an "accidental politician," but Truman took more naturally to politics than to any of his earlier pursuits. In the presidential candidate of 1948 there was still much of the instinctive Truman of 1922, the stubborn Truman of 1924, the rebounding Truman of 1926, the confident Truman of 1930, the

tireless Truman of 1934—and, most of all, the tenacious Truman
of 1940, fighting for his political life against long odds. Anyone
who imagines that 1948 represented the greatest challenge of Truman's electoral career should consider these earlier contests and
even Truman's pre-political life—that is, his first thirty-eight
years, when politics were not at the center of everything.

IN retirement, Truman would often tell groups of students who
visited his presidential library that three experiences represented
the ideal preparation for a career in public service: farming, finance, and the military. This must have seemed archaic to young
people in the 1960s, but it corresponded to Truman's own experiences. Farming was not a matter of choice. The first of three children, he was born in 1884 in the agricultural community of
Lamar, Missouri, to a family more Southern than Midwestern in
its origins and outlook. His parents were in the second generation
of families who had moved to western Missouri from Kentucky,
with antecedents in Virginia and North Carolina, deriving from
the "yeoman gentry" of England. His father, the feisty, restless,
diminutive John Anderson Truman, both a livestock trader and a
farmer, was a man of immense ambition. The one interest he
shared with his shy, bespectacled, bookish elder son was a love of
politics. The two would travel together to the picnics, barbecues,
torchlight parades, and rallies that were staples of turn-of-the-
century political campaigning—politics as entertainment.

Truman's books and spectacles (and piano lessons) reflect the
influence of his strong-willed mother. When Harry was six, Mary
Ellen Young Truman insisted the family move from her own parents' spacious farm in Grandview to the county seat of Independence, a long-established town with excellent schools. Harry
proved a dutiful and conscientious if not brilliant student. Although he won no honors at his high school graduation, he ex-

pected to continue his education. But poor eyesight precluded his appointment to a service academy, and his father's folly finally ruled out college of any kind: John Truman had gambled and lost everything in commodities trading.

The family moved to Kansas City. There Harry held a succession of jobs, ultimately working as a bookkeeper and clerk at major banks, where his industry and demeanor were much praised. The bright lights of the city held an immense attraction for young Truman, especially its music halls and theaters. Settling in a lively boardinghouse, he became more gregarious and with his friends joined a newly formed National Guard artillery battery. If Truman had a plan for his life, Kansas City provided an introduction to both its financial and military components. It was with some regret that Truman heeded his father's call to return with the rest of the family to the Grandview farm. Its six hundred acres had become too much for Harry's maternal grandmother to continue to manage. Harriet Louisa Young lived into her ninety-first year; her unreconstructed sentiments were passed on to her receptive grandson. Truman's Democratic loyalty was as much a part of his inheritance as his Baptist faith.

William Kemper, a prominent banker and investor from Kansas City who supported the emerging Pendergast political organization there, enlisted John Truman to help promote its candidates in the rural regions of Jackson County. Thus when Harry Truman finally ran for political office, even his factional loyalties were inherited. Except for his years in the army and in Washington, Truman lived his entire life within Jackson County. A microcosm of American expansion, its western end was anchored by the metropolis of Kansas City, whose population was already more than 200,000 when the Trumans moved there in 1903. The rural eastern end of the county, homogeneous and Protestant, still included more than 40,000 residents spread over twenty-five towns and villages and more than three hundred farms in the fer-

tile Missouri River valley. The diverse immigration that built
Kansas City was more internal than foreign—poor whites and
blacks moving up from the South. That the Pendergast brothers
and most of their competitors for political power were Catholics
of Irish extraction is more a tribute to their enterprise than their
numbers.

Working in partnership on what was now the Truman farm
forged a closer bond between father and son. Harry invested ten
years in farming, surprising even himself. But he also spent a
great deal of time off the farm, making the rounds of county so-
cials and suppers, and sometimes returning to the diversions of
Kansas City, just fifteen miles away. He renewed his acquaintance with Elizabeth Virginia Wallace of Independence, whom he
had admired since childhood. He joined everything from the Ma-
sons and Farm Bureau to the community band, almost as if he
were running for office.

"I was familiar with local politics," Truman recalled. He had
been a page at the 1900 Democratic National Convention in
Kansas City. He served as Democratic elections judge, a school
director, postmaster of Grandview, and after the death of his father in 1914 he inherited his position as road overseer. By 1915
Harry was a frequent visitor to the Tenth Ward Democratic Club
run by Mike Pendergast, the brother responsible for the eastern
district of Jackson County. At his behest, Truman ran for his first
political office as the Pendergasts' candidate for Washington
Township committeeman. "I got licked," he recalled, "but I
learned how the situation was worked out and profited by it."

Yet when Truman left active farming in 1915 his objective
was not votes but wealth. In partnership with others, he plunged
everything he could scrape up into a series of entrepreneurial ven-
tures—land, lead and zinc mining in Oklahoma, and oil drilling
in Kansas. Remarkably, the last of these risky, undercapitalized
investments nearly made Truman a millionaire. After he sold his

share of the drilling enterprise to a major oil company, their deeper drilling capacity struck immensely profitable pools of oil. By then Harry was a soldier in France, enjoying the first unqualified success of his life. He later wrote, "My whole political career is based on my war service and my war associates."

As a thirty-three-year-old with poor eyesight, ostensibly still engaged in the vital occupation of farming, Truman was under no obligation to volunteer when the United States entered the Great War in 1917. He did so, however, with clear enthusiasm. Rejoining the National Guard, he was surprised to be elected a first lieutenant, one victory for which he was not obliged to campaign. Within a year he was promoted to captain in the regular army and placed in charge of Battery D of the 129th Field Artillery, composed largely of tough Irishmen from areas of Kansas City little less foreign to Truman than France. Somehow he won the respect of these "wild men," and ultimately their affection. The challenges of command and combat confirmed—most importantly to Truman himself—his capacity to lead others. A bond was formed that lasted throughout Truman's lifetime; the veterans of Battery D would be with him in every campaign. A young lieutenant whom Truman saw frequently in France was Mike Pendergast's son Jim.

Within weeks of Truman's return to Kansas City in 1919, he married "Bess" Wallace and sold his share of the farm. With the proceeds and a bank loan, he opened an upscale Kansas City haberdashery in partnership with Eddie Jacobson, an army buddy experienced in retailing. Using the store as a base, Truman pursued other activities, particularly in newly formed veterans' groups. His establishment became a sort of headquarters for former servicemen when they visited downtown. For the first year the store prospered, but in 1921–1922, like many others, it fell victim to a severe business recession. The value of inventory plummeted. Truman would be paying off his debts for the next fifteen years.

The causes of this postwar recession were complex, but to Truman they could be traced directly to the deflationary policies of one man: Warren G. Harding's austere secretary of the treasury, Andrew Mellon. "Old Mellon" became Truman's prototype of Republican reaction and indifference. Clearly the store was "going bust." Truman needed a job.

EIGHT years before Truman was born, an ambitious second-generation Irish-American named James Pendergast traveled downriver from St. Joseph, Missouri, to the more promising environs of an already burgeoning Kansas City. An iron puddler by trade but a risk-taking entrepreneur by inclination, Pendergast bet everything he had on a horse named Climax. With his winnings he opened a hotel and saloon near the Kansas City railroad station. Business prospered, but politics became Pendergast's true vocation. Expanding from his base in the immigrant bastion of "West Bottoms," Pendergast built the first viable political organization in the city, was elected alderman, and sent to St. Joseph for his three brothers to join him. Tom, the most talented, sixteen years younger than "Alderman Jim," would become his brother's true heir. He became known as "T.J." and preferred the urban environs of Kansas City. His brother Mike was dispatched to organize the rural eastern part of Jackson County. "Boss" was a term the Pendergasts always disdained, insisting that political power was based on nothing more complicated than making and keeping friends. In return for the timely distribution of commodities that poor people needed—a load of coal, a Thanksgiving turkey, or even a job—all they asked for was one's vote. As their neighborhood organization expanded, it exercised every form of election-day excess, but it was most noted for block-by-block organization. In time the Pendergasts would outdistance their less sophisticated rivals, become the dominant political machine in the area, and form alliances of mutual benefit with Kansas City's emerging business elite. In 1922, however, this was yet to be realized. The Pendergast "Goats" still vied with the "Rabbits" of the other major faction, run by Joseph Shannon, and with other less colorful Democratic configurations, as well as with the smaller Republican party. Temporary alliances abounded, based on the patronage that fueled all factions. A candidate running on his own had virtually no chance of winning.

In mid-1921 Mike Pendergast joined his son Jim in a visit to "Captain Harry" at the haberdashery. He made Truman an offer. Would he like to run for the Democratic party's nomination for Eastern District judge of the Jackson County Court? An ostensibly incredulous Truman said he would think about it. Even if he was not yet fully aware of his store's imminent problems, Truman recalls, "I liked the political game." It didn't take him long to decide to run.

This judgeship was an administrative, not a judicial, office. The three members of the Board of Judges that governed Jackson County were akin to powerful county commissioners. They levied taxes, built and maintained roads, ran the county courthouse and extensive facilities, dispensed a budget in the millions, and controlled some nine hundred patronage jobs. One judge from each of the eastern and western districts was elected every two years only by the residents of each region, giving the sparsely populated east political clout equal to Kansas City's. The presiding judge, however, was elected every four years by the entire county. In 1922 all three positions were up for election. Winning at least two of the three was the focus of every political faction.

The circumstances were ideal for someone with Harry Truman's credentials. Boasting deep roots in the region, Truman had a foothold in all three areas of Jackson County—farm, town, and city. His exemplary military record and leadership in veterans' affairs could translate into support from an important new constituency. As a former farmer, birthright Baptist, and active Mason, he was everything the Pendergasts were not. And while he had long been interested in local affairs, Truman carried little political baggage. Even his business failure would put him in the sympathetic company of many others who had striven beyond their means and were denied success by circumstances.

Truman's candidacy was announced in March 1922 at a raucous meeting of hundreds of veterans. Official Pendergast support was not confirmed until three months later, but there is no way Truman would have run without it. In future years he would make much of the fact that both his political benefactors, the Pendergasts in 1922 and Franklin Roosevelt in 1944, had come to him. But in 1922 Truman had not even met the true boss, T. J. Pendergast, and Roosevelt's decision was more pragmatic than personal.

However it happened, Truman had found his true vocation. Facing four other candidates in the 1922 Democratic primary, all older and more experienced in government or commerce, Truman demonstrated four characteristics that would mark his future campaigns:

—He devised and carried out his own strategy.

—He outworked everyone else.

—He stuck to a few simple themes.

—He viewed himself, justifiably or not, as an underdog.

Truman turned his inexperience into an asset, censuring the records of three of his opponents who had held county jobs. He campaigned tirelessly from June to August, visiting every precinct and township in the county, traveling in his old Dodge roadster over rutted roads. He made those roads the focus of his campaign, distributing leaflets that read: "My platform: good roads, a balanced road fund, economy, a day's work for a day's pay, fewer automobiles and more work for county employees.

Harry S Truman." He even came to one rally in a friend's airplane; he threw up but managed to make his most effective speech of the campaign. Public speaking was an immense problem for Truman. It was never to come naturally to him, but he learned by constant repetition how to address large audiences with the same apparent simplicity and spontaneity as if he were talking with a few friends. It could be awkward but effective. "Plain speaking" began in 1922, not in 1948.

Truman won the primary by only 279 votes out of a total of 12,071 cast, narrowly defeating the Shannon candidate, a respected banker less vulnerable than the others to accusations of mismanagement. The close race was another precursor of Truman's political future. His victory was literally saved by a former artillery officer Truman had known in France. Now county marshal, he foiled Shannon's attempt to stuff ballot boxes. To the historian James David Barber, this primary election already put Truman's "foot on the first rung of his ladder to the presidency. His style was formed: aggressive rhetoric, swift decision, and, among men of good will, loyalty lasting to the final mile." Campaigning just as strenuously but spending even less money than in the primary, Truman won the general election by a more comfortable 2,749 votes. It was a fortuitous victory for the Pendergasts. Their candidate in the western region, Henry McElroy, also won, but the victorious presiding judge was a Shannon man. Truman's would be the deciding vote in the county court.

Without missing a beat, Truman examined "every road, bridge, lane, and county institution." As his biographer David McCullough writes, "Under McElroy and Truman a county debt of more than a million dollars was cut in half. The county's credit rating improved. So did county services and, most notably, the quality of work on the roads." Truman was also learning the practical lessons of politics, but here he deferred to McElroy. There was no split of patronage among the elected judges. Virtually all the jobs went to "Goat" Democrats loyal to T. J. Pendergast, alienating the other factions.

Even with the support of so normally an anti-Pendergast newspaper as the *Kansas City Star,* Truman faced a formidable challenge to his reelection in 1924. In the Democratic primary he won another narrow victory over a single opponent—6,757 to 5,119. In the general election, opposed not only by the Republicans but by every non-Pendergast Democratic organization and even the Ku Klux Klan (which Truman had refused to join due to its anti-Catholic, anti-Jewish bias), he managed to lose by only 877 votes. Other than his prewar race for Democratic committeeman, this was the only electoral defeat Truman ever suffered. The highlight of 1924 was the birth of the Trumans' only child, Margaret.

Despite making a substantial income selling memberships in the Kansas City Auto Club and attending law school at night, Truman continued to build relationships that would enhance his effectiveness as a candidate—in the Masonic Order, the Army Reserve, and the Old Trails Association. His two years out of office only reinforced Truman's commitment to a political career. In 1926 he finally met Thomas J. Pendergast, whose organization was primed for its greatest years. Their relationship would give Truman as much anguish as opportunity.

When Pendergast and Shannon decided to bury the hatchet in 1926 and form a united party, politics in Jackson County became predictable. That same year voters approved a new Kansas City charter establishing a city-manager form of government. The first city manager was none other than Henry McElroy. Although McElroy was well on his way to becoming a millionaire, Truman was still paying off his haberdashery debts. In 1926 Pendergast slated Truman to run for presiding judge of the Jackson County Court. This time there was no primary opposition and only token opposition in the fall. Under these circumstances even Truman could scarcely feel like an underdog. He beat his Republican opponent by more than 16,000 votes. Running for reelection in 1930, in a contest enlivened only by the use of radio, Truman won by 58,066 votes.

Truman's record on the court, despite having to overcome the mendacity of his associate judges, was one of remarkable achievement. His comprehensive master plan for a modern highway system throughout Jackson County was decades ahead of its time, and he succeeded in passing bond issues to finance it. He organized a Greater Kansas City Regional Planning Association, which was later expanded to the entire state. He promoted tax reform and improved facilities for the black residents of the county. His bond issues financed new hospitals and retirement homes, a remodeled courthouse in Independence, and a new one for Kansas City, fronted by a statue of his childhood hero, Andrew Jackson.

Truman's greatest challenge lay in keeping T. J. Pendergast's hands off these projects, especially in view of Pendergast's concrete company and his commitments to his contractors and cronies. It was an ethical dilemma Truman never fully resolved. He had the patronage to trade for honest contracts, but it was a constant, wearing struggle. Obliged to pad his payroll with hacks and incompetents, Truman looked the other way at their felonies to keep the bulk of his bond money secure. The pressure became more intrusive after the death in 1929 of Mike Pendergast, his buffer with T.J. Although Boss Tom called Truman "the contrariest cuss in Missouri," eventually the two made their own bargain. Truman's achievements rendered more likely the passage of projects run by others less scrupulous.

With increasing frequency between 1930 and 1934, Truman went to his hideaway in Kansas City's rundown Pickwick Hotel, where for hour after hour he would chronicle the emotional costs of this arrangement. "Am I an administrator or not? Or am I just a crook to compromise to get the job done? You judge it. I can't." Writing it all down became a form of self-therapy that Truman carried into his later career. He was concerned not only with moral ambiguity but with his own future. After the election of Franklin Roosevelt to the presidency in 1932, Truman took on the additional task, at no salary, of heading the Federal Reemployment Service in Missouri, reporting directly to Harry Hopkins in Washington. Truman hoped to be considered as Pendergast's candidate for governor or for a congressional seat. Both nominations went to others. The depression had deepened cuts in local programs, and with the rise of organized crime in Kansas City, Pendergast's venality turned more ominous. Having served his maximum two terms as presiding judge, Truman was obliged to leave the court in 1934. His Pickwick papers reveal the state of his mind: "I could have had $1,500,000, but I haven't a hundred and fifty dollars. Am I a fool or an ethical giant? I don't know . . . I'll go out of here poorer in every way than when I came into office." Now turning fifty, Truman had yet to achieve lasting success.

ON HIS fiftieth birthday Truman found himself in the midst of a speaking tour, stumping the state for a bond issue. At his hotel he was surprised by a phone call from the Boss's nephew, his old friend Jim Pendergast, who was with Jim Aylward, Democratic state party chairman. Driving over to meet them in a nearby town, Truman was told that T. J. Pendergast wanted him to run for the United States Senate, an uncommonly ambitious transition for a county judge. Whatever had determined Pendergast to make this extraordinary decision, Truman had the presence of mind to ask a few direct questions. Even with organization support, he realized, he would need all its resources to win a statewide race, including seed money to launch the primary campaign. Aylward assured Truman he would have everything necessary, including the chairman's influence throughout the state. In a matter of weeks Truman had gone from despair to what might well be the culmination of his career.

In 1934 the Pendergast organization ruled Kansas City but hardly all of Missouri. T.J.'s senatorial candidate only two years before had been handily defeated by a rival Democrat, Bennett C. Clark, the ambitious son of legendary House Speaker "Champ" Clark, who went on to win in the general election. It was customary in Missouri to have one senator from the western part of the state, around Kansas City, and one from the east, around St. Louis. In 1934 that was not the case. Clark came from the east, as did the senior senator, a colorless conservative Republican named Roscoe Conkling Patterson. Out of tune with the times, Patterson seemed a vulnerable target to the Democrats. Two popular congressmen vied with Truman for the nomination. Clark induced Jacob L. "Tuck" Milligan, who represented a rural district only fifty miles from Kansas City, to declare for the seat. The later entry of John J. Cochran of St. Louis, even more of a proven vote-getter than Milligan, worked against Aylward's help in the east. Truman would have his hands full, but a three-cornered race also split the anti-Pendergast (or "good government") forces.

Pendergast was the issue in the primary, with Milligan, Cochran, and Clark all charging that Truman was little more than the Boss's office boy, a characterization that would linger long after the 1934 election. If locally the issue was one of independence, nationally it was the opposite. Each of the three candidates fervently supported the New Deal and claimed he could best bring its benefits home to Missourians. The only substantive difference on issues was the veterans' bonus, which Truman favored and his two rivals (and the administration in Washington) opposed. This scarcely handicapped Truman with Missouri's hard-pressed veterans. Just as he had in 1922, Truman turned his lack of experience into an asset, culling the congressional records of Milligan and Cochran for local relevance and denouncing both for their failure "to support the best interests of farmers in bankruptcy legislation."

Once again Truman outworked and outplanned his opponents, delivering six to sixteen speeches a day in 60 of the state's 114 counties, despite fierce midsummer heat, in the automotive equivalent of whistle-stopping. He made perfunctory appearances in Kansas City, where he couldn't lose, and entirely avoided St. Louis, where he couldn't win, focusing his efforts on the rural heartland of the state. Truman's homegrown connections were unmatched—in farm, Masonic, and veterans' organizations, but most of all through his eight years as presiding judge of the Jackson County Court, culminating in the presidency of the Missouri County Judges Association. The support of many of these politically connected judges and their "courthouse gangs" proved of immense value.

The senatorial election was won in the small towns and hollows of the "out country," just as Truman had anticipated. His overall plurality in the Democratic primary was 40,745. Even allowing for the organization's overkill in Kansas City, had there been a single anti-Pendergast candidate rather than two, Truman would have lost. In the general election Truman won by more than a quarter of a million votes. The state's media accorded him little credit for his victory. From the *Kansas City Star* to the *St. Louis Post-Dispatch,* major newspapers lamented this latest manifestation of machine politics. As for the lopsided general election, the popularity of President Roosevelt, the unpopularity of Senator Patterson, and the impact of federal relief funds were viewed as more decisive factors than Truman's skillful and energetic campaign. In his first statewide election, Truman's triumph was widely viewed in the context of another man's electoral coalition. The shadow of Roosevelt dominated in 1934, just as the shade of Roosevelt would dominate in 1948.

STILL, Truman could not be denied an immense satisfaction upon taking his seat in the Senate chamber in January 1935. Although some members of that august body might view him as merely "the senator from Pendergast," he was greeted warmly by most of his new colleagues on both sides of the aisle. Following the admonition of Senator Carl Hayden to be "a workhorse" rather than a "showhorse," Truman sought to earn his place within the inner circle of conscientious men who managed legislative affairs. His major committee assignments, Appropriations and Interstate Commerce, reflected his experience in budget building and his interest in planning. His first term culminated in the writing of the Transportation Act of 1940 and the passage of the Civil Aeronautics Act.

Truman had campaigned on the premise of his support for the New Deal. He was a Democrat, however, who believed in balanced budgets. While he may have blamed the collapse of his own retail establishment on the villainy of Republicans, the experience also cemented his abiding aversion to deficit spending. First and foremost, Truman was a pragmatic politician with one eye always trained on his constituents at home and the other on gaining acceptance in Washington. In a rare instance of public introspection, Truman in his memoirs related his preoccupation from childhood with calculating how to please others. In 1934 Truman's acceptance of the New Deal was based more on its popularity in Missouri and on his sense of party loyalty than on any deep ideological commitment. "Over the next ten years," the historian James W. Hilty writes, Truman "carefully and selectively supported New Deal initiatives, sensibly responded to the interest groups upon which the fortunes of the Democratic Party rested, and patiently and adroitly maneuvered into a position of influence within the Senate."

In this context, Truman's advocacy of civil rights reflected the reality of 250,000 black voters in Missouri. His support of the Wagner Labor Act reflected the influence of powerful railroad brotherhoods at home. His voting record of moderate liberalism encompassed the enactment and perpetuation of Social Security, the Public Works Administration, and housing legislation but opposed the costly expansion of many New Deal programs. Whatever his stance, he was rarely outspoken. Sometimes his loyalty overcame his sentiments, as in his reluctant approval of Roosevelt's 1937 bill to "pack" the Supreme Court by adding justices more sympathetic to New Deal legislation.

By 1939 Roosevelt needed help to pass even a watered-down bill to reorganize his executive offices. Senator Truman was summoned to return from Jefferson City, Missouri, to vote for the bill. A furious Truman, weary from a perilous overnight flight in a snowstorm, complied but informed the president's press secretary that he was tired of being treated as a functionary. The next day the president himself invited Truman to the White House "for a friendly conversation." After expressing his belated appreciation for Truman's support, the president turned to the political situation in Missouri, about which he seemed to know a great deal. He wanted it cleaned up.

Truman's loyalties were about to collide. When he went to Washington he had agreed with Pendergast on a separation of Senate and non-Senate business. Indeed, Boss Tom's only call on "Senate business" was at the behest of the White House—a clumsy attempt to ask Truman to support Alben Barkley as Senate majority leader. Truman had pledged his vote to another, and stuck with it. By the end of his first senatorial term, it was more the residue than the reality of his connection with Pendergast that imperiled Truman's prospects for reelection.

Between 1936 and 1939 everything had collapsed for the Boss. His health had failed. His gambling had turned from an avocation to a runaway addiction. The organization foundered without his hands-on leadership. Both the local business community and the administration in Washington decided against further association with so overtly corrupt a political machine. By 1938 T. J. Pendergast's activities were being investigated by everyone from the Treasury Department and the FBI to a local reform group spearheaded by U.S. District Attorney Maurice Milligan, whose brother had run against Truman in 1934. The probes were supported by Governor Lloyd C. Stark, who had been elected in 1936 with the support of both Truman and Pendergast. In the spring of 1939 Boss Tom was convicted of income-tax evasion and sent to Leavenworth Penitentiary. Released on parole after a year and a day, and barred from political activity, he died less than five years later. Harry Truman said at Pendergast's funeral, "He was my friend and I have always been his."

As 1940 approached, Truman determined that he would run for reelection to the Senate. It is less certain whether Franklin Roosevelt had yet decided to run for an unprecedented third term as president of the United States. Not only Republicans but many Democrats were opposed to the idea—either vocally or, like Harry Truman, quietly. Among the alienated were Vice-President John Nance Garner and Roosevelt's key political strategist, Jim Farley, both of whom had their own ambitions, as well as Secretary of State Cordell Hull. To his confidant Harry Hopkins, a tired Roosevelt revealed the desire to return to his Hudson Valley home at Hyde Park, write his memoirs, and oversee construction of the first presidential library. Only a deterioration of world events would induce him to run again. If this was so, the German blitzkrieg in the spring of 1940 made up the president's mind.

In what looked to be a difficult race, Roosevelt needed allies as reliable as Truman had proven to be, but the president preferred someone in Missouri with less dubious associations. Nearing the end of his term, Governor Stark, a wealthy apple grower who could finance his own campaign, stepped forward to volunteer. Stark and the president determined to get Truman out of the race by offering him a seat on the Interstate Commerce Commission, an overture that Truman bitterly rejected.

Instead he called a meeting of his supporters. According to Truman biographer Robert H. Ferrell, "Half of those he asked did not show up, and the other half saw only defeat facing the senator. Truman then said he would run even if he received only his own vote." Thus began Truman's "loneliest campaign"—in 1940, not 1948. Running on a shoestring, he exceeded even his frenetic pace of 1934, speaking in 74 of Missouri's 114 counties. He ran a positive campaign in the Democratic primary, stressing his record of promises fulfilled—to labor, farmers, and small business—and dwelling on the need for a program of national preparedness. He also emphasized giving every citizen a fair break, including Negroes, a stance that contrasted with Stark's insensitivity and rallied black leaders to Truman. The railroad brotherhoods distributed half a million copies of a special Missouri edition of their newspaper, promoting Truman as a friend of labor and offsetting his scant newspaper support. Despite the tacit endorsement of Stark by their president, Democratic senators from around the nation interrupted their summer schedules to go to Missouri and speak for Truman, illustrating the esteem in which he was already held in that body.

Still, it was an uphill struggle against the well-entrenched Stark until another Milligan came unintentionally to Truman's aid. This time it was the prosecutor of Pendergast, District Attorney Maurice Milligan, who entered the race. He may well have been encouraged to do so, as had his brother in 1934, by Senator Clark. In his desire to dominate Missouri politics, Bennett Clark no longer had Pendergast to worry about but a new opponent in Lloyd Stark, who viewed himself as a personification of reform. In this new three-sided primary, characterized by Truman as "the most bitter, mud-slinging campaign in Missouri's history of dirty campaigns," he wasn't slinging much of the mud. With Clark urging on Milligan and Stark denouncing them both, Truman had the high road to himself.

As Milligan faded and Stark began to blunder, both Clark and the president shifted gears. An ardent isolationist, Clark differed with Truman on policies, but six years together in the Senate had engendered a personal rapport. As for Roosevelt, he knew what he had in Truman, but Stark's irrepressible ambition gave him pause. At the Democratic National Convention in July, which Truman also attended, Stark in mid-campaign also seemed intent on running for the vice-presidency or any other office that might be available. How dependable would he be in the Senate?

It was a most peculiar convention. Apparently also influenced by world events, the Republicans had bypassed such established isolationists as Senator Robert A. Taft to nominate for president a political newcomer, Wendell L. Willkie. An engaging forty-eight-year-old utilities executive from Indiana who had criticized the New Deal but stood for collective security, Willkie had been dubbed "the barefoot boy from Wall Street" by Roosevelt's acerbic secretary of the interior, Harold Ickes. Willkie appeared to be a formidable opponent.

With Mayor Edward J. Kelly of Chicago, Roosevelt now engineered a "draft." Convention chairman Barkley read to the assembled delegates an extraordinary message from the president saying that he had no desire to continue in office and that they were "free to vote for any candidate." With polls indicating Roosevelt to be the only prominent Democrat who could win in 1940, even disgruntled delegates had little choice but to go along with the orchestrated nomination. Yet they still harbored the impression they could name their own vice-presidential candidate to replace the departing Garner. A host of hopeful contenders were lining up support, including Lloyd Stark, busily distributing bushels of his apples. But Roosevelt, who communicated daily only with Harry Hopkins in Chicago, had no intention of relinquishing this decision. Wanting someone who supported his views, and having been rebuffed by Hull, the president settled on his secretary of agriculture, Henry A. Wallace. Wallace, a former progressive Republican, whose loyalty was to the New Deal and Roosevelt rather than to the Democratic party, did not even enjoy the support of his own Iowa delegation. When informed of Roosevelt's wishes, the convention neared a state of insurrection, not even ameliorated by the visit of the president's wife, Eleanor. Roosevelt finally settled the matter by threatening not to accept his own nomination unless the delegates named Wallace as his running mate. A disappointed Stark returned to Missouri, confident that at least he could beat Harry Truman for the Senate.

The Democratic primary in Missouri, however, had tightened to a race that newspapers now viewed as "too close to call." It would be determined, as happened so frequently in Truman's career, by the unexpected intervention of others concerned with their own priorities. The "plain folks" appeal of Truman contrasted with the urbane egotism of Stark, but it was not the farm vote that would resolve the outcome in 1940. The political machine in Missouri that still retained its influence was no longer in bustling, wide-open Kansas City but in staid St. Louis. Just as capable of padding voting rolls and "delivering" districts as the Pendergast organization had been, it was run by Mayor Barney Dickmann and an ambitious young county chairman named

Robert E. Hannegan. Initially the St. Louis bosses favored Stark. Their priority, however, was not the senatorial race but the election of the next governor, the state's prime dispenser of patronage and favors. Their own candidate, a political hack, paled beside his competitor in the primary, a respected state legislator supported by most of the reform elements in Missouri. Truman and Stark endorsed neither, but many of Stark's associates could not contain their enthusiasm for the good-government candidate.

At this juncture Senator Clark intruded. With his own candidate for the Senate, Milligan, almost out of the running, Clark not only took to the stump for Truman, he also took to the telephone. Supported by some of Truman's friends from Jackson County, Clark told Dickmann and Hannegan in St. Louis that if they did not come through for Truman, and if their candidate for governor were to win the primary, "We'll cut his goddamn throat in the fall." Old "Alderman Jim" would have been pleased by how little the tenor of Missouri politics had changed. It is unclear whether Dickmann deserted Stark, but Hannegan took Senator Clark at his word and induced his own supporters to switch to Truman.

St. Louis made the difference, giving Truman a lead of 8,391 votes; his statewide margin was only 7,976. The final result was Truman, 268,557; Stark, 260,581; Milligan, 127,363. Just as in 1934, had a Milligan stayed out of the race, Truman's opponent would have won. As it turned out, the St. Louis bosses' candidate for governor lost in the general election (to a Republican friend of Truman's), but Hannegan had earned the gratitude of both of Missouri's senators.

This time the general election in the fall was a challenge. Stark, who had earned Truman's enduring enmity, sat on his hands. The Republican candidate, Manvel Davis of Kansas City, had no shortage of targets. It must have seemed strange to Truman to be portrayed as the stooge not only of Franklin Roosevelt and the fallen Pendergast but now of the Dickmann-Hannegan machine as well. Would he never be taken seriously on his own? Truman simply ignored Davis, as he would future opponents, and focused on the need for continuity in Washington. Even more than in 1934, Roosevelt was the issue—his accumulated power, the third term, and his increasing involvement in Europe's war. Davis had earlier criticized Truman as a county executive whose predilection for planning bordered on socialism, but his emphasis in 1940 was on the man in the White House. Roosevelt won Missouri by 87,467 votes, and won the election, although by a much smaller margin than in 1936. Truman won by only 44,399 votes out of 1,817,657 cast. In a remarkable reversal of its earlier prediction that "Truman is through in Missouri," the *St. Louis Post-Dispatch* concluded, "Senator Truman has been on the whole a satisfactory Senator. Now seasoned by experience, he should make an even better record in his second term." With his previous benefactor ailing and inactive, and his future benefactor opposing his reelection, Truman's triumph in 1940, not in 1948, was the great upset of his political career.

Taken together, Truman's primary campaigns in 1934 and 1940 are a precursor of his victory in the presidential election of 1948. Missouri's urban-rural mix was more representative of the nation as a whole than that of many states west of the Mississippi. Truman demonstrated his ability to win in both regions. In 1934 the farm vote was vital, in 1940 the support of organized labor. Big-city bosses were significant in both elections, in Kansas City in 1934 and in St. Louis in 1940. In both campaigns Truman enjoyed the backing of minorities, most importantly the black vote, and survived overwhelming media opposition. He took advantage of the mistakes of a smug, overconfident opponent in 1940 and more experienced opponents in 1934. In both elections Truman outworked and largely ignored his actual competitors and faced more than one major candidate. In both he benefited from the aid of people with their own agendas, such as the Milligans, and in

1940 Clark and Hannegan. In both primaries Truman's victory margins were slender.

Dominating in both the general elections in these years was the imposing figure of Franklin Roosevelt, the issue even in absentia. Roosevelt's domestic policy was endorsed in 1934, as was his foreign policy in 1940. Even without FDR's sanction, Truman may have enjoyed something closer to a New Deal electoral coalition in his senatorial contests than in the 1948 presidential election. He slept soundly on that dramatic election night, with the outcome still in doubt, just as he had eight years before. It was hardly a new experience.

EVEN before the end of his first term in the Senate, Truman had little doubt that the United States would be drawn into the war. Since Army Chief of Staff George C. Marshall suggested that fifty-six was rather an advanced age for active duty, Truman determined to aid the cause of preparedness from his Senate seat— or, more accurately, by leaving it to travel throughout the nation. When constituents complained of waste and mismanagement at Missouri military bases and the inability of small firms to obtain government contracts, Truman decided to see for himself. By 1941 an unprecedented national defense program was under way throughout the country. Reflecting public opinion, Congress was still predominantly isolationist but agreed on the necessity for American preparedness. The resulting effort, uniting business, government, and labor, finally helped pull the nation out of the depression. Truman set out to determine how this immense investment was being spent, traveling to factories and military installations as distant as Florida and Texas. His unhappiness with what he saw led in March 1941 to the establishment of the Senate Special Committee to Investigate the National Defense Program. It came to be known as the Truman Committee, and its activities dominated Truman's second term in the Senate. The committee would last until 1948, but its most productive period was under Truman's chairmanship from 1941 to 1944.

Although initially granted only limited funding, by August 1941 Truman's investigators had already uncovered massive fraud and waste in the nation's billion-dollar camp-building program. In 1942 the committee's appropriations increased and its scope widened. The Truman Committee is still viewed as a model for responsible congressional oversight. Truman, who knew something of the value of coalitions, carefully selected the four other Democratic and two Republican senators who joined him, all serious "workhorses" like himself. Still, it was inevitable that media attention would focus on the no-nonsense chairman, especially after the United States was plunged into World War II by the Japanese attack on Pearl Harbor. Truman's face appeared on the cover of *Time,* and he was rated one of the ten most influential men in Washington. Even President Roosevelt, initially suspicious of such intrusive investigation, gave Truman high marks for his evenhanded performance. The Missourian's most notable senatorial achievement was also his most visible.

New Vice-President Henry Wallace was also busy, doing far more than presiding over the Senate. The president entrusted him, unlike his predecessor, with major responsibilities. Roosevelt's first vice-president, "Cactus Jack" Garner of Texas, an experienced politician who held a low opinion of the office, agreed to run in 1932 only to help assure a Democratic victory. He ran again with Roosevelt in 1936 despite his disagreement with most of the New Deal. Garner's presidential ambitions were finally terminated by Roosevelt's decision to run for a third term. But because of his many friends in Congress, Garner had been valuable to Roosevelt as a reliable barometer of congressional sentiment.

The polar opposite of his predecessor, Wallace supported the president unreservedly. Wallace's ideas in fact went well beyond the New Deal, but he was exceedingly uncomfortable in the company of politicians. When Roosevelt named him to the Board of Economic Warfare, Wallace soon fell into conflict with more practical-minded cabinet members. Such disputes were not uncommon in the loose structure of the Roosevelt administration, but wartime conditions impelled greater unity. A more successful experience was Wallace's secret role as the president's direct link with scientists working on the atomic bomb, whose existence Truman would be unaware of until he became president. When his committee's investigators uncovered mysterious installations in Tennessee and Washington State, Senator Truman was warned off by Secretary of War Henry L. Stimson. "I can't tell you what it is," Stimson told Truman, "but it is the greatest project in the history of the world."

Truman admired Wallace's performance as secretary of agriculture but was critical of the Iowan as vice-president, citing his utter lack of rapport with senators. Given Wallace's background, this should not have been surprising. Wallace had inherited his family's farm magazine and progressive proclivities. A skilled plant geneticist, he developed hybrid corn that made him a millionaire but also heightened his concern for a more abundant society. A visionary and something of a mystic, Wallace had little practical political experience when he joined Roosevelt's cabinet.

Particularly during the war, the scope of Wallace's reflections expanded to worldwide dimensions. In May 1942, with the ultimate outcome of the conflict still in doubt, Wallace delivered an address that spelled out his vision of the postwar world. This time, he declared, universal peace must usher in a "people's revolution . . . a better standard for the common man . . . international monopoly under control . . . no privileged peoples," free trade, and subordination of "lesser interest" to the "general welfare throughout the world." Such utterances, as well as articles espousing the "century of the common man," developed a con-

stituency for Wallace that was peculiarly his own: a diverse assemblage of academics, youthful idealists, human-rights activists,
iconoclastic journalists, liberal clergy, left-leaning labor leaders,
and progressives from an earlier era. For a time even Eleanor
Roosevelt viewed Wallace as her husband's logical heir, a man
who could reinvigorate and extend the New Deal and preserve
world peace.

To the leadership of the Democratic party, however, Wallace's
pronouncements were redolent of socialism or even communism,
especially in view of the vice-president's empathy with the Soviet
Union, which went far beyond the acknowledgment of a wartime
alliance. In his only election Wallace had been foisted on the
party faithful by Roosevelt. Democratic leaders such as the new
national chairman, Bob Hannegan, who had taken the job at Truman's urging, were as uncomfortable with the vice-president as
he was with them. When the 1942 off-year elections produced
Republican gains that exceeded expectations, it was, in the words
of the political writer Michael Barone, "taken as a repudiation of
New Deal policies and the mobilization effort at home." Democratic leaders determined to make the highly visible Henry Wallace a casualty of this conclusion.

By 1944 the outcome of the war was no longer in doubt. Unlike in 1940, there was no question that Roosevelt would run for a
fourth term. He was billed as "the indispensable man" who would
lead the nation through to a secure peace. Wallace, however, was
viewed as eminently dispensable by the party bosses and strategists who had supplanted men like Pendergast and Farley—not
only Hannegan but Mayor Kelly of Chicago, Frank Hague of
New Jersey, Ed Flynn of the Bronx, wealthy party treasurer
Edwin Pauley, Postmaster General Frank Walker, and George
Allen. Primarily nonideological, they wanted a vice-president
they knew and could work with. Their motives, however, were

not entirely self-serving. They viewed Wallace as a dreamer, temperamentally unsuited to be president of the United States.

Although concealed as much as possible from the public, it was clear to anyone who saw President Roosevelt with any frequency that he was seriously ill. Whomever the Democrats nominated to run with him in 1944 would almost surely be president before his term ended. Somehow Roosevelt had to be convinced that Wallace would be a detriment to his reelection. But much had changed since 1940. Wallace's idealism helped buoy the nation, and he was far more popular with delegates to the upcoming Democratic National Convention than he had been four years earlier. National party leaders, now virtually conspirators, found a powerful ally in the White House. "Pa" Watson, Roosevelt's appointments secretary, shared their opinion of Wallace. As Roosevelt's gatekeeper, Watson initiated a policy of admitting anti-Wallace visitors to see the president and largely keeping out those with pro-Wallace sentiments.

The Republican party also proved helpful to Hannegan and his associates. Meeting first, as it normally did, the GOP nominated as its candidate for the presidency no political amateur but the youthful, progressive governor of New York, Thomas E. Dewey. The vigorous Dewey had made his reputation as a racket-busting district attorney, and he proposed to put the Roosevelt administration itself on trial. This would be no easy task in wartime, but efficient reconversion to peace would also be on the minds of the electorate. Dewey vowed "an end to one-man government," declaring that Roosevelt "has been able to bury his blunders in foreign affairs under the march of mighty events. He has not been able to bury his domestic blunders." When popular Governor Earl Warren of California declined to join him, Dewey acceded to the nomination of conservative Governor John Bricker of Ohio as his vice-presidential candidate. As in 1940, the Republican ticket thus reflected both wings of the party. Early polls indicated considerable Republican strength. Roosevelt might be well advised to consider a running mate unlikely to alienate any sizable bloc of voters.

That the president was wavering with respect to Wallace is indicated by FDR's decision to send his vice-president on a tour of Asia shortly before the Democrats were to convene. Meanwhile, with his advisers, Roosevelt considered potential replacements. He thought highly of James F. Byrnes, a former senator from South Carolina who had been named to the Supreme Court but left to accept a key post with the administration as a virtual "assistant president" for domestic affairs. But Byrnes was a conservative who lacked labor support, and a Catholic who had converted to the Episcopal church, and thus he would not be well received by many voters in major Northern states. Roosevelt also liked Supreme Court Justice William O. Douglas, but Douglas had little organization support.

At a White House dinner with Democratic leaders in July, the issue was resolved. Even Hannegan's original premise had been more anti-Wallace than pro-Truman, but as the alternatives were considered one by one, Truman emerged as the most viable choice for the vice-presidency. At sixty he was not too old. He had long been active in the party and was well respected in the Senate. His fiscal sanity appealed to conservatives while his close ties to labor, farmers, and minorities made him at least acceptable to liberals. The last thing Roosevelt desired was a recurrence of the 1940 convention debacle. Despite efforts to discourage them, Wallace and Byrnes went to the Democratic National Convention, again in Chicago, convinced they might still be in the running, as did Alben Barkley. Byrnes and Barkley both asked Truman to nominate them. Byrnes asked first, and Truman agreed not only to do so but to try to help bring others to his cause.

It is generally believed that a weary, weakened Roosevelt,

preoccupied with his wartime responsibilities, was agreeable to any candidate approved by the party leaders who would not do the ticket serious harm. Roosevelt is even reputed to have said, "I hardly know Truman." But shortly before his death Hopkins confided to the writer Robert Sherwood that the president had long had his eye on Truman, particularly as someone who could help secure Senate ratification for the peace treaties.

Although Truman went to Chicago intent on helping Byrnes, as described by Truman biographer Richard Lawrence Miller, "Every time he went on a mission for Byrnes, he came away with another endorsement for Truman." The leaders of many delegations already had received the word. In his letters at the time and in his subsequent accounts, Truman claims he didn't want the vice-presidential nomination and did nothing to obtain it, but he had never firmly denied that he would accept it. When Hannegan finally asked Truman to his hotel room to hear the actual voice of the president calling from San Diego and asking, "Bob, have you got that fellow lined up yet?" Truman is reported to have replied, "Why the hell didn't he tell me in the first place?" With the galleries packed by Wallace supporters, it still took some maneuvering by Hannegan and his associates to exercise their control of the convention's machinery and secure Truman's nomination. The whole protracted exercise may seem a characteristic contrast between Roosevelt's deviousness and Truman's straightforward behavior, but as Barkley later remarked to Truman, "You may not have sought this office you have held, but whenever they were out looking for you, you were riding mighty slow."

At an August meeting, one of only three between the convention and the inauguration, Truman lunched with the president behind the White House under a great tree that had been planted by Andrew Jackson. Roosevelt made a rare reference to his mortality. Telling Truman that he would have to do the bulk of the campaigning, Roosevelt urged him not to fly because "one of us has got to stay alive." Thus began Truman's first campaign by train. After lunch Truman told the press that Roosevelt looked robust, was as fully in charge as ever, and had eaten heartily. In fact Truman was appalled by the president's appearance and his trembling hands, but he set out dutifully to reelect the man upon whom "the future of the peace and prosperity of the world depends." He traveled some 7,500 miles across the nation and made fifty-four speeches, but his efforts were overshadowed by Roosevelt's late forays into the campaign and by news from the battlefronts. It was Truman's easiest but also his least satisfying race, as a surrogate talking to modest crowds. In October Roosevelt had himself driven in an open car for 50 miles in the rain throughout the five boroughs of New York City to dispel rumors about his health. A month before, he had made his most memorable address of the campaign at a Teamsters dinner, whimsically scolding the Republicans for attacking even his "little dog Fala."

That address particularly galled Dewey. In a forceful response in Oklahoma City that galvanized his supporters, Dewey attacked the president for his unseemly levity. He accused the administration of having been woefully unprepared for war, quoting not only military leaders but Senator Harry Truman. Roosevelt was indeed indispensable, Dewey went on, but only to party hacks, bureaucrats, Communists, and others of his "motley crew." Previewing their role four years later, virtually the only Republicans who didn't like the speech were Dewey's wife and his closest advisers, who preferred a more statesmanlike stance. This Dewey had tried to effect in ways that would also foreshadow his campaign in 1948. He met with Secretary of State Hull to work out a "bipartisan" (Hull preferred the term "nonpartisan") agreement to take any debate about the role of the United Nations out of the campaign. In the interest of national security, Dewey also reluctantly yielded to a personal plea from Army Chief of Staff Marshall not to reveal that broken Japanese codes had informed the administration in 1941 that war was imminent in the Pacific.

The final Gallup poll before the 1944 election gave Roosevelt a lead of only 51 to 49 percent, with some 3.5 million service personnel an imponderable. As it turned out, Roosevelt won 53.39 to 45.89 percent, with a majority in the electoral college of 432 to 99. Dewey, however, won twelve states, two more than Willkie had in 1940, primarily in the Midwest, and came close in a number of major industrial states as well. Despite positive signs for the future of the GOP, there is no doubt that Roosevelt could have won just as readily with Wallace as with Truman. To try to make it up to his former vice-president, Roosevelt nominated him to be secretary of commerce. The president also tried to mend fences by being especially solicitous of Byrnes. To his new vice-president, Harry Truman, Roosevelt confided little. Two days after the inauguration he was on his way to Yalta to meet for the final time with Winston Churchill and Joseph Stalin. Roosevelt lived only another eighty days.

CHAPTER II

🏳

The Toughest Job
in the World

Following a massive cerebral hemorrhage, Franklin Roosevelt died in Warm Springs, Georgia, on April 12, 1945. His death stunned the nation but could scarcely have surprised Harry Truman. The immense responsibilities he had now to assume were made even more daunting by his utter lack of preparation. Since the inauguration Truman had rarely seen Roosevelt, let alone been privy to his thoughts. It is ironic that when Roosevelt finally had a vice-president who was both as popular in Congress as Garner and as supportive of the administration as Wallace, the president was too weakened and preoccupied to make use of Truman's talents.

Only hours after his hasty swearing in at the White House, Truman assured the nation that he would continue his predecessor's policies—but precisely what were they? Obviously the forceful prosecution of the war against both the Nazis and Imperial Japan came first. Here Truman could rely on the counsel of men like Stimson, Marshall, and Joint Chiefs Chairman Admiral William D. Leahy. Planning for peace was the next priority. Truman announced that the conference in San Francisco to establish what was initially called the United Nations Organization would start as scheduled on April 25. At his first cabinet meeting as president, Truman asked everyone to help him by staying on. After the session Stimson revealed to Truman that "the greatest thing in the world" his senatorial investigating committee had been warned away from was in fact the atomic bomb. Later Byrnes and scientist Vannevar Bush gave their new chief executive more thorough details of how it was intended to work.

Inevitably, as Truman found his way, trying to discern Roosevelt's intentions and adding his own imprint on the office, long-serving cabinet members departed one by one. In less than a year, of those Truman had inherited, only Wallace at Commerce and Secretary of the Navy James Forrestal remained. After the San Francisco conference, Truman replaced holdover Secretary of State Edward Stettinius (who had succeeded Hull in 1944) with Byrnes. Not surprisingly, Truman's personal staff included comfortable cronies, many from Missouri. As cabinet positions opened, a primary consideration was also compatibility with the president. Rather than New Deal ideologues, Truman favored people who were loyal to the Democratic party—hardworking, efficient, pragmatic men like himself, preferably with practical political experience. Many came from the West, with inclinations that were often more conservative than liberal. Some of the more consistently progressive members of the Truman administration began meeting informally on Monday evenings to discuss ways to counter what they viewed as the potentially excessive influence of conservative cabinet members.

IN foreign policy, however, the new president came to rely more on seasoned, nonpolitical professionals, including even some "striped-pants boys" from the State Department, many with Wall Street and Eastern Establishment backgrounds. Truman might complain about them in private, but diplomatic strategy—especially vis-à-vis the Soviet Union—was too important to be entrusted to amateurs. Advice in Washington was not in short supply. Leahy, Forrestal, and many in the State and War departments urged Truman to take a firm line against Soviet expansionism and subversion. Others whom Truman respected, such as former Ambassador to the Soviet Union Joseph E. Davies, urged a policy of conciliation. The president would miss the counsel of Henry Stimson, who in September 1945 finally left government service.

Evaluating all the apparent alternatives, Truman resolved to follow the advice of his experienced ambassador to Moscow, W. Averell Harriman, who urged "a firm but friendly" course toward the Soviets. Initially Truman's implementation seemed more firm than friendly. He abruptly cut off Lend-Lease aid to the USSR, tabled the Soviets' request for a massive loan, and rudely upbraided Soviet Foreign Minister V. M. Molotov when he visited the White House on his way to San Francisco. But Truman also sent Roosevelt's ailing confidant Harry Hopkins on a personal mission to Moscow to assure Stalin of the new president's desire to continue amicable and cooperative relations.

Before he died, Roosevelt had expressed his disappointment and dismay with the Soviets' failure to abide by the agreements reached at Yalta, particularly in regard to the future of Poland. With Russian troops in place throughout Eastern and Central Europe, competing "spheres of influence" might be the only viable arrangement the Western powers could manage, at least until the United Nations developed into the international arbiter that Roosevelt had envisioned. To Winston Churchill, however, the shape of the postwar world was still in question, and there were ominous portents; it was crucial that Stalin be confronted as soon as possible. Churchill urged Truman to consider a "summit" meeting of the sort he, Roosevelt, and Stalin had held in the past. Although immersed in establishing his own administration, after the Germans surrendered on May 7, 1945, Truman agreed. A meeting of the "Big Three" was set for July in the Berlin suburb of Potsdam.

When Truman met Stalin at Potsdam he judged him to be a "straightforward" and skillful negotiator but respectful only of strength. Informed during the conference of the successful testing of the atomic bomb, Truman thereupon told Stalin about a "very powerful" new explosive device that might end the war. The Soviet leader feigned limited comprehension of its immense importance. Churchill pressed Stalin about the curtain of secrecy that had descended over the nations within the orbit of his control, but Churchill was obliged to return to Great Britain for national elections between sessions of the conference. When his Conservative party was soundly defeated, it fell to the new Labour prime minister, Clement Attlee, to assume leadership of the British delegation at Potsdam. At the conclusion of this final wartime summit, of the original Big Three only Stalin remained in power.

On his voyage back to the United States, Truman was informed that, following his approval, the first atomic bomb had been dropped on the Japanese city of Hiroshima. Three days later a second bomb fell on Nagasaki. Soviet entry into the Japanese war, initiated as agreed at Potsdam, was now more a potential threat to American interests than a necessity. The Japanese surrendered unconditionally on August 14, 1945. World War II was over, only to be replaced by a protracted "cold war" that would last seven times as long. Relations with the Soviet Union, generally viewed as the center of worldwide monolithic communism, would dominate the entire period of the Truman administration.

At the outset of his presidency Truman had hoped that, following equitable peace settlements, he would make his mark as a domestic president. In September 1945, nearly five months after he took office, he presented the first of what would become his

annual manifestos to Congress, a lengthy combination of reconversion plans with an agenda of twenty-one domestic proposals.
It encompassed long- and short-range goals: the extension of government economic controls, a permanent Fair Employment Practices Committee, farm price supports, an increase in the
minimum wage, federal aid to housing, unemployment insurance,
and public works. Truman biographer Donald R. McCoy characterizes it as "a party platform, inaugural address, and State of the
Union message all in one package." Most of all, Truman hoped to
avert a postwar recession of the sort that had proven so costly to
people like himself after World War I. He urged that government
and private industry continue their wartime partnership to perpet-
uate full production and full employment. With a Congress no
more liberal than those that had stalled the New Deal since 1938,
Truman's comprehensive program enjoyed little likelihood of enactment. As House minority leader Joseph Martin pointed out, it
was simply too much to absorb—"Not even President Roosevelt
ever asked for as much at one sitting." Truman's address, however, at least for a time certified his progressive credentials and
was generally well received by the press and public. In both domestic and foreign relations, this earnest new president seemed to
know what he wanted to do.

In every way but their abiding interest in politics, Truman
could scarcely have been more different from his patrician predecessor. He didn't look or act or sound remotely like Franklin Roosevelt. Yet in his plain speech, with his awkward gestures and
unfamiliar Missouri twang, Truman seemed accessible, a man of
the people thrust into the toughest job in the world. Perhaps it
represented an amalgam of hope and necessity, but Truman's
Gallup poll approval ratings between his ascension to the presidency and November 1945 ranged between 82 and 87 percent. He
would never approach such a level of popularity again.

Secretary of State Byrnes, who preferred working as something of a lone wolf, persisted in trying to reach agreement with the Soviet Union on the foreign ministers' level. He had his hands full with a growing number of trouble spots, beyond continuing Russian intransigence over what was becoming a string of satellite states throughout Eastern Europe. The Soviets pressured Turkey and Iran, while the Communist government in Yugoslavia pressed its claims for the port of Trieste on the Adriatic. Acting for Stalin, Molotov rejected the international control of atomic energy and demanded a role in Asia and the occupation of Japan. A Communist insurgency threatened Greece. Major Communist parties in Western Europe, particularly in Italy and France, were a source of growing concern.

IN 1946, however, the nation still looked inward. The Pacific war had ended more quickly than anticipated. No comprehensive plan was in place for conversion to peacetime conditions. Yet millions of demobilized servicemen were returning home, anxious to pursue their deferred share of the American dream. By mid-1946 the Truman administration was plagued by domestic problems, some beyond its power to control. Pent-up demand for consumer products, inflation, a severe housing shortage, rumblings of government mismanagement and corruption, the threat of internal subversion, a seeming inability to deal with labor unrest—all were reflected in plummeting confidence in the president. Worst of all, Truman's response seemed inconsistent and uncertain, with policies that confused even his associates. Perhaps the job really was too big for this "accidental" president, well intentioned but overmatched.

The personal qualities of candor and common sense that in 1945 had seemed so refreshing now looked more like bluntness and blundering. Truman preached collective bargaining, for example, but when union unrest was translated into action, the president seized petroleum plants and threatened to draft railway strikers into the army. Settling the steel strike led to higher costs for everyone. Labor strife was matched by rural unrest. Demanding the dismantling of controls, farmers withheld commodities from the marketplace. Consumers, who wanted both low prices and abundance, received neither. In the face of shortages of meat, butter, and other staples, a black market flourished. Truman's confusing stop-and-go policies, culminating in mid-October 1946 with the removal of price controls on meat, came too late to satisfy anyone. High-priced scarcity was no recipe for electoral success. With congressional elections in the offing, Truman's Gallup poll approval ratings had dropped more than sixty percentage points in one year, to 32 percent (with 53 percent disapproving of his handling of the presidency and 15 percent having "no opinion"). Although a man of the Senate, Truman had not even been effective in his relations with a Democratic-controlled Congress, either bypassing its leadership or showing uncommon truculence.

The GOP took advantage of the national mood with an effective slogan in the off-year elections: "Had enough? Vote Republican." Even Truman's old friend, Democratic party chairman Bob Hannegan, prevailed on the president to take no part in the 1946 campaign, vetoing an election-eve broadcast to get out the vote. It was a humiliating rebuff, especially to a chief executive so keen on campaigning. In their rallies, Democratic congressional candidates preferred using the recorded voice of Franklin Roosevelt to sharing the stage with a live Harry Truman. In a light turnout of only 37.1 percent, Republicans gained control of both houses of Congress for the first time since 1928, a fifty-eight-vote edge in the House and a six-vote margin in the Senate. New Republican senators included Joseph R. McCarthy from Wisconsin, John W. Bricker from Ohio, Irving M. Ives from New York, George W. Malone from Nevada, Arthur V. Watkins from Utah, and John J.

Williams from Delaware. Except for Ives, all represented the most conservative wing of the GOP.

Even some Democrats had "had enough." The well-regarded senator from Arkansas, J. William Fulbright (later called "Half-bright" by Truman), suggested that the president name internationalist Republican Senator Arthur H. Vandenberg secretary of state and then resign for the good of the country. Vandenberg would become chief executive and preside over a unified government until the 1948 elections. Despite the hopeful tone of Truman's rhetoric since the start of his presidency, liberals and labor leaders were distressed over the results of the 1946 elections. Their hard-won gains were by no means secure. With a weakened and unreliable presence in the White House and severely diminished representation in both houses of Congress, expectations of future reform measures were equally in doubt. Liberal groups might be best advised to exert their reduced influence through their own institutions, perhaps via a unified progressive voice.

SHOULD that voice also encompass the formation of a new political party? At the outset of his presidency, Franklin Roosevelt had predicted that by its conclusion there might no longer be a Democratic party, but there would surely be a progressive one. (He had first enunciated realignment in 1919.) When, despite his landslide victory in 1936, Roosevelt's attempts in 1938 to purge Democratic conservatives failed, he continued at least to muse about realignment. His earlier triumphs had been enacted and supported by a political configuration as disparate as any in American history, but that was during a period of unprecedented economic emergency. Whether or not the New Deal could be extended in more normal times, it seemed to make sense to bring liberals together either within the Democratic party or through a new progressive entity, and let conservatives settle within the Republican party. FDR reasoned that even with the loss of the solid Democratic South (unless it could be liberalized), reform measures would nonetheless command a majority of the electorate.

The premise of political realignment, in existing or new parties, had long been shared by others, both in and out of government. In 1934 the La Follette brothers had resurrected their father's Progressive party in Wisconsin, intending its eventual evolution to national status. Their hopes were dashed by Robert La Follette, Jr.'s 1946 loss to McCarthy. Walter Reuther of the United Auto Workers was one of many labor leaders who envisioned an authentic Progressive party finally uniting urban, rural, and sectional interests, a challenge that had impeded such earlier efforts as the Populists. Even before the off-year elections of 1946, Reuther was joined by a wide variety of anti-Communist liberals, ranging from philosopher John Dewey to Socialist party leader Norman Thomas, in calling for the formation of a National Educational Committee for a New Party. Their thinking was long range, but other concerns were immediate. Wallace biographer Norman D. Markowitz notes that the conference of progressives who met in Chicago in mid-1946 not only reaffirmed their commitment to an economic bill of rights but promoted "the election of a progressive Congress in the fall." When such efforts failed, their emphasis shifted to trying to strengthen the Democratic commitment to their causes. Expectations of a new party receded further into the future. Yet these progressives were also discouraged with the president—and looking for alternatives. That both the bulk of the American left and the labor union movement would finally come to support Truman in 1948 could not have been foreseen in 1946. That both continued to work with the Democratic party was predicated on a fear they shared: Communist subversion.

The influence of American Communists in labor unions and their success in infiltrating the federal government were immeasurably out of proportion to their numbers. Their influence in the overall liberal establishment was far less significant than the concern it engendered. The left in the United States had never developed along such radical lines as in Western Europe. By the 1930s the staunchly anti-Communist Socialist party (of which the youthful Reuther and his brothers had once been members) was embodied in the increasingly respectable personage of Thomas, its perennial presidential candidate. He ran symbolically for the office six times, most successfully (2.2 percent of the vote) in 1932, the last occasion in 1948. The most forceful manifestation of the American left had been in the efforts of such early unions as the Knights of Labor and the Industrial Workers of the World (IWW). They had attempted to organize American workers irrespective of their skills, gender, or race. The major union that survived, however, was the more conservative American Federation of Labor (AFL), organized in 1886 as an association of "craft" unions—skilled workers such as carpenters and plumbers, not the toiling masses.

With the increasing industrialization of the United States in the twentieth century, union leaders such as John L. Lewis of the United Mine Workers pressured the AFL to organize semiskilled and unskilled workers. These efforts culminated in 1935 with the formation of the Congress of Industrial Organizations (CIO) and in its separation from the AFL three years later. By its nature the AFL was not a likely target for Communist infiltration. The CIO, with its millions of auto workers, steel workers, and textile workers, clearly was.

The rise of fascism in Europe coincided with the growth of the CIO in the United States. Years of struggle amidst the depression had turned American labor leftward. The Moscow-directed Comintern (which coordinated the policies of Communist parties in many countries) encouraged a "popular front" against fascist expansionism throughout the 1930s, but Communist-line leaders in the CIO focused on service to their own locals and to social justice and civil rights. Party-liner Lee Pressman became the CIO's chief counsel. Harry Bridges headed its International Longshoreman's and Warehouseman's Union; Donald Henderson ran the Food, Tobacco, Agricultural, and Allied Workers; "Red" Mike Quill led the Transport Workers Union; Joseph Curran led the National Maritime Union. In the United Electrical, Radio, and Machine Workers Union, known Communists held two of the top three positions. They were also active in the United Auto Workers (UAW) and, most significantly, at CIO headquarters.

The Communist Party/USA (CPUSA) never officially recovered from the massive defections resulting from Soviet purges in the thirties and the ignominious end of the first popular front in 1939 with the signing of the Nazi-Soviet Pact. But party members within the CIO intensified their local emphasis. Their skill at organizing impressed Philip Murray, the soft-spoken former Steelworkers leader who in 1940 succeeded Lewis as CIO president. Murray was convinced he could work with anyone who shared his goals of labor solidarity and growth, curbing their influence if it conflicted with union objectives. Throughout the 1940s UAW president Walter Reuther and CIO secretary-treasurer James Carey warned Murray that Communist influence in individual unions was only in the developmental stage, that their long-range goal was to take over the American labor movement. Sowing dissension within the CIO's councils would likely be the next step, making it more difficult to arrive at union policy, let alone carry it out. Whenever the Moscow line changed, so would the positions of its adherents in the CIO. Political events had already borne this out.

Although not affiliated with the Democratic party, the CIO generally supported its candidates. In 1936 every component union under the CIO umbrella had officially endorsed President Roosevelt for reelection. An immense CIO effort helped get out the vote, and unions replaced business interests as the major source of Democratic funding. But by 1940, when Lewis was eased out as the CIO's president largely because of his bellicose support for the Republican Willkie, a shift in CIO policy had already occurred. There was neither endorsement nor funds for Roosevelt. This was not because of concern over the president's unprecedented bid for a third term but because the Communist line had shifted so abruptly in 1939, making agreement on industrial labor's political endorsements impossible. FDR was now characterized as a stooge for British imperialism in a European war that was of no concern to the working class. CIO leaders who supported Roosevelt did so as individuals.

Reuther and Carey vigorously opposed this turn, but the issue was submerged as events in 1941 made both the United States and the Soviet Union allies of the former British "imperialists." The issue of Communist influence in the house of labor went into mothballs for the duration of the war. In 1943 the CIO founded a Political Action Committee (PAC) under the aggressive leadership of Sidney Hillman. Although officially nonpartisan, it worked closely with Democratic candidates and even a few liberal Republicans with no opposition from Communist sympathizers. Only a year after the end of the war, however, left-leaning CIO activists proposed turning the PAC into a more independent operation, perhaps the forerunner of a new progressive political party.

By 1946 another "popular front" was being formed, directed this time against a new form of "imperialism"—the cold war containment of the Soviet Union being pursued by President Truman. As the call went out to mobilize all "peace-loving" peoples in this effort, the leadership of the CPUSA changed as swiftly as its stance. Genial president Earl Browder was symbolically liquidated in favor of hard-liner William Z. Foster. Discord within the CIO escalated. A number of labor leaders formed their own committee to expose and expel Communists. Philip Murray, however, was still not quite ready to accept the militantly anti-Communist position urged on him by so many associates and growing within the nation as a whole. He supported such Truman initiatives as the Marshall Plan in 1947 more to encourage European recovery, including its trade-union movement, than to combat the Soviets. What led Murray to as fervent an anticommunism as that espoused by the AFL's William Green and George Meany was triggered not so much by internal CIO pressure as by the impact of the 1948 national candidacy of a friend of labor. It was not Harry Truman but Henry Wallace.

Wallace was also in the minds of the founders of both advocacy organizations that competed for the political legacy of Franklin Roosevelt. The resurgence of the Republican right had helped initiate activity along the whole spectrum of the American left. On December 29, 1946, several smaller organizations merged to form the Progressive Citizens of America (PCA). More than three hundred delegates from twenty-one states attended its convention's opening sessions. PCA founders included many intellectuals and entertainers, such prominent black leaders as Walter White of the NAACP and A. Philip Randolph of the AFL's Brotherhood of Sleeping Car Porters, and Philip Murray and Jack Kroll of the CIO. They heard Henry Wallace's keynote address, outlining a "program for political action" and warning against "lukewarm liberals" who would divide and diminish the progressive movement. Calvin B. "Beanie" Baldwin, a Wallace associate, stressed that the American left should not be defined by its enemies. No one would be arbitrarily read out of the PCA, even if they sympathized with objectives of the Soviet Union that were deemed compatible with American liberalism.

The following week the Americans for Democratic Action (ADA) was established, with the blessing of Eleanor Roosevelt and her son Franklin Jr. When Baldwin approached Mrs. Roosevelt to talk of cooperation between the two groups, he was rebuffed. The ADA would preclude anyone with Communist leanings. There would be no unified progressive voice.

The dominant ADA derived not from free-market liberalism but from the Socialist Party of the United States. In 1941 a number of Socialists had broken with the isolationism espoused by Norman Thomas to proclaim their support for forceful opposition to fascist aggression. The group they founded, the Union for Democratic Action, six years later was resurrected as a nonsocialist organization, the ADA, equally opposed to totalitarianism of the left. As James Loeb, Jr., executive director of both organizations, wrote to *The New Republic,* the ADA proclaimed "a declaration of independence from the stifling and paralyzing influence of the Communists and their apologists in America."

The liberal mainstream coalesced into the ADA. Its four hundred founders included most New Dealers who were still active, influential journalists, and such promising young Democrats as Hubert H. Humphrey of Minnesota. Murray attended its initial meeting as an observer, but other leaders from both the CIO and the AFL joined in launching the enterprise. Eventually the most prominent spokesmen of labor and the black organizations who had helped found the PCA, including Murray, White, and Randolph, switched their support to the ADA.

Even before the 1946 congressional elections, the Communist and non-Communist left were being lumped together by such politicians as Martin Dies, the Texas Democrat who chaired the House Committee to Investigate Un-American Activities (HUAC). During his 1946 congressional campaign in California, Richard Nixon accused his opponent Jerry Voorhis of following "the PAC line." To many conservative candidates, radical labor and liberals were indistinguishable from Communists. The historian and political activist Arthur M. Schlesinger, Jr., declared it intolerable that the legitimate, patriotic American left should abdicate the struggle against communism to such rabble-rousers as Dies. The ADA would restore Democratic "nerve," vindicate authentic liberalism, and try to bring the New Deal back to life, "unblemished by foreign ideologies and sympathies." As Murray was to learn in the CIO, the CPUSA, despite its modest size, was a tightly disciplined organization whose members, in the words of Schlesinger, would sacrifice anyone "with fanatical zeal to promote the aims of Russia." The ADA would contest the PCA with all its resources. Eventually President Truman, so scorned by disheartened liberals after the 1946 elections, would be the beneficiary of this ideological struggle.

DESPITE Democratic losses in the 1946 elections, Truman seemed energized. His fortunes improved, and the next two years became the most productive of his presidency. For one thing, the pervasive dissatisfaction of 1946 masked a fundamental economic fact, only later apparent: there was no postwar recession. Truman's Employment Act of 1946 was enacted out of fear that only government intervention could assure economic growth. As it turned out, industry required little incentive to convert swiftly to the production of consumer goods. The GI Bill's provisions, whether in education, low-cost loans, or unemployment benefits, immensely reduced the number of veterans seeking immediate employment. New businesses increased investment in the economy. As productivity grew, real wages, consumer credit, and farm income also rose. Unemployment was negligible, some 2 million versus 58 million who held jobs. In 1947 inflation and labor unrest declined. Food was plentiful and cheaper, and the production of consumer products—from appliances to automobiles—began to catch up with demand.

This upturn in economic conditions, not entirely the province of either party, encouraged Truman to take a more conciliatory approach to the new Republican Congress. He trimmed budget requests, terminated his emergency powers, and cooperated in such areas as public housing with the proposals of Republican Senator Taft. Although both the president and Congress wanted a balanced budget, the legislators preferred that it be balanced at a level low enough to justify tax cuts. Truman vetoed two such proposals, and his vetoes were sustained, but a third veto was overridden, with no apparent harm to the economy. In a forceful confrontation with John L. Lewis, who still headed the now independent United Mine Workers, Truman triumphed, averting a coal shortage and winning general acclaim. By mid-March 1947, Truman's public approval rating was back up to 60 percent.

But few of Truman's domestic proposals emerged from Congress whole. The administration's 1947 appropriations bill was extensively cut, including requests for the school lunch program, conservation projects, rural electrification, and farm ownership loans. The housing act that Truman reluctantly signed was less a public housing and redevelopment measure than one filled with such secondary concerns as FHA loan liberalization, rates for down payments, and eligibility requirements. Truman asked in his ten-point anti-inflation program for highly selective controls on wages, prices, and rationing, hardly the equivalent of wartime powers, but Congress made no substantive response to his requests.

On the other hand, efforts by the Republican-controlled 80th Congress to repeal or roll back aspects of the New Deal—a prospect most feared by liberals—ran into what the political scientist David Plotke defines as the "Democratic political order." Government-sponsored forces built up in the 1930s were so strong by the end of the 1940s that much of the New Deal had be-

come institutionalized. The absence of a postwar recession perpetuated it, and even the efforts of a more conservative Congress
could not materially destabilize it.

The two most notable achievements of the Republican Congress bear out Plotke's premise. Cutbacks in Social Security, re-
moving 750,000 people from the rolls, affected largely such
self-employed categories as newspaper vendors, and were balanced by increased benefits to others. The Labor-Management
Relations Act of 1947, popularly known as the Taft-Hartley Act,
reflected what most legislators in *both* parties viewed as a more
realistic balance between labor and management than the earlier
Wagner Act and other New Deal measures enacted under different circumstances. Although Truman called Taft-Hartley unwork-
able and unfair, vetoed it on June 20, 1947, and denounced it
throughout the 1948 campaign as a "slave labor" measure, the
president privately admitted that it was "a pretty good law." He
would use its injunction provisions many times. His veto of Taft-
Hartley was overridden without debate by the House, 331 to 83
(with 106 Democrats voting in the majority), and in the Senate,
68 to 25 (with 20 Democrats voting to override).

Unions that throughout the war had cooperated with government in accepting controls on wages and working conditions understandably grew restive in the immediate postwar years. There
were more strikes in 1946 than in 1936. Taft-Hartley outlawed
"closed shops," protected the rights of workers to decide whether
or not to join unions, and promoted collective bargaining, mediation, and cooling-off periods to prevent strikes from threatening
national security. In labor-management disputes, the federal government, much as Truman himself believed, would serve as an
impartial arbiter. Reflecting the times, Taft-Hartley obliged union
leaders to sign non-Communist affidavits and forbade certifica-
tion as a bargaining agent of any union having an officer who was
a member of the CPUSA. Taft-Hartley provided neither all that

industry had desired nor broke the power of the union movement, as would be demonstrated in the campaign of 1948, but Truman made it a major issue.

INTIMATIONS of the cold war to come were evident to many observers, even in 1945. The essence of a policy of "containment" of the Soviet Union was presented to Truman before the word itself became generally used. General "Wild Bill" Donovan of the Office of Strategic Services, forerunner of the Central Intelligence Agency (CIA), confirmed in a memo (to FDR) Truman's own conclusion that Stalin was not prepared to bargain in good faith. Soviet expansionism, Donovan wrote, needed to be countered by a policy of patient firmness until the Soviet system evolved into a more benign configuration. The president was on the platform in Westminster, Missouri, in 1946 when Churchill declared that an "iron curtain" had descended from the Baltic to the Adriatic, behind which the Soviets were working their will. There were to be few free elections or long-lived coalition governments in Eastern Europe. In May 1947 non-Communists were ousted from the Hungarian government.

That Truman's administration coincided with the dawn of the atomic age may have made inevitable the president's thinking in global terms, but initially he sought ways to limit direct American involvement in other nations' problems. Believing as firmly as the Republicans in balanced budgets, Truman presided over a rapid demobilization of American armed forces. Republican internationalists, however, had growing concerns about totalitarian expansion around the entire Eurasian rim. Senator Arthur Vandenberg questioned, "What are the Soviets up to?" When Byrnes appeared to favor a more conciliatory approach toward the USSR, Truman exploded, "I'm tired of babying the Soviets!" In a Moscow address on February 9, 1946, Stalin seemed to confirm

Western fears. Echoing the premise of containment from the other side, Stalin stressed the Marxist-Leninist premise that competitive capitalism contained the seeds of its own destruction.

One American reaction came in the form of a "long telegram" sent to his superiors and later distributed throughout the administration by the diplomat George Kennan. Experienced in following the convoluted threads of Russian history, Kennan had been placed in charge of the Moscow embassy when Harriman returned to Washington to counsel Truman. Kennan warned that the USSR still feared encirclement, viewed relationships with the Western democracies as confrontational, and had taken this "neurotic" view of the world to dangerous levels. He concluded that, however sincere the desire for peaceful coexistence, logical agreements of mutual self-interest were impossible with such an implacable opponent. Accordingly the West, and particularly the United States, had to strengthen the unity of its own society and contain the worldwide threat of Communist expansion at the most advantageous places and times, ultimately outlasting the Soviet regime without a new world war. In time communism would collapse or evolve into a more pragmatic entity. Kennan expanded his premise in an anonymous article in *Foreign Affairs*. His words had an influence in Washington transcending his own stature, because they so coherently reinforced the conclusions that many in the State and War departments had urged on the president.

Truman did not start the cold war, but by 1947 he viewed the world much as Kennan pictured it. Initially the president's version of containment was more economic than military. Spreading American bounty and its values were thought to be the best antidote to the appeal of communism. In January Truman replaced Byrnes, with whom his relationship had been less congenial since the confusion over the vice-presidency in 1944, naming George Marshall as new secretary of state. A model of rectitude, Marshall was the contemporary American Truman most admired. Viewed as above politics, Marshall would also be a forceful advocate with Congress.

When the British informed Washington that they were so weakened after six years of war that they could no longer provide aid to Greece and Turkey, Marshall and Undersecretary Dean Acheson persuaded Truman to convene a special meeting of congressional leaders at the White House. Acheson argued that should Soviet pressure on the two nations result in domination, it might lead to further widespread incursions and change the world's balance of power. This early exposition of the "domino theory" had its effect. Aided by the support of influential Republicans such as Vandenberg and an address by Truman to a special joint session, Congress voted on May 15 for $400 million in aid to Greece and Turkey. Bipartisanship worked in foreign policy when a sense of emergency could be established, as it never would in domestic policy. Although the thrust of the aid to Greece and Turkey was economic, the president also gained the right to send in U.S. advisers to train local military forces. The program became known as the Truman Doctrine.

On March 22, 1947, following the advice of a commission he had appointed after the 1946 Democratic defeats, Truman faced the question of domestic Communist subversion. By executive order he established the first loyalty program ever established by a president of the United States. Under Attorney General Tom Clark, cooperation between the administration and Congress attained a level of bipartisanship even in this sensitive area, blunting attempts to label the president as "soft" on communism. The ADA's later reservations about excesses in loyalty procedures would be sublimated in their own zeal to protect national security at all costs while forwarding their liberal agenda at home. Truman assured Philip Murray and others that civil liberties were not compromised by his program, although in fact confidential

charges compiled by the FBI against government employees were
almost impossible to refute.

In June, addressing Harvard graduates, Secretary Marshall
outlined a broader vision than the Truman Doctrine. Unless
granted American aid, he declared, European economies were
threatened with collapse. Totalitarianism thrived in an environment of want and despair. Marshall's call, inviting nations in both
Western and Eastern Europe to draw up a list of their requirements, was answered by detailed plans from sixteen countries. As
the administration had anticipated, the Soviets prevented their
satellites from participating. After extensive testimony by Marshall, a four-year investment of some $17 billion was allocated by
Congress in 1948 to assure European recovery, including that of
the western zones of Germany. Truman insisted that the "Marshall Plan" be named for his resourceful secretary of state.

Throughout 1947 and 1948 the administration forwarded
other foreign policy initiatives, laying the groundwork for alliances in Western Europe and Latin America, setting the worldwide priorities of containment, and affirming the American will
to stay in Berlin. In his 1947 State of the Union address, Truman
vowed support to any nation resisting Communist subversion.
Later in 1947 the National Security Act brought a more unified
command to the armed services under a single Department of Defense. Reciprocal trade was extended, though not for as long a period as Truman desired. The CIA was established, and in 1948 a
peacetime draft was approved.

In any evaluation of the Truman administration, its foreign
policy successes during these two years take pride of place. As he
surveyed what amounted to his first term, the president may have
been disappointed by limited domestic progress, but he must have
been encouraged by the acceptance of his foreign policy and his
high standing in the polls. Even columnists in the Republican-
dominated press praised his seemingly newfound confidence and

command. He had mastered the job in most perilous times. Had he more to prove? In 1948 Truman, though still in robust health, was older than his predecessor had lived to be. He talked of returning to Missouri to more serene forms of service. In comments reminiscent of Roosevelt's in 1940, Truman confided to Forrestal, now the nation's first secretary of defense, that only the pressure of world events could induce him to run for the presidency in 1948. Convinced that he would, Counsel to the President Clark Clifford was already drawing up plans for the campaign, based on the ideas of a canny New Dealer named James Rowe.

CHAPTER III

☙

The Campaign Takes Shape

In 1947 James H. Rowe, Jr., a Washington insider since the 1930s, was not close to Harry Truman. Rowe's law partner, Thomas Corcoran, was particularly disliked by the president. But Rowe was a devoted Democrat, and despite positive signs he was sufficiently concerned about prospects for the 1948 election to set down his thoughts in a thirty-three-page memorandum intended specifically for the president. In "The Politics of 1948," Rowe outlined a comprehensive campaign plan on the supposition that Truman would run and the probabilities that Dewey would be his Republican opponent and that Wallace would contest the presidency as a third-party candidate.

Starting with the proposition that the Democratic party remained "an unhappy alliance of Southern conservatives, Western progressives, and big city labor," Rowe projected that the continued support of these disparate constituencies would enable Truman to win even without the electoral votes of the major northeastern states. "Safely Democratic," the South had no other political home, but labor leaders must be individually courted lest their membership "stay home." The number one priority should be the winning of the West, Rowe suggested, with emphasis on

Democratic achievements in resource management. Although he proposed that the moribund machinery of the Democratic party be revitalized, Rowe observed that its leadership role had been largely supplanted by issue-driven pressure groups and ethnic blocs. Farmers were already favorably disposed toward the administration, but labor support had to be mobilized. Independent and progressive voters must be fed more idealism. Black voters now held the balance of power in populous Northern states. With Italian Americans and other predominantly Catholic voting groups, anticommunism was the major issue; with Jewish voters, support for a new state in Palestine and liberalized immigration policies.

Rowe expected international tensions to escalate in 1948, with Truman gaining political advantage by his opposition to the Kremlin's expansionist aims. But the likelihood that foreign policy would remain bipartisan in an election year seemed remote to Rowe. High prices remained the key domestic issue, for which the Republican Congress should be blamed. The appeal of both Wallace and Dewey could be negated by moving left, with bolder proposals in civil rights, housing, public works, tax reform, and the combating of inflation. Probable congressional rejection of all these proposals would provide a potent campaign issue. Rowe stressed that Truman should appear more presidential and more fully the author of both his domestic and foreign policies.

In terms of specific tactics, Truman could dramatize his role as the nation's unifying commander-in-chief by making the kinds of inspection tours of military installations and federal projects that Roosevelt had, utilizing his presidential power to generate media coverage. Such nonpolitical personages as Albert Einstein and Henry Ford II might be invited to dine at the White House. Prominent progressives should be named to government positions, shoring up liberal support. Once the actual campaign began, Dewey could be largely ignored and Wallace portrayed as a Communist dupe. Rowe proposed the immediate creation of a campaign committee for 1948, closely coordinating its efforts with the administration and the Democratic National Committee. It should begin assembling material for the platform and for Truman's speeches, and provide intelligence through private polling. Rowe concluded that "the presidential election is being determined *now* by the day-to-day events of 1947. In national politics the American people normally make up their minds irrevocably . . . by the end of July [a "law" promoted by FDR's political adviser Jim Farley, who had specified Labor Day as the limit]. If the program discussed here can be properly executed it may be of help in getting them to make up their minds *the right way.*" The memo was dated September 18, 1947.

Rowe gave a copy to his friend, Budget Director James Webb, to present to the president. Without reading it, Truman directed that it be passed to Clark Clifford, who was already gathering suggestions for the 1948 campaign. A fellow Missourian, Clifford had come to the White House as a young naval aide and risen to become counsel to the president, advising Truman in both policy and politics. Although Clifford was a leading member of the Monday night group of administration progressives, his moderate, pragmatic liberalism mirrored Truman's. In the wake of the 1946 election losses, Clifford's influence grew. Some of his associates believed, in the words of the historian Patricia Sullivan, that Clifford was "unencumbered by any strong social philosophy or political conviction." In the 1948 election the forty-one-year-old Clifford would come closest to managing Truman's campaign—though the president was really his own campaign manager. Clifford was so impressed with Rowe's reasoning that only a few weeks later, on November 19, he presented his own "Memorandum to the President" in virtually the same language. This one Truman read.

Making no mention of Rowe, Clifford's version of "The Politics of 1948" reflected his closer relationship with the president. He stressed that "the future of this country and the future of the world are linked irrevocably with [Truman's] election." Clifford added details to several areas, particularly the civil rights proposals, recommending that the president go as far as possible in this direction. Concluding with Rowe's words, Clifford added this reference to his own intended involvement in the campaign to come: "1948 will be a tough, bitterly fought struggle. The issues will be close and the ultimate determination of the winner may well depend upon the type of staff work furnished to the . . . contenders."

What was largely Rowe's memorandum neither influenced Truman's decision to run nor provided a blueprint so compelling that he chose to follow it completely. Rather, it helped to focus the president's thoughts on the election despite all the other concerns competing for his attention. Unlike many presidents, Truman did not object to lengthy communications as long as they offered a clear exposition of alternatives. A good deal of deliberation lay behind his cherished reputation for decisiveness, even in political combat.

Many of the memo's conclusions were obvious; others proved to be mistaken. As it turned out, the South could not be safely ignored; millions of voters made up their minds long after July; and bipartisanship in foreign policy would *not* be a casualty of the contest. The president took those suggestions that fit most naturally into his own campaign style, honed over a quarter-century, and adapted them to his assessment of 1948 circumstances. He discarded the grandstanding and suggestions for photo opportunities. What would be most distinctive about Truman's rhetoric in 1948 was not its idealistic appeal to progressives in either party or to independents, but its partisan stridency—more extreme than in his earlier campaigns. What most separated Truman's strategy from Dewey's, who did turn out to be his Republican opponent,

was that the normally astute Dewey took advice contrary to his
own instincts while Truman did not.

To Truman, good news was always temporary. Whatever the
favorable outlook in 1947, he was as convinced as Rowe or Clifford that the 1948 election would be closely contested. As if on
cue, Truman's cyclical public opinion ratings plunged again.
Only two months after his forceful State of the Union address in
January, Truman's Gallup poll lead of nine percentage points
over any likely Republican challenger in 1948 had reversed into
a deficit of eight points behind the most probable, Governor
Dewey. By the end of June, after Dewey had been nominated
by the Republicans, the Roper poll estimated his lead over
Truman at a whopping twenty-three points. No conceivable
"bounce" coming out of the Democratic National Convention
could make up such a deficit. Truman was not only once again an
authentic underdog, but in the words of the Republican observer
Clare Boothe Luce, apparently "a gone goose." Public approval
of Truman's performance as president was measured by Gallup in
April 1948 at only 36 percent, a drop of twenty-four points in a
year.

What is inexplicable about this decline is the lack of any compelling reason for it. There had been no dramatic dip in employment, income, gross national product, or other economic
indicators. The rate of inflation had declined, yet farmers were
prospering. The Republican-controlled Congress had managed to
make incursions, over Truman's vetoes, in some aspects of the
New Deal. But both its passage of Taft-Hartley and its reduction
of the Social Security rolls turned into Truman advantages. Taft-
Hartley triggered union opposition to the GOP, and polls indicated that the vast majority of Americans favored extending
Social Security coverage. The Communist coup in Czechoslovakia in February 1948 and the confrontation with the USSR over
Berlin in the spring tended to unify the nation behind what ap-

peared to be the firm resolve of its chief executive. What had changed so drastically between January and June?

It could only have been perception. Even in the best of times Truman understood that public confidence in him was not deeply rooted. He used men with the stature of Marshall as virtual co-sponsors of the administration's most important proposals. It took relatively little in 1948 to return popular opinion to a residue of the uncertainties of 1946. The unnecessarily abrupt removal of the last New Deal cabinet holdovers contrasted with the well-publicized excesses of some of Truman's cronies. Republicans charged that administration insiders had made a $4 million killing in the commodities market, benefiting from advance information. The president's inconsistency on Palestine, moving from support of partition to backing a temporary trusteeship, was resolved only on May 14 when Truman granted de facto recognition to the State of Israel within minutes of its declared establishment. By then the action seemed more an expression of politics than policy. In August Truman made his unfortunate "red herring" characterization of charges before the HUAC that Communist spy rings had included government officials. He insisted that such allegations were aimed at distracting public attention from the failures of the 80th Congress. Even the president's plans to build a porch on the south portico of the White House raised the ire of preservation ists. For more than three years Truman had done his best to master the world's most challenging job, for which he was neither ideally suited nor well prepared. Perhaps the nation and its accidental president had both been lucky. Perhaps it was time to turn over the reins to someone more authentically presidential. A quip ascribed to Senator Taft's wife, Martha, made the rounds: "To err is Truman."

Such an appraisal gained credence not only from his Republican opposition but from a widening spectrum in his own Democratic party. A Southern revolt was gathering steam. By the end of

1947 Henry Wallace was already in the field. The Republican national chairman exulted, "With the Moscow wing departed and the racially intolerant wing now threatening to go off in another direction, it looks like the Pendergast wing will be alone next November." Whether Truman's detractors influenced the polls or the polls influenced them, from the spring of 1948 to election day the conviction grew that, whatever else might happen, Harry Truman could not possibly win the presidency in his own right.

WHILE others questioned Truman's capacity, Henry Agard Wallace and Governor James Strom Thurmond of South Carolina were more concerned over the course the president was charting. From the Democratic left Wallace contested the very foundations of Truman's foreign policy. From the Democratic right, Thurmond protested federal intrusion into the rights of individual states. Although they represented opposing political philosophies, Wallace and Thurmond shared a similarly reluctant path to their factional candidacies in the 1948 election. Both had appealed fruitlessly for change within the councils of the national Democratic party. Both came to believe that the party, as they construed it, had abandoned them, not the other way around. When each finally turned to a separatist platform, it was not with a remote expectation of winning the presidency but of influencing the outcome of the election—and demonstrating sufficient strength to ensure that the next administration, whether Truman's or Dewey's, would heed their views.

In Wallace's case these were founded in idealistic antecedents. Both his father and grandfather had merged successful farming, preaching, and publishing into a philosophy of social consciousness and internationalism that transcended devotion to any political party. Although nominal Republicans, the Wallaces of Iowa had recommended a world organization to Woodrow Wilson and had supported Theodore Roosevelt's Bull Moose candidacy for president in 1912, Progressive Robert La Follette in 1924, and Democrat Al Smith in 1928. After young Henry came out for a victorious Franklin Roosevelt in 1932, he was named secretary of agriculture, a post his father had held for two Republican presidents in the 1920s. Not until 1936 did Wallace change his registration to Democratic. His loyalty was to a Democratic party personified by Roosevelt and the New Deal, not to big-city bosses or Southern segregationists. Should the party depart from its progressive path, it would no longer merit his support. In this sense Wallace was always an independent.

As vice-president, Wallace had made so few friends in the Senate that his nomination by Roosevelt as commerce secretary in 1945 was confirmed only with difficulty. After Roosevelt's death, the uneasy relationship between Wallace and Truman resurfaced. It was a speech that finally severed their official ties, just as Wallace's "Century of the Common Man" address in 1942 had solidified the opposition of Democratic leaders to Wallace's renomination as vice-president. And just as Roosevelt was understood to have read that address in advance, apparently President Truman both read and approved the text of the speech Wallace delivered on September 12, 1946, in New York's Madison Square Garden.

Since Truman's ascension to the presidency, Wallace had urged on him a policy of conciliation with the USSR, going the extra mile in consideration of the Soviets' justifiable concerns with secure borders. It was within the province of a commerce secretary to promote free trade, but Wallace's intrusion into foreign policy, recalling the less structured Roosevelt cabinets, antagonized many in the Truman administration. In particular, Wallace believed that the new president, inexperienced in foreign policy, had come under excessive influence by hawkish elements from Great Britain and the State Department. After more than a year of this escalating infighting, matters came to a head in Wallace's New York speech, titled "The Way to Peace." Its sponsorship by such left-wing organizations as the Independent Citizens of the Arts, Sciences, and Professions and the National Citizens Political Action Committee implied its content.

After denouncing racism and isolationism, Wallace criticized the foreign policies of both the United States and the Soviet Union. If cooperation were not always possible, he insisted, let the competition between the two systems be peaceful and open: "Let the results . . . speak for themselves." In view of Soviet realities and of Russian history, the confrontational tone taken by the administration was fraught with peril. "The tougher we get," Wallace insisted, "the tougher the Russians will get." The United States had no more business interfering in the political or economic affairs of Eastern Europe than the Soviets had telling Washington or its neighbors what to do. Senator Claude Pepper of Florida also spoke at the rally, intended to drum up support for liberal Democratic candidates in the November off-year elections. Pepper lashed out at "conservative Democrats and reactionary Republicans making our foreign policy as they are today. It is all we can do to keep foolish people from having us pull a Hitler blitzkrieg and drop our atomic bombs on the Russian people. It is not so far from 'get tough' to 'get rough.' "

In retrospect Pepper's rhetoric sounds a good deal more inflammatory than Wallace's, but the firestorm broke on Wallace. From Paris, where the Council of Foreign Ministers was meeting, Republican internationalist Senator Vandenberg noted the concern of other nations with the degree of American unity. Secretary of State Byrnes threatened to resign if Truman continued to permit Wallace to criticize the nation's foreign policy. Even liberal journals such as *The Nation* noted with dismay the contrast between Wallace's idealistic espousal of the equality of nations and the rights of man in 1942 and his coldly realistic acceptance of repressive spheres of influence in 1946. Truman faced a dilemma. He denied two days after the rally that he had approved Wallace's text, only his right to speak; but Truman admitted to his staff that he had made a "grave blunder." After a confusing exchange of letters and meetings, the president asked for and received Wallace's resignation. On September 20, 1946, Truman wrote, "I found it necessary to dispense with Henry Wallace when I found him interfering with my conduct of foreign policy." It seems rather a belated discovery. It is hard to gauge the motivations of either man in this incident, but both must have felt a sense of relief.

Wallace was now free to speak his mind, unencumbered. That he was still highly regarded by liberals within the Democratic party is evidenced by his many invitations to address pre-election rallies. Introduced by James Roosevelt in Los Angeles, Wallace declared, "I am still a Democrat." On the other hand, Truman, whose prestige was hardly enhanced by the messy Wallace affair, had been induced by party chairman Hannegan not to campaign for congressional candidates. When the results of the 1946 elections gave Republicans control of both houses of Congress, it was not Wallace who was blamed, though Democratic liberals had fallen disproportionately. Four years earlier, lesser Republican gains had provided a tool for Democratic leaders to convince FDR that Wallace was a liability. The message Wallace took out of the 1946 elections was that the Democratic party must be more consistently progressive or die, adding, "I do not expect it to die." In this he was echoing Franklin Roosevelt's sentiments from the 1930s and those of contemporary liberals and labor leaders. Truman also recognized the logic of aligning liberals in the Democratic party and conservatives in the Republican party, but he was far too much a regular Democrat to try to bring it off. The solace Truman took out of the 1946 election was that now the Republicans would have to defend their own congressional record, providing a cudgel he would forcefully wield two years later.

Only three weeks after his ouster by Truman, Wallace accepted the editorship of *The New Republic,* a liberal journal whose prestige exceeded its circulation but which provided a forum for his opinions. In 1947 he embarked on a speaking tour sponsored by the newly formed Progressive Citizens of America. While continuing to preach the liberal revitalization of the Democratic party, Wallace sounded more and more like a candidate. As the subject of a third party gained currency, the New York American Labor party's fiery congressman Vito Marcantonio considered conditions ideal "for the creation of a new party resolving the question of peace and progress on the side of the people," and looked to Wallace to lead it.

Although the line between traditional liberals and Communist sympathizers in the PCA was blurred (the *New Republic* publisher who hired Wallace had been a Communist), Wallace's own domestic proposals differed from Truman's more in degree than in substance. If Truman wanted to raise the minimum wage to 75 cents, Wallace favored $1.25. Truman saw the federal government as the overall arbiter promoting a prosperous and equitable society; Wallace saw it as the more active guarantor of such a society. The overriding issue was world peace. To Wallace, only an accommodation with the Soviet Union would release the resources necessary for social change in the United States. In the spring of 1947 Truman gave Wallace an issue with which to dramatize the differences between them.

When in March Truman asked a joint session of Congress for $400 million in economic and military aid for Greece and Turkey, this was not containment in theory but an affirmation of American will to stop Communist expansion or subversion by any means necessary. Since neither the government of Greece nor Turkey could remotely be considered democratic, and the president's request implied open-ended commitments, the high priority given the "emergency" was questioned by such budget-minded Republicans as Senator Taft and such liberal icons as Eleanor Roosevelt. Its most vigorous opponent, however, was Wallace. Through newspaper ads and a national radio broadcast the day after Truman's request, Wallace suggested that the problem lay not in Greece or Turkey but in the United States. If approved, he said, such aid would lead to unconditional requests from similarly undemocratic regimes around the world, bankrupting and militarizing the United States and ultimately leading to war. Truman's request, Wallace declared, would actually create circumstances that benefited the Communists. The United States could neither prevent change nor police the world. By May, when the Greek-Turkish aid package was enacted into law, Wallace was also attacking the president from cities throughout Western Europe.

The PCA joined with *The New Republic* in sponsoring extensive new tours for Wallace. Their primary source of funding was his American audiences, who paid from fifty cents to three dollars to hear Wallace speak. In London, asked if he would head a third party, Wallace's reply was equivocal, suggesting that Senator Pepper might be a better choice. Back in New York, Wallace repeated that any decision about defecting was not his to make, insisting, "If the Democratic Party becomes a war party, a party of reaction and depression, I'll no longer be a Democrat." In November 1947 a young pro-Wallace candidate allied with the American Labor party won a surprising two-to-one electoral victory over the regular Democratic candidate in a special congressional election in the Bronx borough of New York City, encouraging heightened visions of potential Wallace strength. The Bronx, however, was not necessarily an accurate barometer of urban America, or even of New York State.

In upstate Buffalo in December Wallace made one of those

offhand statements that caused consternation to many who might have favored his cause. He told a group of reporters that he would prefer Senator Taft to either Truman or Dewey, suggesting that despite Taft's "eighteenth century" domestic ideas, he was more likely to keep the nation out of war. The next day, in Albany, Wallace took it all back, claiming he was joking, but later he suggested that Dwight Eisenhower would be less a "war candidate" than either Dewey or Truman. Wallace's true believers, however, could forgive him almost anything. He was, as one of his biographers put it, their "modern Isaiah," whose appearances became rallies not unlike religious revivals, replete with prophesy, joyous music, and collections to help continue the cause. Wallace christened his followers a "Gideon's army," whose strength of conviction belied its size, with trumpets in one hand and illumination in the other. Unfortunately their number did not include a single prominent member of the liberal establishment. Many who admired Wallace personally, and were less than enthusiastic about Truman, came out against the formation of a third party. The only esteemed New Dealer who initially supported Wallace was Rexford Guy Tugwell. The ADA, already far more powerful than its rival PCA, opposed Wallace with a fervor impelled by the affirmation that liberals were no less patriotic than other Americans.

By the close of 1947 Wallace felt he had run out of alternatives: someone had to carry the banner of peace and justice. In December he met in Chicago with the directors of the PCA, which characteristically he had not yet bothered to join. The Truman Doctrine, the Marshall Plan (which at first Wallace had welcomed), and Truman's support of universal military training had apparently sealed Wallace's decision. Despite the reservations of most of his old friends and his family, and little evidence of support beyond fringe groups such as the PCA, Wallace, in the words of Truman biographer Robert Donovan, "allowed himself to be carried along by his temperament, emotions and convictions."

The PCA transformed itself into the Progressive party, in whose name Wallace declared, in a nationwide radio address on December 12, "I shall run in 1948." Rowe had predicted it only three months before. Wallace did not officially accept the presidential nomination of the Progressive party until its national convention in Philadelphia the following July, but by then he had been actively campaigning and the party had been petitioning for space on state ballots for more than six months. They succeeded in forty-five of the forty-eight states. Wallace's initial goal was ten million votes. As always, he would go direct to the people.

One group that had urged Wallace to run was the Communist sympathizers in the CIO, though they did so in their own names. Only a few small unions and affiliates actually endorsed Wallace. Polls indicate that no more than 10 percent of the CIO rank and file ever favored Wallace, no more than 3.5 percent voted for him, and more than half the membership viewed his campaign as Communist-dominated. Norman Markowitz observes that Wallace was never able "to develop the organized liberal-labor support necessary for any successful third-party venture." Three months into the unofficial Wallace campaign, the ADA issued an appraisal of it. Supported by Murray and White, the ADA report noted that Wallace had done next to nothing in his earlier official capacities to help labor or black Americans, and now he proposed to destroy the Marshall Plan, whose aid would help European socialists and trade-unionists. A CIO/PAC radio spot added, "We see a strange combination of the Communist-dominated third party teamed up with notorious reactionaries, with the single purpose of defeating any semblance of real liberal government."

While striving to launch a party, not merely a protest, Wallace's crusade always carried an air of impermanence about it. He repeatedly expressed his willingness to step aside if either of the major parties were to adopt his views, and some evidence suggests that both Democratic and Republican strategists expected

Wallace to find an excuse to do so. His personal antipathy to both Truman and Dewey was not as great as their dislike of each other. The contradictions of this earnest champion of peace would be magnified as he took to the hustings: a millionaire who still had the tousled look of an Iowa farmer, a visionary devoid of small talk, a candidate for the nation's highest office who disdained politicians, and a lover of humanity who could sway multitudes but freeze up when it came to shaking one hand at a time.

SHAKING hands was never a problem for Strom Thurmond, but in 1948 he would be an even more reluctant candidate for the presidency than Wallace. Indeed, Wallace declared first and Thurmond last—the two fringe candidates appropriately boxing Truman and Dewey in the middle. It was a very different Democratic party that claimed Thurmond's loyalty, the party of his Southern heritage, not the personalized entity that Wallace had chosen to join in 1936. That both could call themselves Democrats is a tribute to Roosevelt's extraordinary electoral coalition. Extended by depression and war, it held together precariously as the state of overt emergency receded.

Before 1947 the traditional Southern doctrine of "states' rights" had not really been a concern of Thurmond's. The largesse of the New Deal had fallen on the South throughout the 1930s without visibly affecting its social system. Segregation of the races had been a way of life since the end of Reconstruction. In the context of his time and place, Thurmond was viewed as a constructive progressive. He had been a career politician virtually all his life. Little more than a decade out of Clemson, he was elected to the South Carolina senate and later as a circuit judge before serving in the army during World War II. Determined and ambitious, he successfully took on the entrenched power structure in South Carolina and in 1946 was elected governor. He had just turned forty-four when he made his inaugural address, vowing to improve the lot of all the state's citizenry. He called for streamlining government, eliminating the poll tax for voting, and conducting a more open administration. Near the end of his remarks Thurmond urged that "more attention be given to Negro education. . . . If we provide better educational facilities for them, not only will much be accomplished in human values, but we shall raise our per capita income as well as the educational standing of the state." Bringing up the level of separate schools would benefit both races.

Thurmond added that he also favored greater opportunity and "equal pay for equal work" for the women of South Carolina. Very much his own man, the governor soon gained a first lady by marrying his comely secretary, although she was a quarter-century his junior. Thurmond's "people's inaugural ball," though limited to whites, opened the statehouse to thousands of well-wishers, evoking his commitment to progress in one of the poorest of Southern states. Despite Thurmond's positive message, the forces of change gathering in the South in the late 1940s were no longer to be satisfied with gradual, incremental improvements— especially if segregation remained intact. A. Philip Randolph's threat of a march on Washington in 1941 to protest inequitable hiring practices in defense industries, and President Roosevelt's response in establishing the Fair Employment Practices Committee (FEPC), raised expectations that civil rights might be advanced by mass pressure. By 1944 South Carolina blacks had formed their own statewide Progressive Democratic party, supported by the national office of the NAACP, and the American Civil Liberties Union was looking into violations of minority rights, especially in voting.

Thurmond had been in the governor's chair less than ten months when President Truman's Committee on Civil Rights presented its report. Over nearly the same span of time, this group of fourteen eminently respectable citizens, chaired by Charles E. Wilson, president of General Electric, had labored to fulfill President Truman's charge to get "our Bill of Rights implemented in fact." Their report, titled "To Secure These Rights," was a clarion call to action going far beyond what even the president had anticipated. It made thirty-five specific recommendations to achieve the nationwide "elimination of segregation based on race, color, creed, or national origin from American life." Southern political leaders were stunned. Thurmond joined with other Southern governors in denouncing such sweeping recommendations. Fielding Wright, governor of Mississippi, warned Truman not to play politics with Southern sensibilities. With Wallace threatening Truman from the left, concern heightened that Truman's commitment to civil rights might emerge as a major issue in the 1948 presidential campaign.

During Thurmond's years in public life, the primacy of South Carolina had not been challenged directly by either the federal government or the judiciary. That too was about to change. On December 30, 1947, the United States Court of Appeals upheld a lower court decision that when a black man was turned away from the polls in the Democratic primary in South Carolina, it amounted "to a denial of the constitutional rights of the Negro." The presiding judge of the court was a friend of Thurmond's. The governor refrained from immediate comment. The decision would be appealed to the United States Supreme Court. Unless the Supreme Court reversed the ruling, the black citizens of South Carolina would be legally entitled to vote in the next Democratic primary, the results of which were tantamount to election. Thurmond might be placed in the previously unimagined position of having to choose between fidelity to tradition and his vow to serve all the citizens of his state.

As V. O. Key, Jr., points out, state Democratic parties in the South in the 1940s were not all that different from those in other parts of the country. What was lacking, especially in the deep South, was "the chastening influence of an opposition." This simplified control of the electoral process, as did a generally modest turnout of the electorate. If the national party organization was "merely an association of the various state party organizations," as one Southern governor proclaimed, a candidate for any national office could accept nomination from his state party without ceasing to be a Democrat. Such thoughts were already in the minds of many Southern Democratic leaders, if not Governor Thurmond's. His upbeat message to the South Carolina legislature in January 1948 boasted of many achievements during his first year in office, one of which was substantially increased aid to Negro schools.

Only seven days later, President Truman's State of the Union address included the announcement that he would soon present a comprehensive civil rights program to the nation. On February 2, 1948, before a joint session of Congress—as if to underline the importance of his message—the president recommended many of the proposals outlined in "To Secure These Rights." He endorsed abolition of the poll tax as a requirement for voting (which Thurmond had also favored before considering its relevance to black voting), a federal anti-lynching law, a permanent Fair Employment Practices Committee, and the outlawing of discrimination in interstate commerce. The president's ten proposals encompassed less than a third of the report's recommendations, and not the most controversial ones, but it was nonetheless a forceful message.

Although Truman failed to follow up by sending an omnibus civil rights bill to Congress, his speech exacerbated the already emotional stirrings in the white South. Senator Olin Johnston of South Carolina and others boycotted the Democratic party's Jefferson-Jackson Day dinner in Washington at which Truman spoke, their empty tables providing for the nation's press a graphic picture of Southern protest. Southern governors, meeting later in February in Florida, were uncertain just how they should respond. At one extreme, Governor Wright called for a meeting on March 1 so that "true Democrats" could immediately form their own party. At the other, "Big Jim" Folsom, the colorful Alabama populist, suggested that an overall Southern favorite-son candidate announce for the Democratic nomination for the presidency, using this leverage to bargain over the party's position. Folsom volunteered himself. Finally the governors accepted a compromise sponsored by Thurmond. The administration would be warned in a strongly worded resolution that the South would not mutely accept the dismantling of white supremacy. Thurmond also suggested a "cooling off" period during which an effort would be made to meet with national Democratic leaders, hopefully to find common ground. Without really intending to, by his demeanor at this meeting Thurmond replaced Wright as the governors' spokesman, ostensibly a more reasonable voice for the South. But a meeting in March between Thurmond and other Southern governors, and Democratic national chairman J. Howard McGrath of Rhode Island, who had succeeded Hannegan, got nowhere. Each side viewed the other as intransigent.

In May Thurmond received more bad news. The Supreme Court would not review the earlier decision in his state. Blacks had the right to vote in South Carolina's Democratic primaries. Thurmond denounced the high court's refusal but did not counsel defiance. In mid-May he went to Jackson, Mississippi, to address the first convention of what were now being called "States' Rights Democrats." The name "Dixiecrats," much disliked by those it identified, resulted from a North Carolina editor's inability to squeeze "States' Rights Democrats" into a headline. When "Dixiecrats" first appeared in the *Birmingham News,* former

Governor Dixon of Alabama protested, contending that the movement was in fact returning to the "original concept of the founding fathers of our nation and the Democratic Party."

Thurmond's emphasis was more on federal encroachment on the rights of individual states than on the narrower premise of segregation. The South's sensible Negroes, he declared, did not seek social integration in any case but rather equality of opportunity, "and they will get it through our efforts." Those delegates who remained in the humid hall were presented with a proposal to meet again in Birmingham on July 17, should they be unable to obtain a satisfactory platform plank on civil rights at the Democratic National Convention. The clear implication was a potential bolt from the national party. Many in attendance were upset, still uneasy with the threat of separation however it was phrased. Accordingly the final resolution legalistically disclaimed any intention to hold a "rump convention." After all, with the national party based on the will of the state parties, "the plan of action outlined herein serves to return the party to the people and the principles on which it was founded."

No one felt this dilemma more keenly than Thurmond, caught between conflicting commitments to progress and custom. As recounted by his biographer, Nadine Cohodas, Thurmond uneasily headed to the Democratic National Convention in Philadelphia as "the titular head of a fractious group of Democrats." First, however, he went to New York for a private meeting with Dwight D. Eisenhower, then president of Columbia University, and urged him to accept a Democratic draft to run for president.

THURMOND wasn't alone in calling on Eisenhower. Everyone from Franklin Roosevelt's sons James and Franklin, Jr., liberal labor leaders such as Walter Reuther, and Wallace's favorite sena-

tor, Claude Pepper, to Northern urban bosses and Southern segregationists more extreme than Thurmond had appealed to Eisenhower to lead the Democratic party and the nation. Rarely had
there been a more unified demonstration from every ideological
direction by leaders of the New Deal electoral coalition.
Republicans were making their own, quieter overtures to Eisenhower. That no one knew where Ike stood on any major issue
makes this all the more remarkable. That the esteemed general
could not possibly lose in November makes it understandable. To
Thurmond, Eisenhower, who had never voted, revealed either his
political naiveté or an adroit rejection of any draft by declaring
that he would run only if nominated by both major political parties! Even that statement failed to discourage his many suitors.

In the spring of 1948, with Truman trailing ever more widely
in the polls, his already shallow support began to evaporate.
Those who had never felt altogether comfortable with him
jumped ship first, their unease now mixed with fear. As Truman
biographer Alonzo Hamby puts it, "He was not FDR. His voice
did not resonate with the Northern intelligentsia. He was taking
the party to a crushing defeat." The resentment of many New
Dealers initially had more to do with their residual affection for
Roosevelt, the leader they had served, than with any particular
antipathy for his successor. But with the establishment of loyalty
review boards that Truman found easier to create than to control, the president seemed part of the growing domestic anti-
Communist hysteria that threatened civil liberties. With his failure
to reappoint the respected chairmen of the Federal Reserve Board
and the Civil Aeronautics Board, Truman appeared again to be
tilting to the right. His trust in such advisers as wealthy oilman
Edwin Pauley invited charges of conflict of interest, and the president seemed similarly oblivious to intimations of corruption in
his White House coterie. Even modest incidents were magnified
in the prevailing pessimism over electoral prospects. Of course,

those who sought to replace Truman could succeed only if they provided a successor.

James Loeb of the ADA put it plainly: in April 1948 he called for an "open" Democratic National Convention. Lauding Truman for his apparent fidelity to liberal principles and his proposals in the face of a reactionary Republican Congress, Loeb chided the president for his inability to rally the people behind his programs and for the mediocrity of his appointments. In the best interests of all, Loeb concluded, "We feel strongly that the nation has a right to call upon men like Dwight D. Eisenhower and William O. Douglas if the people so choose." The ingratitude must have reminded Truman of Franklin Roosevelt's abandonment of him in 1940. Later that spring, Truman—recalling how FDR had insisted he run in 1944—berated James Roosevelt in California: "If your father knew what you were doing to me, he would turn over in his grave."

Many liberals, anticipating that Eisenhower would not run, may really have preferred Justice Douglas, as President Roosevelt well may have in 1944 when he named Douglas or Truman as acceptable replacements for Wallace. Douglas, an appealing personality whose liberal and intellectual credentials were a matter of record, could effectively blunt Wallace's appeal to progressives. But Douglas was an avid outdoorsman with a proclivity for escaping to remote locations in the northwestern wilderness, and in 1948 he would be an elusive figure.

Not all labor leaders were as critical of Truman as the United Mine Workers' saturnine John L. Lewis, who considered the president "totally unfitted for the position," but the memory of past problems remained. Truman's veto of Taft-Hartley had been heartening, but only a year earlier he had threatened to draft railway strikers into the army. There was no likelihood that major components of the CIO, let alone the AFL, would have switched to Wallace in 1948—but, as noted, many in the anti-Communist left had pondered the ultimate formation of an authentic progressive party. Ironically it was Wallace's entry into the 1948 race that helped move their thinking back to reform within the Democratic party structure. Eventually labor rallied to Truman, but as late as June, Reuther told reporters that though Truman's "heart was in the right place," he was simply not up to the job. Reuther put his efforts behind Democratic congressional candidates and called a nationwide strategy meeting of his lieutenants for January 21, 1949, the day following the anticipated inauguration of President Thomas E. Dewey.

While not much surprised by the inconstancy of doctrinaire liberals and even the leaders of labor, Truman was deeply disappointed when such old Senate friends as John Sparkman and Lister Hill suggested he gracefully withdraw from the campaign. If there was any hesitation in his decision to take his record to the voters, it vanished in the spring of 1948. With Wallace already being portrayed as a Communist apologist, uncertainty about Douglas's intentions, and the president viewed not only as unelectable but likely to take much of the Democratic party down with him, pressure mounted on Eisenhower. Nineteen prominent Democrats, headed by James Roosevelt, wired every delegate to the national convention, asking them to assemble in Philadelphia two days early for a caucus to select the strongest candidate for president. Although Eisenhower did not finally voice his firm rejection of a draft until the very eve of the proceedings, one man had always been certain Ike would not run. From time to time since 1945 Truman had broached the subject, once reportedly even suggesting an Eisenhower-Truman ticket, but the general had demurred. Truman took Eisenhower at his word. The coolness between the two had not yet developed. Looking around at the possible alternatives, Truman knew he could not be denied the nomination.

Even while riding high in the polls, Truman was no more

comfortable with the New Deal / ADA left than they were with him. The suspicion of many liberals that Truman was more allied with them rhetorically than substantively increased their concerns. Truman had a proclivity for making significant proposals, such as in civil rights, then backing away from implementing them—not entirely by accident. The president's pragmatic political framework was often in conflict with his positive instincts. The historian Nelson Lichtenstein writes, "Truman tried long and hard to accommodate civil rights liberals and Southern white supremacists. 'The strategy,' presidential aide Philleo Nash later explained, 'was to start with a bold measure and then temporize to pick up the right-wing forces.' "

In 1948, however, the opponents of this activist agenda would take Truman seriously enough, especially in the South. Meanwhile the core of the party faithful, including its liberal wing, would come, however reluctantly, to support the president as their only viable alternative.

Unlike Roosevelt, Truman was the product of a political machine. Having experienced factional turmoil, he had been a coalition-builder and compromiser throughout his career, promoting the inclusive "big tent" premise of his party. Deserted by the extreme left and right wings of that party, in 1948 Truman was liberated from the necessity to defend either Communist accommodationists or outright segregationists. He stood solidly in the center, his most comfortable political turf, and needed only to mobilize the Democratic core and widen his appeal to independents. Given his political skills and the nature of his opposition, the 1948 presidential campaign began with advantages for the incumbent.

Truman must have understood that his popularity could return as swiftly as it had declined. Why did he choose to limit his appeal by putting his message into words more extreme than were warranted? Perhaps he too was taken in by the polls he professed never to believe—and determined that the circumstances impelled him to pull out all the rhetorical stops. The most challenging of Truman's earlier campaigns had been in primary elections against his fellow Missouri Democrats. Those primaries had hinged more on perceptions of personalities than on differences of policy. Truman's 1944 campaign for the vice-presidency had been a sideshow. In 1948, for the first time, he found himself at the center of a national election, taking the field against Republicans he still saw in the guise of "Old Mellon." His vigorous personal campaigning would help him win; his strident partisanship would narrow the margin of victory.

SECURE at least in the knowledge that he would be the Democratic nominee, Truman decided to start his campaign early. He had a powerful ally in party chairman McGrath, yet another Irish-American who came to Truman's aid. The senator from Rhode Island (just the sort of professional politician Rowe had recommended against to head the party) had been a stalwart supporter of the president throughout all the dump-Truman machinations. McGrath also controlled the party apparatus, but his coffers were virtually empty.

Thus McGrath was delighted when Truman announced in April that he would accept an invitation from the University of California at Berkeley to receive an honorary degree and address its June commencement. He would travel west not by air but on a special train, with the massive, luxurious *Ferdinand Magellan* at the end. One of a notable series of railroad cars, it had been refurbished and presented to President Roosevelt in 1942 by the Association of American Railroads, and boasted a rear platform ideal for speechmaking. Since the trip was scheduled for an official presidential address, it was billed as "nonpolitical" and was paid for through public funds. In two weeks the president managed to make six major addresses and speak from his rear platform an additional sixty-seven times—forty appearances on the way out and twenty-seven more coming back.

Encouraged by his aides, Truman tried out a more informal style of speaking, initiated earlier in the spring, combining extemporaneous remarks and note cards, and sometimes departing from the text of even his formal addresses. Truman himself refers to adapting new techniques, but in fact he was returning more to the way he had talked to his neighbors in Missouri. At Berkeley his speech was nonpolitical enough, a statesmanlike exploration of American foreign policy. He challenged the Soviet Union to prove its good faith by deeds before entering into genuine negotiations. An earlier address in Chicago to the Swedish Pioneer Centennial Association was only mildly political, stressing the urgency of legislation to admit more displaced persons. Earlier that day in Ohio, however, in his first "rear platform remarks," Truman drew laughter by noting, "On this nonpartisan, bipartisan trip that we are taking here, I understand there are a whole lot of Democrats present, too."

It was those Democrats whom Truman zeroed in on in his other appearances. The trip was not merely a dry run; it was the first campaign swing of 1948. In his other major addresses on the trip, Truman spoke on specific subjects but always wound up excoriating Congress for its inaction—in Omaha on agricultural legislation, in Butte on housing, in Seattle on reclamation of natural resources. Before the Greater Los Angeles Press Club, Truman reviewed the whole litany of an 80th Congress that had "not done very much for the benefit of the people." From the train Truman signed proclamations and sent back to Washington three vetoes of congressional legislation, the most notable being the "Resolution Excluding Certain Groups from Social Security Coverage," which Truman warned were Republican "piecemeal attacks" on the entire system.

In his informal remarks to groups of varying size gathered around the rear of his train at scheduled stops, Truman seemed to be greatly enjoying himself. Citizens in sixteen states saw little of the dignity of the presidency on this tour, but they witnessed a politician honing his message. For most of them outside Missouri, it was their first glimpse of Truman as a campaigner. His emphasis was more negative as the trip progressed, becoming less a recitation of his proposals than a denunciation of the Republican Congress—characterized as not only indifferent to the welfare of the people but almost malevolent. On June 4 in Gary, Indiana, Truman told the crowd, "Your dollar now in the purchase of food is worth only 60 cents of what your dollar was in 1946, when the government was controlling prices in favor of the consumer. . . . The 80th Congress, I am afraid, will adjourn without doing anything about it."

Accepting a gift of spurs from the rear platform at Grand Island, Nebraska, on June 6, Truman remarked, "When I get them on, I can take the Congress to town. Give them a trial just as soon as I get back to Washington." He then expressed his regret that because it was a Sunday it was his habit not to make political remarks. At Olympia, Washington, on June 10, Truman told his audience, "Two-thirds of you stayed home in 1946, and look what a Congress we got. This is your fault. . . . If you people want to continue the policies of the 80th Congress, that will be your funeral."

Such "nonpolitical" talk was getting to be too much for Senator Taft. In a speech in Philadelphia he made an enduring contribution to the American political lexicon by accusing the president of "blackguarding the Congress at whistle-stops all across the country." This observation was received with glee at Democratic national headquarters, which promptly wired mayors and newspapers wherever Truman stopped to inquire whether they viewed their communities as "whistle-stops." Truman also had fun with it, referring to Los Angeles, upon his arrival, as "the biggest whistle-stop of all."

Encouraged to "pour it on" by some spectators, Truman happily obliged. He appealed to class and even sectional prejudice, as in Los Angeles: "You know, Daniel Webster, when the United States was trying to build the Pacific Railroad, made the statement that the West wasn't any good . . . and there are a lot of Republicans now ready to believe like old Daniel Webster did." In Gallup, New Mexico, on June 15 he declared: "The issues are clearly drawn and it's up to you . . . whether you want the special privilege boys to run this country, or whether you want the country to be in the hands of people who are working for your interests." Increasingly Truman recalled the Republican past, as in Newton, Kansas, on June 16: "I don't know whether your memory is good or not, but back in 1932 the farm income was $4,700 million. Last year it was $30 billion, and the farmers had $23 billion on deposit in the bank. . . . Only 33-1/3 percent of the people voted in 1946, and that is the reason we got the kind of Congress we did. . . . It is a minority Congress with a majority against the people." In Harrisburg, Pennsylvania, on June 18, Truman confessed, "I don't know what exactly to expect for the next 3 days from this Congress. . . . They have fixed housing so that the real estate lobby is going to get exactly what it wants."

Returning from California, Truman revealed his definition of legitimate campaign issues. On the domestic agenda, as he suggested in York, Pennsylvania, near the end of his tour, "This is a case of the special interests against the people. We have never had a special interest Congress equal to this one." But, Truman went on, "Everyone wants peace in the world. . . . We are unanimously for the foreign policy of the United States. This is one issue which is bipartisan, and that bipartisanship [sic] should stop at the water's edge." On the one issue that polls indicated a majority of Americans in 1948 really cared about—foreign policy—Truman wanted little discussion and no debate.

Truman learned a great deal from his spring tour, most of all that he needed better-coordinated advance planning. There had been numerous glitches. His speech in Omaha to veterans of his old 35th Division was only sparsely attended. Through a misunderstanding, many more people had been turned away. In Idaho he dedicated an airport to the wrong person. Appearing in so many localities, he was just learning how to use background information on each, provided by William Batt's newly formed research division at the Democratic National Committee. In the fall its work would be invaluable; as Clifford had suggested the preceding November, staff work might make the difference in the election. Meanwhile some problems were of Truman's own making. Speaking informally, he could momentarily forget the media's relentless scrutiny. In Idaho he gloated that his opponents had "never been able to prove" what they said about him. In Oregon he made a more serious gaffe by volunteering that he liked "Old Joe" Stalin, "but Joe is a prisoner of the Politburo. He can't do what he wants to." Truman's advisers subsequently urged the president to be more careful and to limit his rhetorical excesses to Republicans.

After the election a *New York Times* article, headlined "No-Politics Tour Helped Truman Win," observed that "at the outset, President Truman . . . decided that the Eightieth Congress was the Achilles heel of the GOP, and determined to play out the string for all it was worth." Be that as it may, the first document the president signed upon returning to Washington on June 18 was a report to Congress on the establishment of a fact-finding commission. He had used Taft-Hartley to declare an injunction in a Tennessee labor dispute. The Republican National Convention would start the following Monday.

CHAPTER IV

🚩

The Conventions—
Not at All
Conventional

D EWEY was favored to win his party's presidential nomination
despite serious opposition, particularly from Harold E. Stassen,
the vigorous, progressive former "boy governor" of Minnesota,
and the ubiquitous Senator Taft, acclaimed as "Mr. Republican"
by at least the congressional wing of his party. In part to facilitate
television coverage, the first for American political conventions,
both the Republicans and Democrats met in the same Philadelphia hall, as would the Progressive party. As *Time* reported after
the GOP gathering, "Thanks to TV, about ten million spectators
along the Eastern seaboard actually saw the convention in action.
In scattered communities across the U.S., five million others saw
telefilm versions while the news was still warm—three to 24
hours after it happened."

Less extensively than Truman, Governor Dewey had also
traveled the nation in 1948, engaging in a series of presidential
preference primaries. In the last and most significant, in Oregon,
Dewey bested Stassen in a radio debate broadcast nationally from
Portland to more than nine hundred stations. Taking the negative

on a single proposition, "Shall the Communist Party be outlawed in the United States?" (Joseph McCarthy was Stassen's second in the debate), Dewey declared, "There is no such thing as a constitutional right to destroy all constitutional rights" and used his own law-enforcement experience to argue that the most effective way to counter domestic Communists was to keep them out in the open. Dewey's victory in the Oregon primary stopped the momentum of Stassen, who had been viewed by many as a more appealing alternative, and encouraged the supporters of Taft and "favorite sons" to hope for a deadlock at the convention. Despite their ideological differences, perhaps Stassen and Taft could work out a deal. Dewey came to Philadelphia still about 250 votes short of the 548 needed to win the Republican nomination.

The mutual antipathy of Taft and Dewey had deep roots. After his respectable loss to Roosevelt in the 1944 presidential election, when Taft had also hoped to be the Republican nominee, Dewey viewed himself as the titular head of the party. He encouraged his close associate Herbert Brownell to stay on as national chairman and help revitalize and modernize the party structure. With the war winding down, it seemed to Dewey a suitable time to reaffirm Republican principles to the nation—assuming each faction could agree on what they were. After announcing that he would not again contest his party's nomination for president (the arch-conservative *Chicago Tribune* had already proclaimed Dewey's political obituary), Dewey invited Republican congressional leaders to meet with him in New York. When they arrived, led by a dubious Taft, they were presented for their consideration a twelve-point charter outlining Dewey's vision for the Republican party. It included the extension of bipartisanship in foreign policy, freer trade after the war, and aid to devastated nations, but an end to such secret diplomacy as Yalta. Its domestic tenets reflected Dewey's conception of a more efficient progressivism: support for civil rights legislation, equal rights for women, and expansion of Social Security coverage, balanced by reductions in the size of the federal government, cuts in individual and business income taxes, and state control over such programs as unemployment insurance.

Nothing came of the meeting. As Dewey biographer Richard Norton Smith puts it, "The congressional leadership saw no reason to defer to Dewey." Afterward Dewey blamed the influence of Taft. In the view of Brownell, who would at least officially manage Dewey's presidential campaign in 1948 as he had in 1944, the failure of this meeting led to long-lasting tensions. While necessity unified the Democratic core that finally came to support Truman in 1948, Dewey was never able to unify what the historian James MacGregor Burns distinguishes as the presidential and congressional Republican parties.

THE SON of a small-town newspaper publisher, Thomas Edmund Dewey graduated from the University of Michigan and took his law degree at Columbia. Practicing in New York, he attracted the eye of reform-minded Democratic Governor Herbert Lehman, who named Dewey as a special prosecutor to investigate racketeering. Elected New York district attorney in 1937, Dewey became nationally known while still in his thirties by obtaining dramatic indictments of mob leaders and corrupt politicians. After nearly beating his benefactor Lehman in 1938, Dewey was elected governor in 1942 by more than 600,000 votes and won again in 1946. Insisting that "government can be progressive *and* solvent," Dewey built highways and hospitals, offered a workable alternative to federal government domination of reform programs, and pioneered laws prohibiting racial, religious, or gender discrimination in employment and education.

Some of Dewey's most notable achievements occurred in his second term, after his 1944 defeat by Roosevelt for the presidency. Dewey's plan for peacetime conversion in the Empire State was more thorough than Washington's. Classrooms, housing, and support services were expanded to help 100,000 veterans pursue college degrees. Between 1945 and 1947 more than 100,000 new businesses were established in the state. Rent control was continued, and a budget surplus of over $500 million was invested in public facilities. Yet business and personal taxes were cut, and tax forms were simplified. Dewey raised teachers' salaries and supported collective bargaining but spearheaded a bill in 1947 prohibiting public employees from striking, earning praise from the *New York Times* for his "courageous" stance.

Unfortunately Dewey was easier to admire than to like. Stiff in manner, impatient, tactless, arrogant, a calculating perfectionist, he seemed, as one acquaintance noted, capable of strutting while sitting down. Perhaps his precise formality in dress and his dignified demeanor resulted in part from the insecurity of having undertaken such immense responsibilities at so young an age. Dewey's physical appearance didn't help. His large head made his stature seem smaller than five feet eight inches. His old-fashioned, neatly parted dark hair and the "toothbrush" mustache his wife insisted he retain made him an ideal subject for cartoonists. To Alice Roosevelt Longworth, Dewey looked like "the little man on a wedding cake." Yet the energetic Dewey in action was a leader who relied on the collaborative counsel of trusted associates, many of whom stayed with him throughout his career. Ambitious yet realistic, he was also scrupulously honest—in Richard Norton Smith's words, "a complex man molded from simple parts." Dewey's thorough approach as a political candidate embraced the most advanced campaign tools and techniques, including a confidence in scientific polling. His mellifluous speaking voice derived from his earlier ambition, surprising to many who dealt with him, to be an opera singer.

Robert Alphonso Taft, son of a president, and a principled,

brilliant man (first in his class in every elite academic institution he attended), possessed a manner that made even Dewey's seem warm. A practicing attorney in Cincinnati, he served in the Ohio house and senate before being elected to the United States Senate in 1938, where he remained the rest of his life. Although a widely respected Republican senator, Taft, as described by his biographer James Patterson, not only faced "roadblocks to party harmony" but also had to contend with his own personality. In a legislative body that esteemed conviviality, Taft struck "many people as abrupt, cold, and inhumanly efficient." Owlish in appearance and pedantic in speech, Taft in his public utterances rendered Harry Truman a latter-day Demosthenes by comparison. Yet, unlike Truman, Taft never lost an election. But because even Republican leaders who admired him were convinced that Taft's popularity in Ohio would not travel well, voters in the rest of the nation were never granted the opportunity to make their own evaluation.

Taft, who cared as little for public opinion as Dewey valued it, was never really a thoroughgoing conservative. In fact he frequently softened the more extreme opinions of many of his colleagues. Although given to fiscal restraint, he believed in the prudent use of federal investment in the public welfare, issue by issue. For example, he firmly supported and sponsored bills for federal aid to education and public housing—for which he was denounced as a "fellow traveler" of the New Deal and worse by such organizations as the National Association of Real Estate Boards.

In foreign policy Taft's reasoned opposition to Truman's lending and spending plans for Europe was based chiefly on the inflationary effect they might have on the U.S. economy. Taft was not so much a consummate isolationist as a unilateralist who affirmed "America first." Most of all, he believed in the careful examination of every proposal under consideration within a democratic society. Had Taft been the Republican candidate for president in 1948, the premise of Rowe and Clifford that bipartisanship would be a campaign casualty would have been realized. Before the Republican convention, Taft wrote to a friend, "Foreign policy should be one of the main issues in the next election." In this his views appear to have reflected the concerns of most Americans. Despite polls that indicated Taft would be the weakest of the major Republican possibilities to oppose him, Truman considered Taft a far more formidable opponent than Dewey. Meanwhile Taft viewed Dewey as not only too far to the left but also an unprincipled opportunist who could wreck the Republican party.

It took Dewey three ballots to win the 1948 Republican presidential nomination, despite a campaign organization so thorough that one Taft delegate would later recall, "The CIA were amateurs compared to the Dewey people." Brownell and his well-financed staff left nothing to chance. Every delegate's preferences were noted and targeted. Operating from an immense Philadelphia hotel ballroom, dispensing everything from free Pepsi-Cola to perfume, the Dewey forces simply outgunned and outcommunicated Taft's and Stassen's. The victory was not accomplished without residual bitterness. Brownell gained the support of Indiana's delegation by appearing to offer the vice-presidential nomination to their conservative congressman Charles Halleck, but it didn't happen. The Republican ticket in 1948 would not be so ideologically balanced as it was in 1944 or 1940. To stop the Dewey juggernaut, Taft even offered his vice-presidential nomination to Stassen, and Stassen tried to reach Eisenhower and ask him to reconsider, but nothing came of either effort.

In his acceptance speech, Dewey eschewed specifics and repeatedly stressed both party and national unity, setting the tone for the campaign to come. As in 1944, he offered the vice-presidential nomination to Governor Earl Warren of California. This time, after talking it over with his skeptical wife and secur-

ing a commitment from Dewey to make the office more meaningful, Warren accepted. Although the two men were not well ac-
quainted, Dewey shared similar views on most issues with
Warren, a politician immensely popular in his own state. Together
they seemed to represent a coast-to-coast dream ticket.

Time's issue of July 5, 1948, its cover a painting of a trumpet-
ing elephant, represented the views of the nation's press and expressed the yearnings of GOP loyalists who had not experienced
a Republican in the White House since 1932:

> The face of the Republican Party . . . has never appeared so pho-
> togenic, so politically winning . . . smoothly combining the cool
> assurance of Thomas Edmund Dewey, 45, with the genial west-
> ern affability of smiling Earl Warren, 57. . . . The exhausted del-
> egates got just what they wanted; no battle over issues. Even
> though Taft said isolationism is a dead issue, they rallied behind
> Dewey to affirm that the U.S. must accept its leadership in the
> world. . . . The nomination of Earl Warren was a political bull's-
> eye. . . . He will undoubtedly attract millions of independent vot-
> ers. Barring a political miracle, it is the kind of ticket that could
> not fail to sweep the Republican Party back into power.

Dewey's associates had also captured the convention's machinery to hammer out the party platform, which emerged as a
less conservative document than many congressional Republicans may have preferred. On foreign policy, key Dewey adviser
John Foster Dulles, resolutions chairman Henry Cabot Lodge, Jr.,
and especially Senator Vandenberg tried to paper over differences
with congressional isolationists through brief and vaguely
worded planks, but their commitment to bipartisanship was as
clear as their confidence in a Republican victory: "We are proud
of the part that Republicans have played in those limited areas of
foreign policy in which they have been permitted to participate.
We shall invite the minority party to join us under the next Re-

publican administration in stopping partisan politics at the
water's edge. We faithfully dedicate ourselves to peace with justice."

Perhaps in response to Truman's de facto recognition of the
State of Israel, one of the GOP's more specific planks welcomed
Israel into the family of nations, taking "pride in the fact that the
Republican Party was the first to call for the establishment of a
free and independent Jewish commonwealth. . . . We pledge to Is-
rael full recognition, with its boundaries as sanctioned by the
United Nations and aid in developing its economy."

Only in 1945 had Vandenberg turned from isolationism to
internationalism. Like many converts, he became a zealot for
his newfound faith, urging on President Truman a firmer anti-
Communist line. As chairman of the Senate Foreign Relations
Committee in 1947–1948, he was frequently at odds with Taft
and he was immensely helpful in passing the administration's
policies. The egotistical Vandenberg claimed to have submerged
his own presidential ambitions in 1948 in order to make certain
that Republican foreign policy planks did not revert to isolationism or oppose collective security and the European Recovery
Program. He anticipated a fight over the platform, but it never
materialized.

Time may have trumpeted a Republican triumph, but behind
its report on the GOP convention, other news seemed to question
such certainty. In the White House, *Time* reported, President Truman had watched the Republican party's windup on his television
set. Convention coverage provided the "largest gallery" television had gathered thus far, though it was eclipsed later in the
week by the Louis-Walcott fight. People leaving Truman's office
reported the president to be upbeat, even though, with Warren's
nomination, "Democratic strategists gave up any hope of carrying
California."

According to *Time*, the AFL's Bill Green predicted, "The Republicans certainly won't get much labor support." Jake Arvey, Democratic leader in Chicago, felt Truman had "picked up a lot." Congressman John Rankin of Mississippi suggested that secessionist-minded Southern Democrats might "stay hitched" to the party if its 1948 platform went no further on civil rights than 1944's generalities. Poring over a desk clogged with 263 bills, Truman reluctantly signed one to admit 205,000 displaced persons, though he viewed it as "flagrantly discriminatory" against Jews and Catholics. The president also named the first U.S. diplomatic envoy to Israel and signed a major appropriations bill for the foreign-aid program, a one-year extension of reciprocal aid, the draft bill, appropriations of almost $10.5 billion to bolster the armed services, and waterway and flood-control bills totaling $573 million.

Time's International section quoted American General Lucius Clay as assuring Berliners that no Soviet pressures—economic, political, or military—would drive the Western powers out of their city. The Greek army's "Operation Coronet" was reported as making progress in driving the Communist rebels back toward the Albanian border, with "U.S. military mission chief General Van Fleet standing by." General Tito's renegade Communist regime in Yugoslavia was "holding firm" despite threats from Moscow. Everywhere, except perhaps in the uncertain Chinese situation, America and its allies seemed to be standing their ground. At home, despite inflation (though much reduced), a continuing housing shortage, and the scarcity of some consumer goods, *Time*'s reports indicated that everything was either prospering or promising. The magazine's abundant advertising certainly supported this premise. Such was the state of the nation throughout 1948, as presented throughout the American press, however pronounced its Republican inclinations. Yet the consensus persisted that it would take "a miracle" for Truman to remain in office.

DELEGATES to the Democratic National Convention hardly exuded confidence. They assembled in the mid-July humidity of Philadelphia as if attending a wake. The last desultory attempts to nominate someone other than Truman had wilted with Eisenhower's final firm rejection and Senator Pepper's offering of his own name as a last resort. From the ranks of labor, not even Dan Tobin of the Teamsters Union, a staunch Democratic supporter, or the AFL's William Green would agree to share the platform or address the delegates. CIO leaders were little more visible.

Two events shook the gathering out of its torpor. The first was a rousing, old-fashioned keynote address by Senator Alben Barkley of Kentucky that brought the delegates to their feet in the convention's first genuine show of enthusiasm. Unfortunately, in his hour-long denunciation of all things Republican and his glorification of Democratic heroes, Barkley mentioned Truman only once and victory in November not at all. Given the pervasive pessimism about Democratic prospects, the speech launched a brief presidential boomlet for the seventy-one-year-old Barkley. From Washington, Truman glumly watched this demonstration on television, convinced that it was no accident. He had offered the vice-presidential nomination to Justice Douglas in a final attempt to energize the liberal establishment. Douglas took his time deciding, finally declining after the Democrats had already convened. He was reputed to have told friends he would rather not serve as the number-two man to a number-two man, or board the *Titanic*. In any case, Douglas's decision cleared the decks for Barkley.

Although he had been the president's Senate leader, and both came from border states, Barkley and Truman were not especially close. "Why didn't you tell me you wanted to be vice-president?" Truman asked Barkley over the phone, after offering congratulations on his speech. "You do not know it yet," Barkley replied.

If not the presidency, Barkley had fruitlessly sought the vice-presidential nomination five consecutive times. By 1948 he viewed it as a "cold biscuit," but he agreed to run. Qualified candidates were not exactly standing in line to book passage with Truman. It would be a fateful decision for both, leading to genuine friendship and affecting the outcome of the 1948 election more than either could have imagined.

The second jolt to the convention was a genuine debate over the platform. Proposed by the ADA and backed by labor and big-city leaders who were more concerned with the party's congressional prospects, a "minority plank" on civil rights was submitted to the delegates. More specific than the milder plank favored by Truman and platform committee chairman Senator Francis J. Myers of Pennsylvania, it was vigorously contested on the floor. The most memorable oration in its favor was delivered by the youthful mayor of Minneapolis and candidate for the Senate, Hubert Humphrey, who urged the party to "get out of the shadow of states' rights and walk forthrightly into the bright sunshine of human rights." (Humphrey had been one of many who had hoped to draft Eisenhower.) By the narrow margin of 651½ to 582½ votes, the stronger civil rights plank prevailed, leading to a walkout from the convention of the entire Mississippi delegation and half the Alabama delegation—thirty-six delegates in all. Although the civil rights plank was not intended to embarrass Truman, the action was yet another repudiation of his leadership. The president had hoped somehow to placate his Southern critics and keep them within the regular Democratic party.

Comparing the 1948 Democratic and Republican planks on civil rights, it is hard to discern much difference. The most specific paragraph of the Democratic plank asserted:

We call upon the Congress to support our president in guaranteeing these basic and fundamental American principles: (1) the right of full and equal political participation; (2) the right to equal opportunity of employment; (3) the right of security of person; and (4) the right of equal treatment in the service and defense of our nation.

This does not sound very strong until contrasted with the wording of the original "majority" plank: "We again call upon the Congress to exert its full authority to the limit of its constitutional powers to assure and protect these rights."

The 1948 Republican civil rights plank is phrased more like the text of "To Secure These Rights":

> Lynching or any other form of mob violence anywhere is a disgrace to any civilized nation, and we favor the prompt enactment of legislation to end this infamy. One of the basic principles of this Republic is the equality of all individuals in their right to life, liberty, and the pursuit of happiness. . . . The right of equal opportunity to work and to advance in life should never be limited to any individual because of race, religion, color, or country of origin. We favor the enactment and just enforcement of . . . federal legislation . . . to maintain this right at all times in every part of this Republic. We favor the abolition of the poll tax as a requisite for voting. We are opposed to the idea of racial segregation in the armed forces of the United States.

Both the overall similarity of the major party platforms and the adoption of a strong civil rights plank by the Democrats would significantly influence the election. Truman soon capitalized on the first factor; by securing the second, Humphrey and his associates had done the president an unforeseen favor.

Less publicized were the efforts of Southern Democratic delegates to include the kinds of resolutions that had been featured in previous platforms. A typical one reads: "The Democratic Party stands by the principle that the Constitution contemplated and established a union of indestructible sovereign states and that under the Constitution the general federal government and the separate states have their separate fields of power and of permitted activities." It was voted down 925 to 309. Only two Southerners were on the eighteen-member platform committee, but Senator Myers won praise for his skillful handling of potential discord. Some liberals had also threatened to bolt the convention if civil rights were not supported forcefully. At the convention's opening session, Myers also made the most optimistic address to the delegates, encouraging speculation that the Pennsylvanian might be more than a "favorite son" possibility for the vice-presidential nomination. Unlike Barkley, Myers proclaimed that the convention was about to nominate the next president of the United States, that the GOP had picked its "best loser," and that facing "one of the bitterest struggles in American history," the Democrats would prevail.

Truman was denied a unanimous nomination by embittered Southern delegates who remained, including Strom Thurmond's South Carolinians. They rallied around the symbolic candidacy of Senator Richard B. Russell of Georgia, who received 263 votes to Truman's 947½. After Myers's withdrawal, Barkley was nominated for the vice-presidency by acclamation. Wilson W. Wyatt of Louisville described his fellow Kentuckian as the "best campaigner in the nation." Even by the unruly standards of Democratic conventions, 1948 was badly managed. Not until nearly 2 a.m. on Thursday, July 15, did Truman finally stride to the platform, resplendent in a white linen suit, to deliver his acceptance speech to the exhausted delegates. He had arrived from Washington at around nine o'clock the preceding evening and had been sitting on a ramp for hours, catching the air and exchanging stories with Barkley.

Seeing the awkward delivery of Truman's major speeches on film, it is hard to believe so much effort went into preparing them.

For this acceptance speech, Roosevelt's old speechwriter Sam
Rosenman had joined his ideas with Clifford's and others'. Truman straightened the microphones, his opening remarks obviously of his own making: "Senator Barkley and I will win this
election and make those Republicans like it—don't you forget
that." Without a script but supported by sixteen pages of notes,
Truman proceeded to his customary cataloguing of Republican
inaction and indifference. But now he paralleled each failing with
the fresh promises contained in the 1948 Republican platform, so
similar to the Democrats'. Finally he dropped his bombshell: he
would call Congress back into special session on July 26, called
"Turnip Day" in Missouri. "If the Republicans mean what they
say in their platform," Truman insisted, they could immediately
enact legislation to implement it through programs to curb inflation, build housing, expand Social Security, raise the minimum
wage, humanize the Displaced Persons Act, aid education, promote health care, and ensure civil rights—or at least do some of
these things. Almost despite themselves, the delegates went wild.
An emotion suspiciously like hope surged through the hall. They
might not win, but at least there was a fighter carrying their banner. Truman sustained the initiative he had seized in his State of
the Union address in January and reinforced by his spring tour.
Throughout the entire campaign, he would never relinquish it.

Two weeks after the Democratic convention, Truman issued
executive orders 9980 and 9981. The first called for regulations
governing "fair employment practices within the federal establishment." The second established a committee to achieve "equality of treatment and opportunity in the armed services." Both
aimed at ending segregation. Wallace immediately attacked their
lack of detail, but the black press was enthusiastic. As he had with
Roosevelt and FEPC in 1941, A. Philip Randolph may have influenced Truman's decision to issue these orders. Randolph had
threatened that unless desegregation was initiated in the armed

forces before the implementation of the new draft law in August, there might be civil disobedience and young blacks might not report. In June Truman replied that it was a matter for Congress to decide. With his Southern flank turned by the Dixiecrat walkout, however, Truman the politician again motivated Truman the president. On July 26 he took direct action to implement the stronger Democratic civil rights plank he had so recently opposed.

FOLLOWING the dramatic conclusion to the Democratic National Convention, many Southern Democrats, as prearranged, met in Birmingham, Alabama. Thurmond had said in Philadelphia that if Truman were renominated, South Carolina Democrats could not support him. What was their alternative? To the most respected Southern senators, such as Richard Russell of Georgia and Lister Hill of Alabama, trading their seniority and influence in Washington for a protest that would likely prove futile was too great a risk. Even the sacrosanct issue of states' rights did not play all that well after sixteen years of federal investment in the South. As a typical newspaper reaction from South Carolina put it, "We stopped talking about states' rights and state sovereignty when we saw the gravy train headed our way." South Carolina's Senator Olin Johnston, who had snubbed Truman at the February dinner but remained quiet through November, added, "The South's fight against the civil rights program can be blocked in Congress." Whether Truman won or lost, "Democratic control of Congress giving Southerners key posts would turn the tide." A segregated South could continue to thrive. For that matter, might not Dewey, if elected, prove a more aggressive implementer of civil rights than Truman? Governor William M. Tuck of Virginia summed up the views of most responsible Southern leaders about the Dixiecrats: "What's the sense of jumping out of a fourth-floor window if it isn't going to save someone's life?"

Of all the Southern senators, only the two from Mississippi went to Birmingham to attend what became the nominating convention of the States' Rights Democratic party. Governor Strom Thurmond, despite his anti-Truman sympathies, had also planned to stay home. Only the pleas of old friends induced him to alter his schedule to see what was transpiring in Birmingham. Arriving on the afternoon of July 17, Thurmond learned that a number of others, while professing their support for the cause, had declined the honor of running for president on the States' Rights ticket. With time short, Thurmond's friends insisted that, having become a Southern spokesman, he make the race.

Thurmond spent an hour weighing his political future against championing a principle he had already espoused. Running, he knew, would also project him into the national spotlight, but how would he be portrayed? On the other hand, if everything fell into place, his efforts might determine not only the outcome of the election but the future relationship between Washington and the states. Were Dewey elected, Thurmond's influence might be enhanced—after tempers cooled and a new Democratic structure took shape under someone reasonable, such as Alben Barkley. As the *St. Louis Post-Dispatch* predicted, Barkley would be the "best possible choice to weld the scattered fragments of the party together and rebuild it for 1952." Even if the election went into the House of Representatives (where each state would have a single vote) and Truman finally won, the South would have demonstrated its power, precluding federal interference for the foreseeable future.

Thurmond decided to run, even if he was to be viewed a "candidate by default." He had no competition for the nomination. With little time to prepare his acceptance speech, Thurmond nonetheless made a forceful presentation. Stressing the issue of states' rights over segregation, as he would throughout the campaign, Thurmond later told newsmen, "We do not need the sup-

Clifford Kennedy Berryman, *Washington Star*

" . . . They've Already Gone, Howard."

port of . . . rabble-rousers who use race prejudice and class hatred to inflame the emotions of the people." Fielding Wright of Mississippi agreed to run with him. What the two governors saw when they entered the arena, packed with six thousand enthusiastic, largely self-appointed delegates, illustrated the problem they would face throughout the fall campaign. A large American flag and state banners decorated the hall, but the cheering crowd, far more like a Henry Wallace rally than the Democratic convention some had so recently exited, were waving Confederate battle flags. The brief States' Rights platform called on "all Democrats and upon all other loyal Americans . . . to join with us in ignominiously defeating Harry S. Truman and Thomas E. Dewey, and every other candidate for public office who would establish a police state in the United States of America."

Technically Thurmond and Wright accepted nominations ten-
dered by the state Democratic parties of Alabama, South Carolina, and Mississippi. In Alabama, electors had been chosen in
May, pledged in advance not to vote for Truman. After the convention these electors, whose names appeared on the ballot in the
regular Democratic column, announced their support of Thurmond and Wright. In Mississippi the state Democratic convention
directed its electors to vote for the States' Rights Democratic candidates. After the Birmingham convention, the state Democratic
committees in South Carolina and Louisiana designated Thurmond and Wright as the party's official nominees. In Alabama,
Truman and Barkley's names did not even appear on the fall ballot. In South Carolina, Mississippi, and Louisiana they were replaced in the regular Democratic column. In the absence of
substantial Republican opposition in these four states, the decisions reached within each virtually guaranteed the States' Rights
presidential ticket, running as Democrats, a total of thirty-eight
electoral votes. The question was, could Thurmond and Wright
expand their geographical base?

THE challenge for Wallace and his Progressives was to expand
their *ideological* base. They had already overcome two of the
customary problems of launching a third-party movement—financing and exposure to the electorate. Only in three states was
Wallace not on the ballot—Nebraska, Oklahoma, and Illinois (the
one absence that would prove significant). In California his supporters had presented more than 400,000 signatures in their petitions, well over the required number. In a luminous aura of
optimism, the Progressives held an extraordinary and truly national convention late in July. More than 3,000 delegates and al-
ternates descended on Philadelphia, as diverse an assemblage in
age, race, gender, and occupation as had ever gathered for a polit-

ical meeting in the United States. The delegates were frugal; merchants and food vendors complained that they bought even less than the Democrats, and far less than the buoyant Republicans of the previous month. Yet they contributed $80,000 to their party on the spot, nearly three times the convention's cost.

Entertained by Pete Seeger and a host of other folksingers, the faithful moved from Convention Hall to an outdoor baseball stadium, Shibe Park, for the acceptance speeches of their uncontested nominees. Wallace's running mate was the colorful Senator Glen Taylor, dubbed (appropriately enough for these Progressives of 1948) the "singing cowboy" of Idaho. More than 32,000 paid admission to hear them. Wallace made his finest speech of the campaign, proclaiming his pride that, unlike the disavowals of other candidates, he had many commitments—to all the working people of the nation and to peace-loving people everywhere.

But problems had already developed over the wording of the platform. The rejection of a relatively innocuous "Vermont resolution," denying "blanket endorsement" of *any* nation's foreign policy, indicated control of the proceedings by Communist activists. On local levels the Wallace campaign seemed refreshingly open, but a tight cadre of men like Pressman, Marcantonio, and John Abt pulled the national levers. All were to the left of Wallace himself, who as usual was uncomfortable in the company of inflexible professionals of any ideology. Taylor humanized the campaign without bringing in any new constituencies. Dwight Macdonald wrote in 1948, "It is not true that Henry Wallace is an agent of Moscow. But it is true that he behaves like one." Wallace himself wistfully revealed to friends before the Progressive convention that he wished the Communists would just go away. If they had a ticket of their own, Wallace reasoned, his Progressive party "would lose 100,000 votes but gain four million." However that may be, Wallace's inability to control his handlers and the PCA-derived policy of excluding no one led to results in 1948 that, as Norman Markowitz concludes, "removed the last serious opposition to Truman's foreign and domestic policies from the left."

The platform finally emerged as by far the longest of any party's in 1948. The Progressives identified the root cause of America's problems as big-business control of every facet of the nation's economy, its foreign policy, and both major political parties. While calling for a comprehensive program of government action in guaranteeing full rights and benefits for every segment of the population, the platform was most specific in denouncing "anti-Soviet hysteria as a mask for monopoly, militarism, and reaction." It urged immediate negotiations with the Soviet Union, arms reduction, the repeal of the peacetime draft and the National Security Act, the rejection of universal military training, the repudiation of the Truman Doctrine, the abandonment of American bases around the world, the phasing out of the Marshall Plan, an end to relations with Franco's Spain and other "reactionary and fascist regimes" and to colonialism, the "peaceful application of atomic energy," and the use of the United Nations to provide economic, not military, assistance to needy nations.

With the Berlin airlift in full flight to overcome the Soviet blockade of the city, and resistance to Stalin's threats enjoying evident public support, July 1948 was not an ideal time to launch a manifesto extolling peaceful coexistence with the Soviet Union. Gallup measured Wallace's potential support in June 1947 at 13 percent of the electorate. A year later it had dropped to an estimated 5 percent. The official start of the Progressive party's campaign, the exuberant high-water mark of "Gideon's Army," would also prove to be very nearly its last hurrah.

AS THE Progressives left Philadelphia, a smaller, more homogeneous, and far more disconsolate group gathered in Washington.

Many people took credit for suggesting to President Truman the idea of a special congressional session. It is clear from campaign memos that it was not a sudden formulation. Precedents were cited from past administrations, especially in New York State, and interest groups were mobilized to put pressure on the legislators. Of course, the risk was that the Republican-controlled Congress would enact just enough meaningful legislation to put the president on the defensive. Truman felt confident they would not.

On July 27 he went to Capitol Hill to outline what he wanted in even a short session. His priorities were "relief from high prices and the housing shortage," largely based on his earlier proposals, but he enumerated many other areas of concern. The president spoke for only six minutes to a chamber even less receptive than the one he had faced in January, insisting that "the vigor of our democracy is judged by its ability to take decisive actions. . . . The legislative and executive branches of our government can meet that test today. The American people rightfully expect us to meet it together."

Dewey recognized the session for the blatantly political ploy it was, but he also saw its ominous implications. He dispatched Brownell and Republican national chairman Hugh Scott to huddle with their party's congressional leadership, especially Senator Taft. Brownell suggested the passage of a bill revising the Displaced Persons Act, a bill expanding Social Security, and the passage of a $65 million loan to help establish the United Nations in New York City. It seemed little enough and would effectively call Truman's bluff. Unfortunately the senator whose committee oversaw refugee problems balked at any reconsideration of the Displaced Persons Act. And Taft is reported to have said, "I'm not going to give that fellow [Truman] anything," though in fact he tried to move his resentful colleagues to action, largely in vain. Congress agreed to authorize limited consumer credit controls and an increase in bank reserve minimums. No action was taken

on the thrust of Truman's anti-inflation program, housing legislation, or any other major domestic proposal. As Richard Norton
Smith writes: "On August 7, the Congress packed its bags and
went home to campaign. In eleven days it had given Truman only
two of the eight points in his anti-inflation program. Dewey got
even less: the UN loan, which survived a House-Senate conference committee only because Taft agreed to defer to the right
wing of his party and withdraw his housing assistance bill."

Dewey was denied the ammunition he could have used to
wage an aggressively unified campaign. Congress's inaction
drove a deep wedge between Dewey and the congressional wing
of his party. Most important, it played into Truman's hands. His
gamble had worked. Whatever the conflicts to come, he could re-
monstrate that the "do-nothing" summer session accurately represented a "do-nothing" Republican-controlled Congress, against
which even the party's own standard-bearer was powerless. As always, the GOP offered only promises of progressive programs
while Democratic action resulted in prosperity and progress.

Nevertheless in August the Gallup poll indicated that Dewey
continued to lead Truman by 48 to 37 percent, with Wallace at 5
percent and 10 percent of the respondents undecided. Roper's
margin in favor of Dewey was wider. At least in the perception of
the polls, the preliminaries and conventions had changed few
minds as the candidates approached Labor Day, the traditional
kickoff for the real campaign. If, as James Rowe maintained, few
votes shifted after July, the race was already over.

CHAPTER V

🏴

Truman's Leverage

AFTER the election, when Harry Truman was asked his opinion of television as a campaign medium, he replied, "It didn't cover enough territory was the only trouble." Covering territory was always Truman's conception of campaigning, no less in 1948 than in 1922. Only the dimensions had changed. Truman told his key advance man in 1948, Donald Dawson, that he wanted to go personally into every county in the United States so that people "would see I don't have horns and a spiked tail." That he didn't actually get to all 3,000 counties wasn't for want of trying. Truman estimated he traveled about 31,700 miles in his train tours after Labor Day, delivering 356 speeches to "twelve to fifteen million people," from one end of the country to the other. The actual number of his appearances was undoubtedly higher, depending on what constitutes a speech. One analyst of the rhetorical campaign of 1948 estimated the average length of Truman's informal remarks at 860 words, about a third of the length of his major addresses. But if a crowd were to gather at an authentic whistle-stop around midnight, more often than not Truman would come out on the rear platform to say a few words, even in his dressing gown and slippers.

Vowing the most vigorous campaign in the history of the presidency, Truman made as many as sixteen stops a day in only thirty-five full days of speechmaking (he did not really campaign on Sundays) between September 17 and November 2. In three extensive train tours, following appearances in Michigan and Ohio on Labor Day and separated by brief stays in Washington, Truman visited twenty-eight states. He conducted the nation's business from the train, equipped with advanced electronic equipment, and even held press conferences on board. Seen off by Barkley on his first campaign tour in September, the president added his own enduring phrase to Taft's contribution of "whistle-stop." Together they have come to define the 1948 election. Encouraged by his running mate to "mow 'em down," Truman responded, "I'm going to give 'em hell."

Eleven days earlier, in his nationally broadcast Labor Day address in Detroit's Cadillac Square, Truman served notice that he was not about to soften the rhetorical tone of his spring swing. Sharing a platform with, among others, Walter Reuther, Truman warned that "The Taft-Hartley Law is only a foretaste of what you will get if the Republican reaction is allowed to continue to grow," headed by people who "hate labor." "The reactionary of today is a shrewd man," Truman added. "He is a man with a calculating machine where his heart ought to be."

Clifford had been doing some calculating of his own. He viewed the president's position as that of a quarterback starting from his own end zone. As with his earlier recommendations, Clifford's August memo to the president on the conduct of the campaign reflected the views of others, particularly his closest associate, George Elsey, and Democratic research chief Batt (who was active in the ADA). They stressed four objectives: (1) presenting the president as a "crusading" leader carrying forward the gains of the New Deal and a firm foreign policy leading to peace; (2) winning "a large majority of the estimated 15,000,000 independent voters"; (3) linking Dewey with the 80th Congress; and (4) especially aiming appeals at the three constituencies that

Walt Kelly, New York Star

"They're off."

could swing the election—"working people, veterans, and Negroes." Clifford retrospectively amended this to "labor, farmers,
blacks, and veterans (which in today's terms would mean, to a
considerable extent, consumers)." Virtually the only people
not targeted were corporate Republicans. The memo recommended that Truman concentrate on the 17 states, containing

274 electoral votes, most closely contested in 1944, and make his major addresses in the nations's 23 largest cities.

Truman characteristically adapted this memo to his own conception of the campaign. He talked little in 1948 of foreign policy or civil rights, rarely referred to Dewey, and keyed his "vote for yourself" appeals to whomever had benefited most from the New Deal. He campaigned for all or part of five days in Ohio, five in Illinois, and three in California, where he had previously aimed his spring tour. In November the electoral votes of these three states sealed the election.

Although generous in giving credit to others at the time, Truman wrote in his memoirs, "My one-man crusade took effect. The people responded with increasing enthusiasm as the day of the election neared. I never doubted that they would vote for me, although my advisers were still not optimistic." This view has been perpetuated by such journalistic accounts of the election as Irwin Ross's *The Loneliest Campaign,* referring to Truman, and Jules Abels's *Out of the Jaws of Victory,* referring to Dewey. With the passage of time, historians have painted a more complex picture. Herbert Parmet, agreeing that "Truman worked hard and fully deserved his triumph," adds that "his success came from a number of factors beyond his control." Richard Kirkendall points out that "while in touch with some of the realities" of the 1948 campaign, the premise of "a brave man, fighting against great odds . . . and emerging as the winner in the greatest upset in American political history" is an interpretation that "obscures at least as much as it reveals."

Democratic victory in 1948 had many fathers and was based on many factors. Some of the most critical are infrequently cited. Beyond the thoroughly documented contrasts between the personalities and campaign styles of Truman and Dewey, and sheer luck in the timing of specific events, four factors particularly influenced the outcome: (1) the unusually important role of the

Daniel Fitzpatrick, St. Louis Post-Dispatch
Westward Ho!

major-party vice-presidential candidates; (2) the limited appeal of
the separatist parties; (3) prosperity at home and peril abroad—
both favoring the incumbent; and (4) the unsuspected superiority
of the Democratic campaign organization.

AMERICAN political history is replete with vice-presidential candidates who position themselves for presidential bids of their own.
The congenial contest between Barkley and Warren, however,
had an immediate impact on the outcome in 1948. To some extent

this was based on how each was viewed by the top of his ticket. Late returns from three major states secured the ultimate outcome of the election, but their importance was determined by earlier returns from two regions of the nation—the states bordering the deep South, and the Farm Belt of the Midwest. In both regions Barkley's efforts were pivotal.

Truman may have made more personal appearances, but Barkley undoubtedly covered more ground in 1948 than any other candidate. He campaigned by air, having convinced the reluctant Democratic National Committee to charter and adapt a DC-3 from United Airlines. Dubbed the "Bluegrass," Barkley's flying headquarters comfortably carried the candidate, a small campaign staff including two speechwriters whom Barkley rarely required, airline personnel, and two media representatives. Barkley claimed his "prop-stop" campaign covered 150,000 miles, equivalent to flying coast-to-coast fifty times, enabling him to visit thirty-six states and carry out a more flexible schedule than could his train-bound contemporaries. Between major addresses the tireless septuagenarian went by motorcade or bus to smaller rallies nearby and then flew off to another state. Barkley was fond of contrasting his own practice of writing speeches in the air and delivering them on the ground with the style of his Republican opponents, whose bland presentations were written on the ground but "were always up in the air."

Meeting shortly after the Democratic convention, Truman and Barkley had little difficulty in coordinating their campaigns. As both president and presidential candidate, Truman understood that he was obliged to make major addresses in cities within states such as New York and Pennsylvania that he was unlikely to carry, hoping his message would resonate widely. Of the seventy-four speeches Truman made that were broadcast on radio, twenty were heard nationally. Of his four television appearances, two were shown throughout the existing network of stations. Largely limited to regional radio, Barkley was able to tailor his appeals to more localized issues. He focused his attention not only on the South and later on the Midwest but also on states with key Senate races. This strategy embodied the conviction of Democratic leaders that, even should Truman lose, the party had a realistic chance of regaining control of the Senate. Like Truman in 1944, Barkley in 1948 was acceptable to Democrats in all parts of the nation, but under far more demanding circumstances.

As a youth, Alben William Barkley was so certain he wanted to be in politics that he changed his given name of "Willie Alben" as soon as he could legally do so, on the grounds that it wasn't likely to win him many votes. The oldest of eight children, Barkley was born in 1877 in a real log cabin to a tobacco-farming family near Paducah, Kentucky. Unlike Truman, Barkley won early renown for his oratorical skills and his physical strength. Working his way through two colleges, he read for the law, became a prosecuting attorney, and won election to Congress in 1912 at the age of thirty-five. Sworn in on the same day as the inauguration of his (and Truman's) political hero, Woodrow Wilson, Barkley befriended other freshmen congressmen who would go on to notable careers, such as Sam Rayburn of Texas. In 1926 Barkley was elected to the United States Senate from Kentucky. He had networked so successfully in the House that he was already being talked of as a vice-presidential candidate in 1928 (Barkley envisioned running with Al Smith in an "Al and Al" campaign). Barkley's reputation as a public speaker led to well-received keynote addresses at the 1932 and 1936 Democratic National Conventions.

It came as little surprise in 1937 that Barkley emerged as President Roosevelt's choice for Senate majority leader upon the sudden death of Joseph Robinson. After first-term Senator Harry Truman, despite White House pressure, honored his commitment to vote for Pat Harrison of Mississippi, Barkley won the post by a single vote, 38 to 37. There was no apparent enmity; both Barkley and Harrison were among the senators who journeyed to Missouri to urge Truman's reelection in 1940, though Barkley reflected, "I have often wondered how I would have felt about Harry Truman if I had lost the majority leadership by one vote." An ardent New Dealer and an effective floor leader during difficult times for the administration, Barkley broke with Roosevelt in 1944 over a controversial tax bill. After Truman's ascension to the presidency in 1945, he and Barkley worked reasonably well together, though Truman's congressional relationships were not so close as might be expected of a chief executive who cherished his earlier status as a man of the Senate. Barkley's biographer, Polly Ann Davis, writes that despite often being caught unawares by Truman's domestic proposals, Barkley was "undismayed by imperfect communications with the White House" and "provided outstanding support for the European Recovery Program."

Barkley's first important decision as minority leader after the Republican congressional sweep of 1946 would resonate in 1948. He worked out a compromise with Senator Taft regarding the seating of Democratic Senator Theodore G. Bilbo of Mississippi, an especially virulent segregationist who had been accused of fraud. Bilbo died in 1947 while his credentials were still "on the table without prejudice," confirming in the minds of many Southerners that Barkley was a man whose word they could trust. Although a border-state senator, Barkley supported his party's civil rights program without ever quite seeming to share in its sponsorship. He consistently voted for anti-lynching legislation and to outlaw the poll tax. But as a party leader he stressed compromise. In 1945, for example, he skillfully steered through the Senate a funding bill for the Fair Employment Practices Committee that fully satisfied neither liberals nor segregationists but impressed both sides with Barkley's evenhanded approach. The trouble with Truman's later comprehensive civil rights proposals, Barkley wrote to a friend, was that they "threw a whole basketful of matters in the lap of Congress at one swing and the result has been that it has injured him . . . in the South and it is doubtful whether it has helped him much in the North."

Although long established as the indefatigable "iron horse" of campaigners, after twenty years of fruitlessly seeking higher office Barkley in 1948 was resigned to ending his career in the Senate, well regarded on both sides of the aisle. When the call came to deliver yet another keynote address, he made the most of it. That address, more than Truman's response to it, truly nominated the Kentuckian as the president's running mate. Recently widowed (he would go on to enjoy a second happy, if brief, marriage), Barkley found the campaign a tonic. Beneath his affability and old-fashioned charm lay, as the political analyst William S. White observed, "a serious man of politics," capable of "reaching for the jugular vein of his enemies" yet conciliatory enough to bring wavering Democrats back inside the tent. In 1948 Barkley duplicated Truman's strength as an energetic campaigner, without Truman's weaknesses of political positioning and rhetorical stridency. It is instructive, for example, to compare Barkley's reasoned explanation of why the Republican tax cuts were "the wrong kind of tax reduction at the wrong time," and benefiting the wrong people, with Truman's emotional denunciations of an "outrageous . . . rich man's" tax bill, among the worst "things that has ever happened in our country."

Earl Warren was fifty-seven, fourteen years younger than Barkley, when he agreed to run with Dewey. The son of Scandinavian parents, Warren grew up in Bakersfield, California, where his father was employed by the Southern Pacific Railroad. Like Barkley, Warren had few doubts about his future—law leading to politics. Working his way through the University of California at Berkeley, he was among the first graduates of its new law school. As district attorney for Alameda County, he earned a record for prosecuting crime and corruption that was only a bit less impressive than Dewey's in New York. Warren was even broader in stature than Barkley and boasted an appealingly photogenic family. His outgoing geniality nevertheless masked a complex personality. As his biographer Ed Cray puts it, "Warren's career was a tangle of seeming contradictions." Neither eloquent nor particularly original, Warren had a dogged thoroughness that could seem plodding, yet Cray quotes one veteran California politician as observing, "Warren . . . always was about two jumps ahead of where you thought he was."

Whatever the basis of his popularity, Warren was unbeatable in California. Elected attorney general of the state in 1938 and governor in 1942, he conducted a prudently progressive administration that mirrored Dewey's in New York. He favored cost-conscious but vigorous government involvement when and where private enterprise could not or would not do the job. *Kiplinger Magazine*'s premature election issue of November 1948 touted the "new vice president" as "a big friendly Westerner" who, even while reducing taxes, "got one of the highest old-age pensions in the United States, set up a $450,000 postwar planning program [and] overhauled the decadent prison system." But Warren, in the tradition of California's Hiram Johnson, was more a popular than a party leader. His proposals, particularly for health-care reform, upset many of his fellow California Republicans. Conservative opposition hampered his efforts to effect a transition to the national stage. Still, Warren was renominated for governor on both the Republican and Democratic tickets in 1946 (Ike's premise was possible, at least in California), ultimately winning 90 percent of the vote. It is little wonder that, nonpartisan or not, Warren was sought by Dewey as a running mate. Together in 1948 their two states accounted for 72 of the 266 electoral votes needed to win the election.

Once his offer had been accepted, though, Dewey seemed to

lose interest in Warren. Their meeting in Albany after the Republican convention was much different from Truman's with Barkley. It resembled a briefing. Dewey and his aides informed Warren and his campaign manager, Senator William F. Knowland, that the New Yorker's plans were already set. Dewey's major speeches had been fully prepared and separated by subject. Initially Dewey would go west by train; Warren would come east. Dewey assigned to Warren some speechwriters he had no use for, and wished him well. Warren not only had no input into overall strategy, he considered himself "entirely separated from the main campaign" and left to his own devices. Truman and Barkley thereafter treated the Californian more like a victim than an opponent. Truman labeled Warren "a Democrat who is unaware of it"—a sentiment undoubtedly shared by many conservative Republicans. Barkley suggested that Warren "had no choice but to go along" with Dewey. The "loneliest campaign" in 1948 was not waged by Truman but by Warren.

WALLACE and Thurmond also had reason to feel increasingly isolated. As September turned into October, they seemed to be preaching either to congregations of the already converted or to the indifferent. Wallace campaigned vigorously throughout the nation, but his symbolic, courageous forays into the South, turned into near riots by egg- and tomato-throwing white supremacists, were more relevant for the future. Wallace was not the only candidate who insisted on speaking before desegregated audiences; Warren was haunted for the rest of his life by the "searching look" of blacks he saw in Savannah. Wallace, however, insisted that his audiences not be racially separated into sections but mixed indiscriminately, as at his Northern rallies. He characterized one week-long tour of the South—by bus, train, and car, encompassing thirty appearances in seven states—from Virginia to

Mississippi, enduring late-summer humidity and the real threat of violence, as the most memorable experience of his life. Many of Wallace's idealistic young supporters, black and white, helped lay the groundwork and learn the techniques that would enable their causes in the 1960s to reach fruition outside of political parties: civil rights and the women's and peace movements. In 1948, however laudable his intentions, Wallace might more profitably have invested his time in a few major states, particularly California, if his realistic goal was to deny Truman the presidency.

The theologian and social activist Reinhold Niebuhr, who had helped to inspire the founding of the ADA, circulated an appeal to liberals in October 1948, supported by such prominent friends of Wallace as former New York governor Lehman, that all but sanctified "cold war liberalism." Comparing the appeasement of Stalinism to the earlier mistakes of Munich, it further excluded Wallace from the liberal and intellectual mainstream and denied the legitimacy of his arguments. Wallace refused the Socialist Norman Thomas's challenge to a debate on communism, branding it a diversionary tactic by a marginal candidate who was only a stalking-horse for Truman.

The concession of the Progressives as a full-fledged political party came early. On September 21 a frustrated "Beanie" Baldwin formally withdrew Progressive candidates in races against such liberal Democrats as Hubert Humphrey in Minnesota and Chester Bowles in Connecticut. Henceforward the Progressives, like the Dixiecrats, would be more a protest than a party. Patricia Sullivan adds a telling comment from a contemporary voter. Truman's "standing up to Southern threats stopped the swing of many towards the Progressives because now thousands of colored and liberal white voters can vote the Democratic ticket without apology." Many "colored" voters obviously admired Wallace, but fewer than 10 percent of those who were enfranchised voted for him. By making the most of such circumstances as the stronger civil rights plank, Truman appeared more steadfast than he had been. It would happen again in foreign policy.

Thurmond's fate was sealed by the failure of all the other states of the old Confederacy to follow the example of the four who had slated the States' Rights candidates as the sanctioned Democratic ticket. Tennessee rejected a proposal like Alabama's to pre-commit its electors to vote against Truman. One by one the Democratic leadership in Virginia, North Carolina, Florida, Arkansas, Texas, and Georgia resisted attempts to replace Truman-Barkley as their endorsed slate. A stronger Republican presence influenced several of these decisions; the desire to preserve party harmony and relationships influenced them all. Most disappointing to Thurmond was his failure in Georgia, where the staunchly segregationist Herman Talmadge held sway. Richard Kirkendall writes, "Where Truman was able to run as the Democratic candidate, he was able to win."

The president made one brief excursion into the South at the end of his second train tour, but it consisted of only three appearances. He addressed the American Legion in Miami, not as a candidate but "as a comrade in arms," and praised the efforts of both major parties in supporting peace through strength. The next day Truman's remarks at the North Carolina capitol in Raleigh, dedicating a monument to former presidents Andrew Jackson, James K. Polk, and Andrew Johnson, included a telling reference to Jackson's knowing "that the way to correct injustice in a democracy is by reason and debate, never by walking out in a huff." That evening, at the Raleigh fairgrounds, Truman made his one thoroughly political address south of the border states of West Virginia and Kentucky, other than in Texas. Dealing mainly with agricultural policy, it differed little from his customary attack on the 80th Congress and the remote residue of Hooverism except for this clear reference to the Dixiecrats near the end: "A vote for a third, fourth, or fifth candidate is the same as a vote for the Re-

publican candidate. . . . I think you know who your friends are."
Uncharacteristically, there were no whistle-stops on the way back
to Washington.

Barkley was entrusted with carrying out a policy of domestic
containment, designed to limit the Dixiecrats to their four-state
base. In New Orleans, speaking to probably the least enthusiastic
"party rally" of his life, Barkley served notice that the national
Democratic ticket was abdicating no section of the country. After
enumerating all the beneficial administration programs for the
port city—from reciprocal trade to flood control—Barkley
launched into his main theme, repeated throughout the region: the
South "would still its own voice in government if they voted for
anyone but Harry Truman." Normally Barkley, an instinctive ora-
tor, found that "the words came to me as I went along." In the
South, however, and even in safer border states, his addresses
were carefully prepared, tailored to his specific audience, and devoid of the humor he usually employed. Farther north in
Delaware, for example, when it began to rain, Barkley cut short
his speech, insisting that not only did he not want his listeners to
get wet, he didn't even want them to get "dewy." On another occasion he suggested that the motto of the 80th Congress might be
"We feel for you, but we just can't reach you."

In his serious Southern speeches, Barkley made no mention
of civil rights or Strom Thurmond, except by inference, and denounced only the Republicans. In New Orleans he claimed that
the GOP "in the long years since the War Between the States has
neglected the South and has permitted and even encouraged the
exploitation of the South by those same plutocratic interests
which have always dominated the Republican Party." This reads
like Truman rhetoric, but Barkley's speaking style had a way of
softening any message he delivered.

More frequently he spoke in terms of conciliation, reminding
Southerners of their own interests, as in Asheville, North Car-

olina: "It would be a tragic thing if the partnership between the Democratic Party and the states of the South were to be destroyed. It would leave the South without effective means of promoting its own high aspirations and without a voice in the councils of the nation." Or in Tennessee: "The Republican Party does not understand the South and is not interested in its problems. . . . It is a fear justified by their record that the Republican nominee in this campaign will terminate our great natural resources. . . . The men and women of the South are searching their hearts. I have faith in their judgment. I believe in their future." In Barkley's appeals, the Dixiecrat threat became a Republican appendage. At the other end of the ideological spectrum, Truman was applying the same technique to Wallace's Progressives.

Barkley's most important exercises in persuasion were conducted off the podium, in private talks with Southern officeholders, many of them old acquaintances. A Republican victory might cost them their influence, if not their jobs. Already inclined toward neutrality, the most prominent required little entreaty to remain safely and unobtrusively sidelined for the extent of the campaign—but Barkley was better suited than Truman to deliver the message.

Thurmond got his national publicity, but it was phrased in the racial context he had feared. *Time* put him on its cover under the heading, "The Dixiecrats' J. Strom Thurmond—Is the Issue Black and White?" Ralph McGill of the *Atlanta Constitution,* like most major Southern newsmen opposed to the Dixiecrat movement, wrote a prophetic piece for the *Saturday Evening Post* predicting that Southern conservatives would ultimately wind up in the Republican party. "The revolt has no place to go," he concluded. "The South has."

The suspicion of some mainstream Democrats that the Dixiecrats would receive substantial support from oil companies because of their stand in favor of state control of offshore drilling never materialized. With little money and limited organization, Thurmond sensibly made only a token appearance or two in the North but extensively toured the states contiguous to his base— from Texas to Maryland. He would lose them all, except for a single Tennessee elector who could not bring himself to vote for Truman. Unlike the hostility Wallace faced in the white South, Thurmond was invariably treated with courtesy as a visiting governor, but few dignitaries showed up to be seen or photographed with him. In Houston, for example, only the mayor performed his official function by greeting Thurmond. All other officeholders— local, state, and national—stayed away.

Reporters complained that Thurmond seemed only to have a single stock speech, one theme suitable for all occasions. They could not induce him to express opinions on the other pressing issues of the day, beyond voicing his opposition to communism at home and abroad. Thurmond maintained to the end that his motivating concern was federal encroachment on the rights of the states. He could no more escape the issue of race, however, than Wallace could overcome the issue of communism.

FOREIGN policy was the overriding issue in 1948, yet it was rarely raised by any candidate other than Henry Wallace. The polling organizations that proved so unreliable in predicting the election's outcome appear to have been closer to the mark in measuring the mood of the American people. Throughout 1948 all pollsters agreed that fear of a new war was by far the greatest concern of those they interviewed, irrespective of their political preferences or any other variable. For example, the Gallup poll issued on April 19, 1948, asked, "What do you think is the most important problem facing the country today?" Thirty-eight percent of respondents volunteered answers such as "preventing war," "peace," "danger of war," or "working out peace." Twenty-seven percent provided such responses as "foreign policy," "getting along with Russia and other nations," and "helping Europe." Only 9 percent mentioned such areas as "domestic politics" or "presidential election"; only 8 percent, "inflation," "high prices," or "cost of living." When Gallup asked the same question in July, responses under "foreign policy" totaled 44 percent, those under "high cost of living," 23 percent. No other issue came in at over 9 percent. A companion poll, with third parties excluded, asked, "Which political party do you think can do a better job of handling the problem you have just mentioned?" Democrats were favored over Republicans by 52 to 48 percent.

Surveys by Roper and Crossley, the other major polling organizations in 1948, confirmed these conclusions. Elmo Roper wrote that his own findings indicated that Truman's secretary of state, George C. Marshall, who was viewed as "above politics," was more respected than any likely Republican replacement. At this time Dewey still led Truman in all three major polls by an average margin of 12 percent. Prominent pundits such as the Alsop brothers and Walter Lippmann, who accepted the proposition that Dewey was as good as elected, also reflected the view that the pivotal issue of 1948 was whether Truman or Dewey could better lead the nation in a dangerous world.

The message of these mixed polling signals was misread by both candidates. Truman was drawn into more than a cursory review of foreign policy only late in the campaign, and in a generally negative context. Initially he seemed to view not only his secretary of state but the whole subject of foreign policy as above politics. It should not have been off-limits for Dewey, but his most consistent criticism of the administration's foreign policy complained only of its confused and inefficient management. He lamented the millions lost to communism in Eastern Europe without detailing what might have been done to prevent it. He declared that Asia should be given attention equal to Europe but conceded that the matter was complex and needed more study. He vowed to clean up the mess in Washington, including ridding the government of Communist sympathizers, but Truman's loyalty program and Wallace's presence in the race blunted the impact of such appeals.

With the pervasive theme of national unity dominating Dewey's carefully prepared public utterances, it was particularly difficult to separate foreign relations as an area of contention. With Dewey's poll numbers high, Vandenberg and Dulles, who was slated to become Dewey's secretary of state, urged states-manlike caution. Dewey would need Democratic cooperation to conduct his own foreign policy; in terms of objectives, the cold war consensus had already formed. When Truman proposed aid to Greece and Turkey, Senator Vandenberg told the president that "it is necessary to scare the hell out of the country." He, Dulles, and other Republicans, while dedicated to Dewey, had helped shape Truman's foreign policy. For his part, Dewey needed little encouragement to support bipartisanship. After all, in his mind he had initiated it in 1944.

Dewey continued to take credit for Republican foreign policy leadership despite former Secretary of State Hull's complaints about the New Yorker's "extravagant claims" for "achievements that were the fruit of joint patriotic efforts by members of both parties." Dewey's major speeches may have been carefully pre-pared (Truman's proclivity was to talk all over the lot), but as Earl Warren could testify, they were united by their imprecision. Some even seemed contradictory. In Louisville, for example, Dewey accused the administration of "clumsiness . . . weakness . . . wobbling," and failing "to consult the Republicans before making sudden and vital policy commitments." Nonetheless, Dewey contended, when laudable steps were taken, "the names in the headlines were Senator Vandenberg, Congressman Eaton, Harold Stassen, and John Foster Dulles." Dewey concluded with the hope that a genuine "bipartisan peace policy could be brought to effective practice not by the present administration, which cannot understand the Communists, but by new Republican leadership. Strong and united, we will wage the peace together."

Not all Republicans concurred with this bland approach. Young Hugh Scott, the Philadelphia congressman who became Republican national chairman in 1948, urged Dewey shortly after the convention to "come out fighting," as he had in 1944 with his Oklahoma City address accusing the Roosevelt administration of all but criminal negligence in failing to prepare the nation for war. Dewey answered Scott, "That was the worst speech I ever made," and declared his intention to conduct an affirmative campaign "focused toward moral issues." Even Vandenberg, echoing the Republican platform he had helped shape, said, " 'Bipartisan foreign policy' applies only where cooperative consultation and mutual cooperation exist from start to finish. . . . This has not been the case in China, Palestine, or Japan."

The flashpoints throughout 1948, however, were in Europe. It is unknown whether Joseph Stalin had a preference in the presidential election of 1948, but his actions strengthened Truman's stance as a commander-in-chief who not only talked national unity, as did Dewey, but personified it. From the Soviet threats to Iran and Turkey in 1946, through the inception of the Truman Doctrine in 1947 and the debate over European recovery in 1948, the nation seemed to face perpetual emergency. As one international crisis followed another and focus shifted from domestic concerns, the *Wall Street Journal* spoke for many Americans in lamenting, "We have had too many 'crises,' too many promises that this or that action would save the day. . . . We have a right to expect more than that from our leaders." Apprehension and uncertainty were shared on both sides of the Iron Curtain. If the Russians legitimately feared encirclement, as Wallace and his followers maintained, Truman's concern in 1948 was not so much the threat of overt Soviet aggression (they already held most of the territory their armies had occupied in 1945) but Communist subversion.

The coup in Czechoslovakia in February 1948 confirmed Truman's worst fears. This was not Bulgaria or Albania or even Hungary but a Western-inspired nation with democratic antecedents, formed after World War I under the enlightened leadership of Thomas Masaryk and brutally sold out to the Nazis in the 1938 Munich accords. No nation better represented the perils of appeasing despotism. After World War II, Czech president Eduard Beneš, who well remembered Munich, extended the hand of friendship to both Washington and Moscow. Beneš wanted to participate in the Marshall Plan but also allowed free elections in which the Communists polled more than any other party and were invited to form part of a broad coalition government.

In a complex series of events in February, twelve ministers from several parties resigned from the Beneš cabinet, fearful that the powerful Communist interior minister would rig upcoming elections. The Czech Communist leader Klement Gottwald then demanded that Beneš name a new Communist-controlled government. For the second time in a decade, Beneš unhappily presided over the dissolution of Czech democracy. How much direct Soviet pressure was exerted is uncertain, though Truman later wrote that the takeover was "supported by the Russian army at the border," and the Soviet deputy foreign minister was in Prague at the time. On March 10 Czech Foreign Minister Jan Masaryk, son of the republic's first president, fell or was pushed from his apartment window to his death. That this last nation to "fall" to the Soviet Union had held such promise of peaceful coexistence made the shock all the greater throughout Western Europe. The Czech Communists moved swiftly and brutally to crush all opposition and form a satellite state as subservient to the Soviets as any of their neighbors to the east.

Truman also moved quickly. The Czech crisis validated his view of the postwar world. As he had written his daughter, Margaret, in 1947, "The attempt of Lenin, Trotsky, Stalin, et al. to fool the world and the American Crackpots Association . . . is just like Hitler's and Mussolini's so-called socialist states. Your pop had to tell the world just that in polite language." The president called a joint session of Congress and urged a restoration of the draft for five years, the passage of universal military training, and prompt enactment of the European Recovery Program. As the historian Melvyn Leffler writes, the Czech crisis "altered congressional sentiment. Everyone was afraid the Communists would try to seize power in other countries." This was the cold war in a hotter dimension, but atomic threats were irrelevant to subversion. A buildup in conventional armed forces followed, supplementing the economic component of containment. Even in budget-minded Washington, Truman noted to an aide, "Every department of the government has now gone warlike." The representatives of five European nations were already meeting in Brussels to discuss military as well as economic cooperation.

In a rare mention of the only presidential candidate already in the race, Truman declared on March 17 to the Friendly Sons of St. Patrick in New York that he did not want and would not accept "the political support of Henry Wallace and his Communists." The Czech coup was also a crisis for Wallace. He handled it clumsily, insisting at first that it was an all but inevitable outgrowth of Truman's truculent foreign policy, "not a tempest in a vacuum." Later he speculated that Masaryk's death might well have been a suicide and noted rumors that a right-wing coup had been brewing in Czechoslovakia with the collusion of the American ambassador. Once again the liberal media was incensed, *The*

Nation reminding Wallace that "Beneš and Masaryk had stood for democratic socialism, for the new Europe that liberals had hoped would emerge from the war." Many within the Progressive party questioned their leader's views. Months before Wallace's official nomination, Norman Markowitz observes, "the Czech coup did much to undermine Wallace's contention that long-range cooperation was possible with the Soviet Union."

Truman's view of Wallace was more ambivalent than his outright disdain for the Dixiecrats. He feared that Wallace, despite all his gaffes, would preempt the peace issue. This apprehension ultimately led to some peculiar decisions, resulting in unusual discord in the Democratic camp, even given the conviction of Clifford and his colleagues that they were engaged in an uphill struggle against long odds and short time.

The Czech coup extended and exacerbated the crisis atmosphere in Washington in the spring and summer of 1948. The historian Martin Walker characterizes the early years of the cold war as akin to a tennis match in which each side felt obliged to return serve with a volley of its own. Western policymakers, unlike some legislators, were convinced that the Soviets, whether momentarily on the offensive or the defensive, did not want a direct military confrontation. Leffler writes, "The key task for U.S. and British leaders was to find the proper mix of prudence and toughness." Truman genuinely desired to de-escalate international tensions, but he did not trust Stalin sufficiently to enter into direct negotiations. His immediate concern in April, shared by his military and diplomatic advisers, was how to head off a probable Soviet response to the most recent Western successes—victory by Christian Democrats (covertly funded by the CIA) in the Italian elections, and the Greek government's rolling back (supported by American advisers) of Communist rebels. From the State Department, Marshall and Undersecretary Robert Lovett, counseled by Russian experts George Kennan and "Chip" Bohlen, instructed

American Ambassador Walter Bedell Smith to convey to the Soviets U.S. resolve to resist any precipitous retaliatory action, but to phrase the message in conciliatory terms. Truman concurred.

The Soviet response ignored American firmness but seized on the prospect of mediation. On May 11 Radio Moscow announced a statement by Soviet Foreign Minister Molotov, replying to a "proposal" from Bohlen of which the American public knew nothing. The Soviet government agreed to a full "discussion and settlement of differences between us." After the nerve-wracking months of "war scare," as the historian Frank Kofsky puts it, a "peace scare" seemed to have broken out. The ball was in Washington's court. Truman must have been dumbfounded. He hurried to issue an equivocal statement the same day, suggesting that Molotov had not been very specific, that there was "no new departure" in American policy, and that "the United States has no hostile or aggressive designs whatever with respect to the Soviet Union."

Wallace, perhaps still smarting from the reception to his comments on the Czech coup, grasped the opportunity. It happened that he had a major rally scheduled on the very next evening in New York City. Wallace issued his own invitation to the Soviets, which he claimed to have prepared earlier but had revised "to take into account the events of yesterday." Blaming both sides for misunderstandings, Wallace made six specific proposals for immediate action to end the cold war: (1) a reduction and ban on the development of all armaments, leading to (2) general disarmament; (3) free trade; (4) free travel; (5) free exchange of all scientific information; and (6) the establishment of a United Nations agency for the distribution of international relief. In effect this was an open letter to both Stalin and Truman. Again the Soviet response was not long in coming. On May 17 a second statement was broadcast over Radio Moscow, this time quoting Premier

Stalin himself, acknowledging that "Mr. Wallace's program could serve as a good and useful basis for such an agreement."

Wallace's intrusion gave Truman the excuse he needed to distance himself further from a summit meeting. The day after Wallace's speech, Secretary Marshall declared that no useful purpose would be served by holding talks with the Soviet Union since the American position was well understood by both. On May 13, four days before Stalin's response to Wallace, Truman used his news conference to back Marshall. The president wanted deeds, not words. His answers to most questions were blunt and brief, not uncommon in Truman's meetings with the press. He reiterated that his longtime invitation to Stalin to visit the United States had never been withdrawn, and that Marshall had responded "adequately" to the exchange of notes. In Moscow, Ambassador Smith suggested that there be no "misconceptions" about political speeches in the United States. Whether Wallace gained support through his initiative would be determined by the American electorate in November, but both he and Stalin had Truman on the defensive—something Dewey was never able to do.

On June 24 the Kremlin abruptly terminated any peace overture by cutting all surface traffic to and from West Berlin. The Soviets seemed intent on driving the Western powers out of the city, even at the risk of war. Truman made no further reference that spring to meetings with Stalin, except to instruct Ambassador Smith to make clear American insistence on Western rights in Berlin. Conciliatory proposals receded into irrelevance. After some indecision, the president agreed to the "temporary" expedient of an airlift to bring food and fuel to more than two million marooned Berliners. The American military governor, General Lucius D. Clay, who oversaw this enterprise, had little confidence in it. Supported by some members of Congress and the British Labour government, Clay favored sending U.S. armored columns from Western Germany into the Soviet zone to clear the roads, whatever the risks. Truman rejected such a confrontational stance and continued to consider other options. The airlift's extraordinary success, exceeding all expectations, made other action unnecessary. American and British cargo planes supplied the city until the Soviets quit their blockade the following spring. The morale of all Western Europe had received an immense lift.

These dramatic events formed the international backdrop to the 1948 political conventions. As in civil rights, the president had not been as decisive as he appeared, but his calculated firmness had stalemated the Soviets and avoided war. In the long term, as Walker writes, "an astonishing display of the West's industrial weight and political determination . . . also settled into place the strategic permafrost which was to settle over Europe for a generation." In immediate political terms, it became more difficult for Dewey to depart from bipartisanship, even had he wanted to.

The Republican candidate, traveling west on his "Victory Special," now outdid himself in effusions of national unity. (Warren's train, dubbed the "Victory Express," also implied optimism, though with its frequent stops it was more like a local. Truman's "Presidential Special" was the immense *Ferdinand Magellan,* attached to an engine and fifteen normal-size railroad cars—to the very limits of permissible length for a passenger train.) On September 22 Dewey said in Denver of the United Nations General Assembly meeting in Paris, "Our country will make an immense contribution to the success of that conference by a mighty showing of the action that binds us together." In Los Angeles he told a large audience, "In Berlin our planes and our men are giving the world fresh proof that America has what it takes." Even while using two of his favorite lines, "With your permission, we are going to have a big housekeeping in Washington—the biggest untangling, unsnarling, weeding and pruning operation in our history," and "The head of our own government called the exposure of Communists . . . a red herring," Dewey uttered no criticism of Truman's foreign policy. He wound up with his customary call for "a new unity for all America and with every American."

In Salt Lake City on October 1 Dewey delivered an entire address devoted to "our greatest domestic issue. . . . It is the problem of the peace of the world." Then he added, "It is one which should only be dealt with entirely without partisanship, and in the highest realm of statesmanship." Before turning to the nebulous eight-point program that followed, Dewey decried the Soviets' "easy victories" and "concessions made by our government," but, he declared, "these things are done. . . . The question is: what lies ahead?" The gist of what lay ahead was the bold assertion that "it is not too late to develop and pursue a consistent and effective foreign policy and to make the Soviets understand that just as we intend to deal fairly and honestly with others, so we insist that others deal honestly and fairly with us."

Even that bromide was too much for Harry Truman. Late in the campaign, when he finally began to speak more about foreign policy, Truman invariably blamed Dewey for bringing the subject up, as if it were tantamount to disloyalty. The president extended this tactic to domestic issues with international implications. For example, on October 14 in Milwaukee he made his most thoughtful address of the campaign, limited to the question of atomic energy. He initiated it by saying, "Tonight I'm going to talk about something that ought not to be in politics at all, but the Republican candidate has brought it in, and I have to tell you about it. When he did this, he displayed a dangerous lack of understanding of the subject." Truman proceeded to explain the Atomic Energy Act of 1946 and why the Atomic Energy Commission should be controlled by government rather than private industry. He examined how civilian leadership worked with the military and spelled out his hopes for international control and inspection in the future. It was a rare departure from his attack mode. In Oklahoma

City he returned to the offensive, accusing Republicans of maligning the loyalty of government employees, despite his own program in this area. Truman declared, "I should like the American people to consider the damage that is being done to our national security by irresponsible persons who place their own political interests above the security of the nation."

ALTHOUGH he dismissed the renegade Democratic splinter parties with fine impartiality, whether the "crackpot forces of the extreme right" or the "contemptible Communist minority" of the far left, Truman continued to be concerned about Wallace's "shrill campaign." Although the Progressives' strength was visibly shrinking, what effect were Wallace's accusations of "warmongering," directed at both major party candidates, having around the world? Dewey, who continued to lead comfortably in the polls, wasn't about to take on Wallace. Particularly in view of the Berlin crisis, even Dewey's foreign policy contest with Truman became more muted. Publicly Truman exuded confidence, despite every indication to the contrary, that he would win in November. On the train he even outlined to a fascinated George Elsey how it would go state by state, finally yielding the Democratic ticket 340 electoral votes. Still, Wallace's accusations rankled. Perhaps after the quick demise of the "peace scare," some positive initiative from the president might help to secure the election. Having demonstrated his willingness to stand up to the Russians, Truman mused about a dramatic gesture to enhance the peacekeeping side of the equation.

The president's October surprise was not the result of a long-nurtured plan. Clifford considered it "the worst mistake of the Truman campaign." Apparently it was the idea of two young staffers, David Noyes (who later helped Truman write his memoirs) and Albert Carr, who took it to Truman's influential appointments secretary, Matt Connelly. Despite his earlier opposition to negotiations, Truman (perhaps assisted by Noyes) wrote in his memoirs that he had been pondering "some new approach to the Kremlin in an effort to ease the tensions and get on with our many unfinished negotiations."

Personal diplomacy might be most effective, but Truman could hardly leave the country in the final stages of a political campaign. In the face of strenuous opposition from his staff, he decided to send his old friend Fred M. Vinson, chief justice of the United States, on a Harry Hopkins–like mission to Moscow to talk personally with Stalin. Somehow the president was convinced that "Old Joe" might be inclined to "unburden himself to someone on our side he felt he could trust fully." But why Vinson, who had no diplomatic experience and had never even met Stalin?

At the time, Secretary of State Marshall was in Paris at the UN meeting, over which the perplexing issue of Berlin still loomed. Marshall knew nothing of a Vinson mission. On October 5, as soon as an incredulous Lovett in Washington had seen a copy of Truman's proposed announcement of the mission, he requested an urgent meeting at the White House. By then word of the plan had leaked to at least one newspaper. Lovett cautioned the president that the Vinson mission would not only inhibit policymakers but at the very least would result in Marshall's resignation. Truman abandoned the idea, undoubtedly to the relief of Vinson, but endured the double embarrassment of having both his secret plan and its abrupt cancellation revealed to the nation.

The press had a field day. *Time* called the intrusive proposal "shocking." The *Buffalo News* labeled it "amateurish electioneering." In a particularly patronizing column titled "What Next?" Walter Lippmann all but suggested that Truman resign before the election so that he could do no further harm to the nation's prestige. Republicans in Congress were more restrained; Truman's blunder was so obvious that it hardly called for a partisan attack. Dewey was most restrained of all, counseled by Dulles that only a steady demeanor would reassure the country's "jittery" allies and the confused Soviets that Truman's unpredictable meddling would soon be over.

Other observers differed. In an article titled "Try Again, Mr. President," the columnist Thomas Stokes faulted not the idea but the failure to carry it out: "The peace of the world is worth it." Even Elsey, who had opposed the mission, commented retrospectively, "I think the people said to themselves, 'Harry Truman is trying to do something for peace, but the State Department has blocked him again.'" Anti-Wallace liberals had no objection to the president making an end run around the diplomatic establishment. With only a gesture—in this instance, even a failed gesture—Truman made his point, particularly with some constituencies that had been notably "mild about Harry."

Truman's behavior in the final days of the campaign encourages speculation about his confidence in victory. He escalated his rhetoric to new heights—or depths, implying that somehow Dewey was related to both Communists and fascists. Just as Dewey was occasionally obliged to find a way to defend the domestic record of an 80th Congress that had denied him effective ammunition to do so, Truman's dilemma was to claim success for the nation's bipartisan foreign policy without excessively crediting Republicans. His customary conclusion, as in a Brooklyn speech, was to welcome "the real contributions made to our foreign policy by certain Republicans"—but then to remind his audience that "these contributions must not blind us to the fact that the Republican Party . . . is a late convert to the cause of international good will and cooperation." As for the election itself, Truman insisted that Stalin really hoped Dewey would win.

Truman had implied this throughout the campaign, but in its last week he became more explicit, as if trying to goad Dewey into finally taking the gloves off. In rear-platform remarks in Indiana, Truman declared, "If anyone in this country is friendly to the Communists, it is the Republicans [by financing] the Communism-inspired third party to beat the Democrats." In Boston Truman accused the Republicans of doing everything possible to get "a third party candidate" on the ballot. He further claimed that the American Communist party, under instructions from Moscow, supported Wallace's divisive candidacy so that the Republicans could win. Why? "The Communists don't want me to be president," Truman said, "because this country, under a Democratic administration, has rallied the forces of all the democracies in the world to safeguard freedom." Apparently bipartisanship wouldn't be the same with a Republican at the helm. "The Communists want a Republican administration," Truman stated, "because they believe its reactionary policies will lead to the confusion and strife upon which Communism thrives. . . . The Democratic Party has been leading the fight to make democracy effective, and to wipe out Communism in the United States." Truman never deigned, any more than Dewey did, to debate the merits of Wallace's specific proposals. In view of ongoing international events, the administration had a strong case for its anti-Communist policies, but it was rarely advanced in detail or with suitable restraint to an electorate that would have been receptive to a positive discussion of foreign affairs.

Truman's most inflammatory attack on Dewey was made on the evening of October 25 in a major address at the Chicago Stadium, broadcast on nationwide radio. He again accused the 80th Congress of religious prejudice by passing a "shocking displaced persons bill . . . which cruelly discriminated against Catholics and Jews," and he censured cynical Republicans for using left-wing extremists to get themselves elected. Then he ventured into new ground, tying Dewey not only to the customary "gluttons of privilege" but also to "undemocratic forces" of the right. The dangerously concentrated economic power of a few men in the United States, Truman asserted, required a "front man to run the country for them." In Germany such interests had found Adolf Hitler; in Italy, Mussolini; in Japan, Tojo. The implication was clear. It was one thing to brand Wallace a naive Communist dupe or Thurmond a supporter of segregation. It was quite another to call Dewey the potential stooge of a fascist elite.

The Republican candidate, hearing Truman's speech in Albany as he was about to depart for his final campaign swing, was predictably infuriated. Richard Norton Smith writes, "Realizing that Truman had afforded him a final chance to abandon sweetness and light, Dewey wanted to make the most of it." As luck would have it, Dewey was to make a major speech the following evening in Chicago, in the same hall where Truman had spoken, but it was slated to be on domestic policy. For once in his carefully calibrated campaign, Dewey considered having an entirely new speech prepared. At that moment, which might have changed the outcome of the election, Dewey's "organizational instincts betrayed him." Everyone close to him agreed that he should stay the restrained course they were still convinced would lead to victory. The candidate's wife, Frances, for whose opinion Dewey had considerable regard, "reminded him of the horror of Oklahoma City. 'If I have to stay up all night to see that you don't tear up that speech, I will,' she told her husband." A survey was taken of the national committeemen, even of the journalists on the train. "Chastened by a solid front of certainty," Smith writes, "Dewey wavered, then gave way, concluding, 'I can't go against the whole Republican Party.'" It was too late to change strategy—or even the thrust of a speech.

Instead Dewey went partway. As he began speaking in Chicago, heard nationwide over NBC radio and seen regionally on ABC television, Dewey devoted one paragraph to foreign policy:

We all know the sad record of the present administration. More than three years have passed since the end of the war and it has failed to win the peace. Instead millions upon millions of people have been delivered into Soviet slavery while our own administration has tried appeasement one day and bluster the next. Our country desperately needs new and better leadership in the cause of peace and freedom. It needs a government that will lead from strength to build peace in the world so that your sons and mine will not have to go through another war.

That was it. The remainder of the speech catalogued how the Truman administration had "failed even more miserably at home"—except for one further reference. Dewey took to task his unnamed opponent who had now "reached a new low in mudslinging," and added, "This is the kind of campaign I refuse to wage." Even in this instance, echoing the tone of pundits like Lippmann, Dewey patronized Truman as more inept than evil, more worthy of pity than of anger. Dewey's own polls indicated that Truman, the battling underdog, would benefit from attacks that seemed too personal.

Dewey's next major address, the following evening in Cleveland, fortuitously was to be about foreign relations. Dewey and his advisers had a full day to reconsider its wording. Unfortunately that meant ignoring the crowds that had gathered to see the candidate along the way. One of the most disappointed of the thousands who had hoped to hear from Dewey trainside in Ohio was John Bricker, Dewey's running mate in 1944. Bricker could not help comparing Dewey's seeming indifference with the intensive campaigning Truman had recently done along the same tracks. That evening Dewey dined only with his aide Paul Lockwood, refusing even to invite Senator Taft, who was left to ponder why Dewey so disliked him. On his campaign train, Dewey frequently ate alone.

Taft nonetheless gave Dewey a gracious introduction at the Cleveland Auditorium. Early in the campaign, Dwight Eisenhower, perhaps in the process of discovering he was a Republican, had privately told Dewey that a six-week tour of the nation convinced him that the election would come down to just two questions, "Russia and inflation." Russia undoubtedly was the more important. Dewey soberly intoned to his Cleveland audience that "towering over every other cause is the burning question of world peace." He continued by enumerating all the nations that had been swallowed up by the Soviet Union since 1945, and those presently threatened. He did not limit his list to Europe, declaring, "It is very late, and all China is in grave peril." How might China be saved? Only by American resolve under more consistent, more focused, and more determined leadership. Only a unified America could unify the free world, leading to security and ultimately to peace. No more specific solution to any international problem was spelled out. There had been no changes to the original text, delivered in advance to the media. The candidate might have more profitably invested his day in campaigning.

The most elaborate of the "What Dewey Will Do" projections at the close of the 1948 campaign, a thirty-four-page special section of the new *Kiplinger Magazine,* encompassing the efforts of twelve reporters over six months, predicted: "The Dewey-Dulles Republican foreign policy will not be drastically different from the policy of the past." *Kiplinger* continued, "It will be more consistent, more businesslike . . . more aggressive, yet less truculent. . . . The Marshall Plan will be continued. Reciprocal trade will be extended. . . . Dewey will . . . strengthen the Truman Doctrine . . . [and] push for a broad European alliance," including integrating a reindustrialized West Germany. Defense spending would likely be increased, but within a balanced budget. "Patience and firmness" described both the Dewey and Truman foreign policies. *Kiplinger* noted only one probable point of departure: Dewey would quickly implement "a new policy for China . . . [consisting of] military aid for a year or two, but prime emphasis on more economic aid, long haul."

China had a special place in American sympathies, including those of normally isolationist Republican conservatives. What became known as the "China Lobby" originated as an amalgam of respect for high Chinese civilization, the dreams of Christian missionaries, the lure of immense economic potential, and admiration for Chinese fortitude in the face of sustained Japanese aggression. Earlier personified by the enlightened Sun Yat-sen, the vision of a unified, democratic China had ostensibly been inherited by Nationalist leader Chiang Kai-shek and his charismatic American-educated wife. Despite a deteriorating economy and an unstable political situation, in February 1948 Congress appropriated $463 million for aid to the Nationalist regime. Marshall warned that no amount of aid could assure the continuation of Chiang's government in the face of concerted attempts to overthrow it by the Chinese Communists, who had actually done more fighting against the Japanese than had the Nationalists.

The question came down to how and where in the world the American government proposed to carry out its policy of Communist containment. As Lovett warned in the summer of 1948, "vital" interests had to be separated from "peripheral" interests: "The fine line must be drawn somewhere or the United States would find itself in the position of underwriting the security of the whole world." The Truman administration made the difficult determination that, although communism was still viewed as a monolithic worldwide conspiracy, the vast mainland of Asia was not as vital as the bastion of a rebuilt Japan and a mutual defense alliance with Western Europe. On the overall premise of priorities, in the words of the historian Wilson D. Miscamble, even a Communist-controlled China "could not threaten the security of the United States." The case of Korea, however, was complicated.

Originally seen as a prime candidate for containment, southern Korea had been run by the American military between 1945 and 1948, then turned into a client state, the Republic of Korea. Only after Truman's victory was South Korea viewed as outside the American "defense perimeter," but in 1948 it was not a focus for discussion.

Truman was so concerned about the domestic consequences of an immediate Chinese collapse, however, that in March 1948 he denied he had earlier recommended Communist participation in the Chinese government. If a coalition government could not work in Czechoslovakia, what chance would it have in China? As a practical political strategy, had Dewey seized on the China issue and the whole question of the extent of America's commitment in Asia, he could not have been accused of abandoning Europe-based bipartisanship, and his examination of this policy would have enjoyed uncommonly unified Republican support. Had Dewey made even the dramatic announcement "I will go to China," he might have secured the opportunity to do so as president. He needed to do more than protest Truman's inconsistencies with pious platitudes.

James MacGregor Burns succinctly summarizes the 1948 campaign: "Dewey, seeking to soften memories of his blatant linking of the Democrats with communism in 1944, took the high road, and lost his fighting edge . . . to the degree that he could not exploit Truman's chief vulnerabilities." No one put it better than the New Deal's Harold Ickes, out of power but not out of adjectives, who referred to "Thomas Elusive Dewey, the candidate in sneakers," who rather than contest for any constituency simply dodged his way to defeat. Despite high regard for the loyalty of his associates, in politics Truman kept his own counsel and followed his own instincts. They betrayed him at the end of October, just as did Dewey's "organizational instincts." A fighting Dewey, sufficiently experienced to retain his controlled demeanor, would have won the election—but Truman's luck held. Dewey refused to accept the gift.

Years later Dean Acheson reminisced in a letter to Truman, "You remember that we used to say that in a tight pinch we could generally rely on some fool play of the Russians to pull us through?" There were at least two "fool plays" during 1948—the Czech crisis merged into the Berlin crisis, underscoring the American electorate's deep concern with issues of war and peace. That neither Truman nor Dewey adequately addressed this concern is indicated by the millions of voters who stayed home on election day.

CHAPTER VI

🚩

The Upset
That Wasn't

AT THE outset of the 1948 campaign, Truman's most obvious advantage was that there were more Democrats in the nation than Republicans. Despite the GOP sweep in the congressional elections of 1946, the "normal" Democratic vote during this period was computed at 57 percent of the electorate, including 10 percent "independent Democrats." On that premise Truman could afford to lose a percentage point or two to both the Dixiecrats and the Progressives, as long as he retained the Democratic core and the separatists' strength was bunched in a relatively few states. The outcome might be very close, however, unless Truman's appeals registered more forcefully than Dewey's with independent-minded voters. Both major parties expected a record turnout. Even Elmo Roper, so convinced of the certainty of a Dewey victory that he ceased polling the outcome of the presidential race early in September, predicted that more than 51 million Americans would vote in 1948. Less than 48 million had done so in 1944. Roper's competitor, George Gallup, continued his organization's efforts on the presidential contest right up to the election, but his 1948 polling results were based on interviews initiated as much as two weeks earlier.

Gallup made a cogent point after the election: an "unexpected economic development" had helped decide it. "Events again turned the tide in the late stages of a campaign," Gallup noted, refuting "Farley's Law" (most voters decided by Labor Day) and its acceptance by Rowe and Clifford. "Few political observers are aware of the important role that events play in presidential campaigns," Gallup continued. Events in this instance might also be defined as luck.

Truman should have benefited from both his leadership role in a perilous world and general prosperity at home. Yet even with employment and profits high, inflation and strikes reduced, the president was regarded as unelectable. Convinced that he could only beat himself by going on the offensive, Dewey coasted. The most compelling of the all-but-unanimous predictions on the outcome in 1948 was the celebrated *Newsweek* poll near the end of the campaign. *Newsweek* consulted fifty of the nation's most astute political observers, including Marquis Childs, Arthur Krock, and Raymond Moley (himself a former New Dealer). They unanimously predicted a Dewey victory.

Perhaps they should have gone to Iowa. The "unexpected economic development" to which Gallup referred was based on a decision not late in the campaign but quite early. Its significance was only later appreciated. If there is such a thing as too much prosperity, farmers in the grain belt of America's heartland experienced it in the fall of 1948.

Before the New Deal, the Midwest had been traditionally Republican. Between 1880 and 1932 the only Democratic presidential candidates to make inroads were Cleveland in 1892 and, more extensively, Wilson in 1912. In 1932 and 1936 Franklin Roosevelt won virtually everywhere. In 1940, however, Wendell Willkie achieved a return to the Republican column of much of the Midwest, as well as some Great Plains and Mountain states. He won Indiana, Iowa, Michigan, North Dakota, South Dakota,

Daniel Fitzpatrick, St. Louis Post-Dispatch

How to Get That Guard Down?

Nebraska, Kansas, and Colorado. In 1944 Dewey won these same
states except for Michigan (which he lost by only 22,476 votes),
while adding Ohio, Wisconsin, and Wyoming. In planning the
1948 campaign, Truman and his advisers were uncertain how
much emphasis (despite Clifford's retrospective addition of farmers as a target group) to place on pursuit of the farm vote. Although farmers in general were viewed as well disposed toward
the administration, its agricultural policy, like Truman's efforts to
contain inflation, seemed to cut both ways, giving the Democrats
no evident advantages.

Within Truman's cabinet, farm issues were a source of contention. Federal price supports, which Dewey also favored in modified form, buttressed agricultural prosperity. But they could result in higher food prices for American families. Harold Stassen, after meeting with Dewey, asserted shortly before the fall campaign got under way that the Democratic administration was "doing all in its power to keep consumer prices artificially high." Truman's commerce secretary, Charles Sawyer, seemed to agree. Only two days after Stassen's remarks, Sawyer ordered a curb on grain exports to reduce domestic prices on agricultural products, declaring, "I think it's time the housewife got a break." This move upset Truman's secretary of agriculture, Charles F. Brannan, but he publicly took aim not at Sawyer but at the Republicans, stressing the inadequacy of the Hope-Aiken flexible farm price supports bill passed by the ("do nothing") 80th Congress. To Brannan the Republicans' real aim was to "scuttle the entire price-support system." Truman was caught in the middle.

Before the fall campaign both parties were slow to recognize a potentially crucial farm issue. Good weather made 1948 a bountiful year for the harvest of wheat, corn, oats, and other staple crops. The provender was so abundant that farmers needed additional storage space until they could sell their harvest at peak market value. Under the Commodity Credit Corporation (CCC) the federal government had provided such storage facilities for agricultural surplus. In June the CCC charter came up for automatic renewal. In a cost-cutting move little noted at the time and not criticized by the administration, Congress revised the charter, making it impossible for the CCC to lease any facility except office space. Farmers, especially in the Midwest grain belt, who did not have excess storage facilities of their own were obliged to sell any surplus quickly, at whatever price they could obtain, or watch their crops spoil. An obscure journalist with Democratic inclinations supplied his own explanation, headlining his article, "Congress Acts to Force Down Farmers' Price at Behest of Grain Lobby."

By September Clifford was fully alert to this almost providential new issue. Truman was already scheduled to speak at the National Plowing Contest at Dexter, Iowa, on September 18 before an audience exceeded only by his Labor Day crowd, an expected 80,000 to 100,000 people. He and his strategists decided to launch a "preemptive attack" on Dewey in the Farm Belt before the Republican candidate arrived. (Whether by design or happenstance, Dewey's train often seemed to be following Truman's around the country, permitting the president to proclaim near the end of the campaign that one place Dewey wouldn't follow him was into the White House.)

At Dexter, after demonstrating his residual skill in plowing a straight furrow, Truman used the storage bin controversy in the same way he exploited Taft-Hartley before labor audiences. In a speech most remembered for the graphic accusation that "this Republican Congress has already stuck a pitchfork in the farmer's back," Truman also introduced to the sea of faces before him the notion that GOP stood for "gluttons of privilege." Then he spelled out his newly discovered conspiracy:

> Most growers have sold their wheat this summer at less than the support prices, because they could not find proper storage. . . . Big business lobbyists and speculators persuaded the Congress not to provide the storage bins for the farmers. They tied the hands of the administration. . . . Now they have attacked the whole structure of price supports. . . . They are obviously ready to let the bottom fall out of our farm prices . . . but the price of bread has come down not one cent. . . . There is only one way to stop the forces of reaction. . . . I'm not asking you just to vote for me. Vote for yourselves! . . . Vote for your farms! . . . Vote for your future!

The response, perhaps due to the widely scattered nature of the audience, was only polite applause. Public opinion polls in Iowa changed little after the president's address, retaining a gap of fifteen to twenty percentage points in favor of Dewey. But perhaps a seed had been planted.

It would be cultivated by Alben Barkley, making his impact on the second critical region that determined the outcome of the election. He sometimes traveled in tandem with Secretary of Agriculture Brannan. (Truman later insisted that "very few members of my cabinet made any political speeches." He must have overlooked Brannan, who made more than eighty.) Barkley's tour of the Midwest, the Mountain states, and the West Coast during the first half of October convinced him for the first time of the possibility of victory. He later told an interviewer, "When I got out into the corn belt . . . the great agricultural states, I began to feel the tide was in our direction." If the Republicans had already taken away farmers' storage facilities, what else might follow in Dewey's promised housecleaning in Washington?

Barkley's wit, largely absent from his speechmaking in the Southern and border states, returned in the Midwest. Compare the overkill of Truman's Dexter oration with these excerpts from a typical address of Barkley's in farm country, this one delivered in Mankato, Minnesota:

> On the one hand the Governor of California has been quoted as saying that farm policy, like foreign policy, ought to be removed from the realm of political discussion. . . . The Governor of New York . . . couched his discussion in such vague and general terms that I am unable to determine just what his views are. . . . I do not believe that the farmers of the United States are willing to allow themselves to be taken in by doses of New York soothing syrup, accompanied by the faint odor of California orange blossoms. . . . It has been reliably reported that the Republican lead-

ership of the state of Minnesota is deeply disturbed about what the next Congress, if it is a Republican Congress, will do in the field of farm legislation. . . . They have watched the dead hand of the Republican leadership in the 80th Congress do its work on segment after segment of the Democratic farm program. . . . Thousands of farmers have had to sell their grain at distress prices. . . . Right here in Minnesota, your corn crop is 75 million bushels larger than it was before the war . . . but the Republicans have seen to it that storage capacity will stay small.

Barkley also blamed the GOP for playing politics with agricultural conservation, the Rural Electrification Administration, and the Farmers Home Administration, praised Truman for extending New Deal policies, and closed with an appeal similar to Truman's but phrased quite differently: "The Democratic Party has a right to expect the gratitude of the farmers of the nation. But we do not ask for gratitude. We ask only that the farmers apply the practical common sense for which they are noted to the issues of this election. We have no doubt that if they do, the Democratic Party will sweep the farm sections of the nation."

On the other side of the fence, Brownell was fuming. So were such leading Republicans as Vermont senator George D. Aiken and Kansas governor Frank Carlson, who urged that Dewey depart from his prepared speeches to make a vigorous, definitive address validating his enlightened views on agricultural policy. Despite his urbane appearance, Dewey was the proprietor of a working, profitable dairy farm on his "Dapplemere" estate in Pawling, New York. He knew about farming. His advisers on agriculture, however, were theoreticians from Cornell University rather than practical Midwestern farm leaders. In both 1944 and 1948 Brownell had urged more input from real farmers, understanding the crucial importance of the farm vote to any national

Republican victory. In 1948 he nearly resigned over Dewey's indifference to the storage bin uproar, where in fact the Democrats were equally vulnerable. John Burton, the alert Republican equivalent of Bill Batt, volunteered his own draft of a new farm speech for Dewey. But all Burton, Brownell, Aiken, or Carlson could get out of Dewey's campaign handlers was that their candidate wasn't about to discuss anything controversial. Apparently unity had more appeal, even in the Farm Belt and in the face of this new crisis, than did self-interest.

In his own account of the election, Brownell made the farm issue part of his lingering dissatisfaction with the whole nature of the Dewey campaign, over which he was supposedly presiding:

> Near the end of the campaign, agricultural prices fell nearly 50 percent, and farmers had to sell their grain at depressed prices. Truman capitalized on this development by showing that the Republican-dominated Eightieth Congress had refused to appropriate government funds for the construction of grain-storage facilities. . . . The Dewey campaign was again stymied by the shortsighted actions of the Republicans in Congress. . . . Our problem in this instance was another result of our earlier decision not to break with the conservative Taft Republicans on the hill. Vice-President Alben Barkley, the popular "Veep" and an orator of great repute from Kentucky, then went on the hustings to dramatize the issue. Secretary Charles Brannan joined in the fray. The media did not get the significance of the drop in farm prices, but the October crowds in the farm states surely did. I have always credited Barkley with putting the Truman ticket over the top in the last days of the campaign.

After the election, a *Washington Post* editorial criticized Barkley for resorting to the same "slashing methods of attack" as those employed by Truman, implying that these tactics were unworthy of Barkley. The *Post* hoped Barkley would return to his customary gracious demeanor back on the Hill. Whatever his campaign methods, they had certainly worked.

DESPITE the apparent certainty of Republican victory, it had taken Earl Warren seven hours to decide to run with Dewey. Warren's wife, Nina, wondered whether her independent-minded husband could conduct a campaign directed by others. The problem turned out to be less a matter of dictation than indifference. By the Californian's very presence on the ticket, it was assumed that the Far West had been secured. Before 1948 Dewey had campaigned largely in the image of the relentless prosecutor he had been. It was a past shared by Warren, who could also be tough in political combat. Nonetheless Warren took more naturally to the moderate Republican themes of 1948. His emphasis on the blessings of unity, however, while an appropriate message for the governor of so diverse a state as California, did not effectively counter Truman's scare tactics on a national stage.

Warren and Dewey both spoke at whistle-stops on their train tours, though Dewey stressed his major addresses, rarely made stops before 10 a.m., and is estimated to have spoken on perhaps 170 occasions during the entire campaign. In a single month-long swing through 29 states, Warren probably made twice as many appearances as Dewey, "eight or ten stops each day." The opening address of Warren's transcontinental campaign, delivered in Salt Lake City on September 15, was titled "A More Perfect Union." He took gentle swipes at Truman's already evident rhetorical excesses but went on to emphasize the need for national unity, transcending politics. His speech was replete with such laudable statements as "Good Americans are to be found in both parties," "There are progressives and conservatives . . . in both parties," "No party has a patent on progress," and "Our campaigns must be vigorous, but friendly."

When Warren referred to the "precarious" world situation and to such problems as the cost of living and dissension at home, he cautioned that they were not "entirely the fault of any one individual, any political party or any national administration. Much of it has been caused by world forces beyond the control of the American people." Elect Republicans in 1948, he urged, because of their greater unity and competence. The experienced Dewey, Warren promised, would lead a "progressive" administration, combining "efficiency and humanity." Warren's most solid shot at the opposition—a good applause line he would use many times—was, "It will be no problem for Tom Dewey to get communists out of government—because he'll never let them in."

Overall Warren hardly exemplified the customary attack role of vice-presidential candidates. On the Democratic side, the top of the ticket had taken on this task himself, complemented by the more restrained appeals of his own running mate. Warren, who finally decided to prepare most of his own speeches, dispatched them to Dewey's headquarters for approval. Ed Cray quotes Warren's secretary as reporting, "A lot of stuff got knocked out." A generally exhausted Warren who, unlike Dewey, made a point of meeting with local Republican leaders wherever he went, later wrote, "I was speaking not for myself but for Tom Dewey, and was always conscious . . . of avoiding anything that might conflict with his policies." How effective the genial Warren of 1948 might have been as a bare-knuckles contestant is open to conjecture. Both his and Dewey's speeches would have benefited from more aggressiveness, but what they needed most was more specificity.

Constrained or not, Warren's approach to the campaign was warmly welcomed by the press. Under the heading "Something New Under the Sun," the *New York Times* appraised the Salt Lake City kickoff:

Jay Norwood (Ding) Darling, Des Moines Register
Counting His Chickens

Governor Warren of California has chosen to open the Republican national campaign in a highly unorthodox manner. He does not find all the good on one side, all the evil on the other. . . . It is Governor Warren's thesis that over the course of history both political parties in the United States have served the country well . . . that the question before the independent voter . . . is to make his appraisal of strengths and weaknesses . . . giving his support to that vehicle of the two which offers the best hope for the solution of current problems. . . . Mr. Warren's own appraisal leads him, not unnaturally, to choose the Republican side. . . . He himself has given an excellent example of how to go about this . . . in a mood of simple and unadorned sincerity. . . . Governor Warren has set an admirable pattern of the way to conduct a political campaign without jeopardizing the unity of a free people at a time of danger.

Whatever Warren's protestations to Dewey, the rhetorical results continued to represent the bland leading the bland. In Pueblo, Colorado, on September 17, Warren obliquely criticized Wallace's Progressives for subverting a "wholesome name" and suggested that all parties should stress "what's right with America." He even praised the 80th Congress, noting it had appropriated "more money for reclamation in these states than any other Congress in the history of our country." In Albuquerque Warren denounced government "through political trickery and chicanery," without naming any names. In St. Louis he replied to Truman's farm address in Dexter, Iowa, declaring (an assertion Barkley subsequently questioned) that "agriculture isn't a political issue." Without referring to Congress, Warren did in this instance enumerate his, and Dewey's, record of approval for price supports, agricultural co-ops, rural electrification, and improved roads to connect farms and markets.

In Columbus, Ohio, Warren warned other nations "not to mistake a political campaign as evidence of disunity" and called on Republicans and Democrats alike to "stand shoulder to shoulder regardless of the outcome of the election." Warren went on to make the difficult point that "everyone knows . . . our country is now riding the crest of the biggest boom in history, and it is going to take a steady, sure hand at the tiller to keep us on an even keel." Apparently the Democratic administration, now in the process of "breaking up," had little to do with bringing on the boom. In Detroit Warren promised that victorious Republicans would amend the Taft-Hartley law "if any of its provisions are oppressive." Speaking in Louisville, Warren repeated Dewey's claim to have initiated the nation's bipartisan foreign policy, pledged it would continue, and paid tribute to Senator Barkley in his home state as "a fine American who has made many contributions to good government." Finally, at the end of September, Warren's "Victory Express" reached the East Coast. Accompanied by his wife and their eldest daughter, Virginia, Warren pledged in a Newark rally that a "progressive" and "forward-looking" Republican administration would guarantee a "reasonable floor of economic and social security" without sacrificing individual freedom or imposing governmental regimentation. During the campaign Warren may well have used the word "unity" even more than Dewey and "progressive" more frequently than Wallace. Riding in a motorcade through rush-hour mid-Manhattan to party headquarters at the Hotel Roosevelt, the Warrens enjoyed one of their more exciting days in the campaign.

Warren reported "fair crowds" throughout his trip but observed that while they were friendly they showed little enthusiasm. From his train he repeatedly called Dewey's lieutenants, urging a more vigorous campaign. In New York he confided to an equally disconsolate Herbert Brownell, "I wish I could call someone an S.O.B." Brownell, who had been retained as Republican national chairman after the election of 1944 at least in part through Warren's moderating influence, little appreciated Warren's efforts, noting after the election that the Californian simply didn't register as a national candidate. Warren's accumulated frustrations boiled to the surface before his arrival in Manhattan, but his anger was directed at his fellow Republicans. In upstate New York the party organization didn't even bother to greet him. Demanding of Dewey, "Is this any way to run a railroad?" Warren found a better-planned reception in New York City.

Warren returned to California with two weeks left to campaign. He was asked by his wife, "Honey, do you really think you will win this election?" At about the same time Bess Truman was inquiring of her husband's aides, "Does he really think he is going to win?" More Americans would have shared Mrs. Truman's doubts, but Warren knew that, at least in California, the Republicans were in trouble.

Two decisions inhibited Warren's campaigning in his own state and raised his ire as nothing had previously. First, the Republican leadership, agreeing with the Roper poll that the outcome of the election was a foregone conclusion, and anxious to save money, had taken the extraordinary step of closing GOP campaign headquarters in San Francisco and other California cities in mid-October. The second decision, reached earlier, was Dewey's personally and reflected the way he conducted the entire campaign. In the great Central Valley of California, where the Sacramento and San Joaquin rivers flow, the key local issue was water and power development. Warren had made his progressive reputation there by championing reclamation and conservation efforts. Dewey entrusted to his running mate the issue of federal irrigation assistance to the West's water-dependent growers. But when Dewey toured the Central Valley, while Warren was at the opposite end of the country, many of its residents and newspapers wanted to know more about the New Yorker's specific commitments to their own welfare.

Although Warren's memoirs were unfinished at the time of his death, they deal fully with the 1948 campaign and this localized aspect of it:

> Where people [were] interested in the manner of development of the water and power of these rivers, [Dewey] was pressed for an answer to particular phases of that project. His only reply was to refer them to his speech on water conservation made, I believe, in Oklahoma some weeks before. Some of the press was greatly annoyed. . . . I called Tom on the phone and suggested he discuss

the matter with the California press. He refused to do so but said, "You tell them what you think the policy should be, and I will stick with you on it." I told him they knew what my policies were, but they wanted to know from him what his were. He was adamant, and he lost the state by less than one vote per precinct—about 18,000—but we lost the Central Valley alone by about 200,000 votes.

Nothing Warren could say rectified Dewey's silence. The most popular governor in the history of California watched helplessly in 1948 as his state slid into the Democratic column.

By the end of the campaign it is likely that Warren, Truman, and Barkley shared at least one opinion—a personal antipathy to Thomas E. Dewey. Despite the similarity of their experiences and political positions, the Republican dream ticket simply didn't work. Nevertheless Warren always viewed Dewey as a superb administrator who would have made an excellent president. Dewey's graciousness in defeat heightened Warren's sense of regret. A month after the election the enigmatic squire of Pawling revealed an unexpected self-deprecating wit at the Gridiron Club dinner in Washington. As Warren recalled, Dewey "was more relaxed, genial, humorous, and even folksy than I had ever seen him. I have often thought that if he had displayed a little humor in a relaxed way during his successive campaigns . . . he might have become president." It would have taken more than humor for Dewey and Warren to have won in 1948, but in view of the final figures, not very much more.

ALMOST overlooked at the time was the superiority of the Democratic campaign organization. Even if staff work didn't fulfill Clifford's prediction that it would prove decisive in determining the election's outcome, it helped make possible the coordinated effectiveness of the Truman-Barkley campaign. Many of those involved, like men in battle, were not fully cognizant of the importance of their contributions. They were focused on the next crossroads and the next news release, and were running largely on adrenaline. Most of what they heard from the media made their efforts seem futile. To the press, the pervasive Republican theme of unity was exemplified by the sheer efficiency of the GOP campaign. Dewey's train ran on time, Truman's was chaos on wheels. But the Republican machinery was not as well oiled as it appeared. And the reality of Democratic unity could only be found beneath the surface.

The overwhelming majority of the nation's newspapers, including many that were normally disposed to support Democrats, in 1948 chose to endorse Dewey. Even that voice of GOP conservatism, the *Chicago Tribune,* which only four years earlier had been delighted to declare Dewey's political demise, grudgingly gave him their nod. At least he wasn't Truman. Those in the press who favored Dewey had little need to color their coverage: Truman's actions seemed to speak for themselves. His frenetic campaign—attacking Congress and a Hoover administration that had left office almost sixteen years earlier, instead of his actual opponents in the race—drew press reactions ranging from condescension to contempt. Walter Lippmann spoke for many of his journalistic colleagues in labeling it "a palpable absurdity" that Truman and his administration were more liberal than Dewey and Warren. The traditionally progressive *Oregon Journal* voiced its dismay at the public spectacle of a president "descending to the level of his Missouri training in campaign vilification." In fact, Truman had immense respect for Hoover; but 1948 was an election year.

In marked contrast, the dignified challenger campaigned more like an incumbent. Dewey had already been anointed by publisher Henry Luce, whose *Time* magazine of October 25 reported that little remained beyond counting the votes to compute Dewey's victory margin, and whose *Life* magazine a week later featured a full-page photograph of Dewey and his wife, captioned "The Next President Travels By Ferry Boat Over The Broad Waters Of San Francisco Bay." Even Dewey's lifeless campaign was defended on the premise that it prefigured a nation no longer at war with itself. Democrats for Dewey included everyone from the prizefighter Joe Louis to the daughter of Al Smith. No record survives of an organization called Republicans for Truman.

But the apparent unity of the Republican effort covered deep divisions, not only between the candidates and Congress but between the titular party leadership and the tight little group who were really in charge. Truman's "Missouri Gang," some of whose members were indeed secluded during the campaign, consisted largely of comfortable cronies who exerted little influence on policy. Dewey's "Albany Gang" of long-term acquaintances exercised real power, both within New York State and in planning Dewey's rise to national stature. Republican chairman Scott discovered just how much power when he met with some of them after voicing his "disquiet" with Dewey's projected high-level campaign. New York committeeman J. Russell Sprague and upstate leader Edwin F. Jaeckle bluntly told Scott that his role was to keep the party faithful happy, not to suggest Dewey's strategy. Scott writes of being invited to only one joint meeting during the entire "harmonious" campaign and of hearing the already apprehensive Brownell express his wish "that the election were that very day." Scott's Republican national headquarters exerted its modest influence from a different Washington building than the one in which Dewey's campaign headquarters were located, with little contact between the two.

Dewey had a sizable campaign staff, bigger than Truman's, but it was largely composed of functionaries employed in such

tasks as catering to the press. His inner circle of trusted New
Yorkers, including Sprague, Jaeckle, executive assistant Paul
Lockwood, and speechwriter Stanley High, was headed not by
Brownell but by Elliott V. Bell. A Columbia classmate of
Dewey's, Bell was not only his closest adviser but his best friend,
godfather to both of Dewey's sons. In 1948 Bell was also superin-
tendent of banks for New York State, readily accessible to the
governor. Previously a successful journalist, the well-organized
Bell coordinated the preparation of Dewey's addresses. More
than anyone else he was responsible for their consistency and the
inflexibly bland quality of the campaign. Confidence based on
the two men's earlier political successes influenced Dewey's re-
luctance to shift his strategy when he felt the 1948 race drawing
tighter near the end.

This small group of insiders was certainly unified, but it was
not entirely insular. A second, much larger tier of people helped
sustain the tone of the campaign—Republican state chairmen,
committeemen, and other political professionals throughout the
country. Although they enjoyed little personal contact with
Dewey, they fed consistently supportive information to his staff.
Often they seemed mesmerized by their own local polls and cautioned against changing strategy. A disgusted John Burton, who
tried to "raise hell" about the low-key effort, observed, "Twenty-
five years earlier, the professionals would have recommended a
front-porch, rocking chair campaign." To Burton, "Dewey turned
around his good public image by not being himself." Scott concurred but directed his blame at those closest to the candidate.
Dewey had won in the past by fighting. In 1948, however, Scott
recalled, "He switched. I now suspect that Dewey's inner circle
had no stomach for a battle of personalities with Harry Truman.
There was an acute sensitivity in the Dewey camp." Even if he
had chosen to express such views, it is doubtful that Scott would
have found much support for them as he dutifully visited with

Republican leaders in all forty-eight states. Placid or not, the strategy seemed to be working.

The most memorable account of the visible contrast between Dewey's and Truman's efforts came from Richard H. Rovere, writing for the *New Yorker* directly from each candidate's train. In his lengthy "Letter from a Campaign Train—En route with Dewey," Rovere observed, "Candidates notoriously promise better than they ever perform, but if Governor Dewey manages the presidency half as well as he is managing his campaign for it, we are about to have four, eight, twelve, sixteen years of cool, sleek, efficiency in government." Rovere, who had previously traveled on the Truman train, went on to compare the two: "The difference is . . . thirty or forty years. It is the difference between horsehair and foam rubber, between the coal-stove griddle and the pop-up toaster." Aboard Truman's "Presidential Special," correspondents missed deadline after deadline while waiting for advance copies of speeches Truman didn't follow anyway. "Dewey's speeches, which reporters can put on the telegraph wires twelve to twenty-four hours before delivery time, are as smooth and glossy as chromium."

The atmosphere in the press section of the Truman train reminded Rovere of the back room at a district party headquarters, redolent of bourbon and poker. Dewey's was more like a country club, with the relaxed patrons enjoying martinis and manhattans. Creature comforts were provided by the accommodating Dewey staff. When the train stopped for the night, "luggage vanishes from your berth and is waiting for you in the hotel room you have been assigned. Good Republican caterers have hot coffee and thick roast-beef sandwiches waiting in the press rooms at every stopover." Life with Truman was catch as catch can. Reporters had to scramble off to hear Truman's whistle-stop remarks. Dewey's were broadcast throughout the train.

Yet what was it all for? On either train or anywhere else, Rovere was unable to interview "a single impartial and responsible observer of national affairs who is willing to defend the thesis that this tearing around will affect the electoral vote in even one state." Still, Rovere found the image of a battling Harry Truman peculiarly affecting. At many stops the president insisted on bringing his exceedingly reluctant family onto the rear platform to join him, introducing his wife as "the boss" and his daughter Margaret as "the one who bosses the boss." Rovere wrote, "The three traveling Trumans . . . will be a picture to cherish, and it will stand Harry Truman in good stead for the rest of his life. Traveling with him you get the feeling that the American people . . . would be willing to give him just about anything he wants except the presidency."

Charter Heslep of Mutual News, who spent weeks on the Truman train, noted the enormous crowds the president was drawing but recalled that former losers such as Wendell Willkie had also enjoyed large, enthusiastic crowds. Perhaps people were simply curious to see a president in the flesh. Heslep also remarked on Truman's extraordinary energy but added that about half of the nearly fifty "weary" newsmen, radio reporters, and photographers on board were planning to jump to the Dewey train when the two overlapped in Los Angeles. At its peak Dewey's "Victory Special" carried about a hundred media representatives, hardly surprising in view of the quality of its amenities and the apparent certainty of the Republican's election.

Along the smooth Republican route, only once did the "old" Dewey resurface in a major address. His October 11 speech in Pittsburgh, focused on labor relations, had everything his other orations in 1948 lacked. It was specific, hard-hitting, and effective. Dewey began by recognizing that the Taft-Hartley law needed revision—but why, he asked, in over three and a half years hadn't Truman offered any positive programs of his own to deal with labor unrest? Perhaps, Dewey suggested, Truman's solution was still simply to draft strikers. Dewey pointed out that "116 million workdays were lost to strikes in 1946," but Taft-Hartley "had reduced time lost to strikes by 50 percent." In fact Truman had invoked Taft-Hartley's provisions seven times in just over a year. Dewey went on to outline his own twelve-point labor program in plain language and denounced Truman's prediction that a depression would follow a Republican victory as "an infamous falsehood."

The audience loved it, as did Burton and Stassen. Influential columnists such as the *New York Times*'s James Reston lauded Dewey's rediscovered vigor and clarity. Only the candidate's staff objected, as they had in Oklahoma City four years before. When Dewey reboarded his train that night, he was asked, "Are you trying to lose the election?" It is a mystery how such a forceful address got past Elliott Bell, but for the remainder of the campaign its style was never repeated, beyond Dewey's half-hearted response to Truman's mudslinging late in October. By failing to contest even Truman's wildest charges, Dewey lost by default.

It was scarcely necessary for the Dewey train to be wired for sound; his whistle-stop remarks varied little. Truman's, on the other hand, were not only more numerous but always different. Of course they invariably stressed preserving Democratic programs and thwarting Republican reaction, but each started with local references meticulously compiled by Batt and his eight-man research team and relayed to Elsey on the train. Building on experience gained during the preliminary tour in the spring, the staff were well prepared for the main event in the fall. The voluminous files of Clifford and others at the Truman Library are filled with specific instructions. For example, in terms of advance work: "A trained observer should precede the president at every stop . . . [and] prepare a brief on the town . . . explaining the local issues of importance and how they tie into the national issues.

These reports should be obtained from friendly editors, Democrats, and other such sources, and telegraphed to the train daily." This work was to start in each locality at least two weeks before the arrival of the president's train.

The chief advance man, Donald Dawson, provided sound advice early in October. Dawson suggested to Clifford, "I think the president would do well from this point forward to stop attacking . . . and start talking about what he had done and what he is going to do. His record is superb and his action fits the Democratic platform." Alas, Dawson's advice was little more heeded than Burton's on the Republican side. While their approach to the campaign was diametrically opposed, both Dewey and Truman allowed themselves to be hemmed in by inflexible strategies, though Truman's was more of his own making.

Unlike Scott, Democratic national chairman McGrath worked closely with Truman's campaign team. Indeed, he was part of it. He faced a difficult task of maintaining party cohesion in the face of ominous predictions, but at least Democratic prospects for the Senate appeared promising. Truman was aided throughout 1948 by an uncommonly appealing array of Democratic candidates in congressional and gubernatorial races. Many of them were fresh faces, little allied with Truman in the eyes of the electorate. In the key state of Illinois, for example, Adlai Stevenson, running for governor, and Paul Douglas, a University of Chicago economics professor running for the Senate, were demonstrating immense strength in the polls. Near the end of the campaign, McGrath pondered how so many favorable reports from so many states could fail to have an impact on the presidential contest as well.

Nowhere was the effectiveness of the Democratic campaign organization more crucial than in fund-raising. Initially there wasn't enough even to launch the campaign. Bernard Baruch, C. V. Whitney, and other affluent Democrats found reasons not to head Truman's finance committee. Almost by default, former Democratic finance chairman Louis Johnson accepted the responsibility. Johnson may have been a divisive failure in his government service before and later, just as McGrath would prove to be as attorney general, but in 1948 he was a superb fund-raiser for Truman. With a dozen key associates, including the ubiquitous Ed Pauley and wealthy Oklahoma oilman Robert Kerr, who ran successfully for the Senate, Johnson's first task was to induce the president to ask personally for contributions. Truman detested pleading for anything but recognized that if he did not, his train might never leave Washington. The campaign nearly ran out of funds again in Oklahoma City, but Kerr and his friends pulled out their own checkbooks to keep things moving. In between, speeches had to be cut, radio time curtailed, and plans altered, and Truman suffered all the other afflictions common to an enterprise in apparent trouble.

Dewey's campaign, ostensibly so amply financed throughout, ran into monetary difficulties at just about the time Truman's financial support was picking up. With Dewey's supporters the problem was overconfidence. It led to such precipitous decisions as the closing of California campaign offices and ultimately (at least in Dewey's mind) to more lethal forms of overconfidence— millions of Republicans who saw no need to vote on election day. On Truman's part, it is little wonder that the first opinion he voiced the morning after the election was that "labor did it." Once mobilized, not only did the unions provide thousands of volunteers to supplement and in some districts take the place of Democratic party workers, both the AFL and the CIO were major contributors to Truman's campaign chest. Complacent Wall Streeters saw no need to finance Dewey, who in their eyes was already elected.

In his biography of Truman, David McCullough documents the surprising conclusion: "It would turn out that the Democrats had spent more on the campaign than the Republicans . . . $2,736,334 to $2,127,296—though many of the largest donations to the Democrats came pouring in . . . after November 2, some $700,000 in post-dated checks."

With so much of the press arrayed against him, Truman needed money to broadcast his message. Radio was vital to his campaign, and he invested more in it than Dewey did. Although Truman was scarcely a master of the medium like Franklin Roosevelt, his clipped sentences and direct delivery often registered better over the airwaves than in person. He believed in intensive, old-fashioned, personal campaigning, but he was never averse to technology. In 1947 he made the first televised speech from the White House. For years he had worked with specialists to improve his radio delivery, and in 1948 he made it an important component of plain speaking.

Reading or listening to many of Truman's bellicose remarks throughout 1948, it is hard to believe that so many people worked with remarkable harmony to help prepare them, often finishing at virtually the last minute. Truman's most prominent speechwriter was Charles Murphy, who later succeeded Clifford as presidential counsel. Murphy wrote a ninety-five-page memoir of how it was done. As many as seven or eight separate drafts were prepared. Even whistle-stop remarks had an outline or draft put together by Elsey, Batt, and others. Not all administration loyalists took to the hustings, as did Brannan, but such specialists as Leon Keyserling of the Council of Economic Advisers provided their expertise in specific areas. The president would read drafts aloud to get the reaction of people he trusted, such as press secretary Charlie Ross. Truman's contribution was almost always to reduce and simplify the verbiage. Whether he was using a text or cards or speaking with a degree of spontaneity, simplicity was always his style.

Ross, Truman's closest friend from his youth, was his equivalent of Dewey's Elliott Bell. Like Bell, Ross had been a successful journalist. Unlike Bell, Ross merely advised Truman; he didn't run his campaigns. Ross's reluctant departure from the editorship of the *St. Louis Post-Dispatch* editorial page in 1945 had been motivated entirely by loyalty to the new president. Despite Truman's esteem for the man he called "the old philosopher," Ross wasn't always able to moderate Truman's rhetoric before or after 1948, but he made a solid contribution to the candidate's more thoughtful utterances. Another who bridged all components of the campaign team was Jack Redding, publicity director for the Democratic National Committee. Redding was a font of ideas, adroitly convincing motion picture theater owners to run a ten-minute documentary film on Truman free of charge and putting press releases into foreign languages for local newspapers and radio stations. Few Republicans understood, as Burton did, what a "competent staff" they were up against.

Perhaps the cohesion of Truman's team escaped the notice of even such seasoned observers as Rovere and Heslep because the Democrats' efforts were placed behind their candidate rather than in placating the press. When *Life* brought over David Low, the renowned British cartoonist, to portray his impressions of the campaign, Low's most memorable cartoon illustrated the chaotic scene in and outside of Truman's train. This was generally viewed as a suitable subject for satire. Even when the election was over and Ross wrote an article for *Collier's* outlining the unacknowledged teamwork behind Truman's triumph, he concluded that the real credit belonged solely to the president himself.

BY THE last week of October it was clear that the presidential race was narrowing. In California that belated Truman loyalist James Roosevelt had been astonished by the size and enthusiasm of Truman's crowds. In Ohio, Democratic candidate for governor Frank Lausche was so buoyed by a similar spectacle that he couldn't bring himself to leave Truman's train. Even staff members did not grasp the point of the president's insistence on stopping everywhere he could in Ohio. On October 26, for example, Truman made one rear-platform appearance at 3:37 p.m. in Sandusky and another at 4:24 p.m. in Elyria, between major speeches in Toledo and Cleveland. A week later Truman's aides would better appreciate what it was all about. So many local politicians, once lukewarm to Democratic prospects, now wanted to board the train that Connelly joined with staffers Bill Bray and Jonathan Daniels in making them feel comfortable. (Daniels would later write the first biography of Truman.) Truman was at least afforded some time to rest, see his family, and dispatch directions to Washington through his secretary, Rose Conway. The president's personal physician, Wallace Graham, was on hand to monitor his health. Murphy, Clifford, and Elsey had been supplemented by David Bell, Bob Carr, Franklin Carter, and others in preparing drafts of speeches. Ross provided daily press briefings. By the end of the campaign, Truman's train, despite the exhaustion of virtually everyone on board, took on an aspect of greater efficiency, even if never quite the equivalent of Dewey's.

The sense that Dewey's lead was diminishing brought even Roper back to survey the voters, but his final presidential poll was not of preference but of expectations. He found, not surprisingly, that a substantial majority of those interviewed still expected Dewey to win. The final Gallup poll, though predicting a "wide electoral vote margin," had Dewey ahead by 49.5 to 44.5 percent in the popular vote, a lead of only five points. Wallace was at 4 percent, Thurmond 2 percent. Clifford felt that given only another week or two, the Democrats might actually have a chance to pull it off.

Burton finally caught up with his candidate in Buffalo on October 18, on board the "Victory Special." He was surprised when Dewey came into his compartment, sat down next to him, and asked, "Johnny, we are slipping, aren't we?" Burton replied that the campaign "was not in the best shape." It was only a week after Dewey's stirring labor speech in Pittsburgh. Yet he had concluded, as he would again the following week, that it was simply too late to change course. Dewey rather plaintively recalled Franklin Roosevelt's coming through Buffalo at about the same stage of his campaign in 1932, when he too seemed to be slipping. "But he won, didn't he?" Dewey asked, as much to himself as to Burton.

Just as he had rediscovered foreign policy, at least in a fashion, near the close of his campaign Truman finally resurrected civil rights, the issue that had loomed so large earlier in the year. He spoke outdoors in Harlem shortly before 4 p.m. on October 29, exactly one year after the report of his Committee on Civil Rights had been issued. After receiving the Franklin D. Roosevelt Memorial Award from the Interdenominational Ministers Alliance, Truman reviewed his record of civil rights recommendations, the promise represented by his two executive orders, and his encouragement of judicial initiatives. He restated his intention "to attain the goal of equal rights and equal opportunity" and vowed to pursue it "with every ounce of strength and determination that I have." His speech wasn't very long or specific, but it proved to be more than sufficient.

Truman's final remarks of the 1948 campaign were not delivered at a rally but broadcast on election eve, November 1 from the living room of his Independence home to a national radio audience. He was introduced by Barkley, speaking from his own home in Kentucky, a final affirmation of the coordination of their campaigns. Many people provided the president with ideas and phrasing for this talk, but Murphy recalls that Truman wrote much of it himself. Friends of Murphy later viewed it as "the most effective election eve broadcast they ever heard." It was a lofty conclusion to what on Truman's part had rarely been a high-minded campaign. While repeating that a Democratic administration was the "best insurance against going back to the dark days of 1932," the president concluded, "Go to the polls tomorrow and vote your convictions, your hopes, and your faith . . . in the future of a nation that under God can lead the world to freedom and to peace." After completing his introduction, Barkley put his head in his hands and then walked into his bedroom and closed the door. Whether tired or dispirited or both, he did not emerge for many hours.

The final pre-election newspaper accounts, though virtually all agreeing that Dewey was merely awaiting the expiration of Truman's White House lease, gave the president his due, reflecting Truman's own suggestion of an epitaph for himself: "He done his damnedest." In an uncommonly perceptive article in the *Washington Post* of October 31, Robert C. Albright observed that Truman's personal vilification almost induced Dewey to get mad at the end and return to his natural "prosecutorial stance." The whole campaign had been a study in contradiction. "Harry Truman, by nature a kindly man . . . stepped completely out of character. He said mean, angry, ruthless things about Dewey that shocked Main Street." It is difficult to accept the premise that Truman, however hard-pressed, ever brought himself to believe such accusations as the "pitchfork" remark or the fascist innuendos. Obviously he felt such excoriations were necessary. Yet a *Post* editorial seemed almost sorry to see it all end, suggesting that "if the campaign could have gone on a few weeks longer it might have become one of the most exciting in history instead of one of the dullest."

Wallace had at least tried to inject some life, warning in the face of a solid phalanx of establishment liberal opposition that Truman's political compromises were in no way like Roosevelt's. Roosevelt's had always been to advance a progressive program; Truman's were merely for self-preservation. Toward the end,

Wallace largely abandoned policy for prophesy, vowing that if the world were to be saved, it must ultimately come to his conclusions. Thurmond never succeeded in varying his campaign or broadening its appeal. After Pittsburgh, Dewey returned to Olympus. Following the election, the irrepressible H. L. Mencken, having covered his final political campaign, put the rhetorical contrast between Truman and Dewey about as well as anyone: "Truman . . . assumed as a matter of course that the American people were just folks like himself. He . . . appealed to their self-interest. . . . Neither candidate made a speech . . . that will survive in the schoolbooks, but those of Truman at least had some natural warmth in them." By targeting "the groups that seemed to be the most numerous," Mencken concluded, Truman proved to be "a smart mathematician."

AFTER voting on November 2, Truman took everyone by surprise. He reverted to his days of introspective solitude at the old Pickwick Hotel and, accompanied only by the Secret Service, drove twenty-five miles to the Elms Hotel in the resort town of Excelsior Springs, Missouri. There he enjoyed a steam bath, a rubdown, and a modest repast. After hearing the early returns on the radio, he went to bed around 9 p.m. From all indications, the election looked to be as much a cliffhanger as had his 1940 senatorial primary. Back on Delaware Avenue in Independence, his wife and daughter also listened to returns. Margaret emerged to tell incredulous reporters surrounding the house that no, her father was not within. They, like she, would have to wait to hear from him.

Around midnight Truman awoke, turned on the radio again, and heard the authoritative voice of H. V. Kaltenborn of NBC reporting that while the president's lead in the popular vote was increasing, he could not possibly win in the electoral college. Truman went back to sleep. By that time Dewey, in his suite in

New York City's Roosevelt Hotel, was probably protected by a larger Secret Service detail than Truman's. Shortly after six o'clock the following morning, a refreshed Truman strode into his headquarters in Kansas City's Muehlebach Hotel. Although the conclusive returns would not be in for several more hours and Dewey's official concession came even later, Truman, the most composed man in Missouri that morning, knew he had won.

Final results in the three states that sealed the election were so close that Truman's confidence is all the more remarkable. He won Ohio by 7,107 votes out of nearly 3 million cast, a minuscule 0.3 percent; Illinois by 33,612 votes out of nearly 4 million cast; California by 17,865 votes out of more than 4 million cast. A shift of fewer than 30,000 votes in these three states, totaling 78 electoral votes, would have given the election to Dewey. It would have taken less to put the contest into the House of Representatives. Truman won 28 states with an electoral total of 303—37 less than he had predicted to Elsey. Dewey won 16 states with an electoral vote total of 189. Thurmond won only his four-state Dixie base, plus one disaffected elector in Tennessee, for an electoral vote total of 39. Wallace won no electoral votes, but his popular vote total prevented Truman from taking New York, Michigan, and Maryland.

Truman received just under half the popular vote, 49.51 percent, finishing with a total of 24,179,345. Dewey ended with a popular vote total of 21,991,291, or 45.12 percent, doing marginally poorer in both respects than he had in 1944. Wallace and Thurmond wound up in a disappointing dead heat, Wallace at 2.38 percent and 1,157,326 votes, Thurmond at 2.40 percent and 1,176,125 votes. Other candidates received 289,739 votes. Truman's plurality was 2,188,054 out of 48,793,826 votes cast.

Ohio, Illinois, and California provided the drama, but the real story was in the two regions of Barkley's special emphasis. In the four states of the deep South, predictably Thurmond won. His

Jay Norwood (Ding) Darling, Des Moines Register
The One Man Army

share of the popular vote there ranged from 49.1 percent in Louisiana to 87.2 percent in Mississippi. But in the other seven states of the old Confederacy, all overwhelmingly won by Truman, the highest popular vote percentage for the Dixiecrat ticket was 20.3 percent in Georgia (Truman's percentage was 60.8). These seven states (minus that one stubborn Tennessee elector) gave the regular Democratic ticket a total of 88 electoral votes, 10 more than the total of Ohio, Illinois, and California.

Other than the Dixiecrat defection, the most remarkable turnaround from 1944 was in the farm belt of the Midwest and in the Mountain states. Truman won Iowa and Wisconsin, Wyoming, and Colorado, and everywhere west of the Dakotas to the Pacific, with the exception of Oregon. Of the twelve states Dewey had won in 1944, he lost five in 1948. On the other hand, Dewey was dominant in the major Northeastern states—New York, Pennsylvania, and New Jersey—and he reclaimed Michigan. He won nine states in 1948 that he had lost to Roosevelt in 1944, containing 146 of his 189 electoral votes.

More than half of Wallace's vote, 509,559, was in New York State, largely centered in New York City. In only one other state, California, did it rise above 4 percent, and Wallace's popular vote total there—190,381—was less than half the number of Californians whose petitions had originally put him on the ballot. Still, had Wallace succeeded in being placed on the Illinois ballot, and had Dewey campaigned more strenuously in Ohio and responded more effectively in the Central Valley of California, Dewey and Warren would almost certainly have enjoyed a narrow victory of their own. All in all, it was a very close thing.

Truman's razor-thin survival would hardly have been seen as an extension of the New Deal electoral coalition by Roosevelt's 1932 strategist, Louis Howe. Could anyone imagine a Democratic president winning without New York, Michigan, or the Solid South? As it turned out, someone could. After the election, George Gallup, overcoming his embarrassment, suggested that Truman's triumph was more evocative of Wilson's New Freedom than of Roosevelt's New Deal. At least in terms of the electoral college breakdown, it resembled no other presidential election so closely as that won in 1916 by Woodrow Wilson. Of course, this analysis failed to take into account the absence of women's suffrage in 1916 and the subsequent black migration and enfranchisement in the North, but it did underscore the possibility of another political realignment.

Beyond that, perhaps the 1948 presidential election also presaged something more fundamental about American political parties themselves, and about the nature of party loyalty. The Bronx garment worker who voted for Wallace in 1948 and the Mississippi cotton grower who voted for Thurmond would both have been considered members of reliable components of the New Deal electoral coalition only four years before. Iowa farmers who voted for Willkie in 1940 and Dewey in 1944 were not likely to justify their switch to Truman in 1948 on the basis of a Democratic epiphany. In that generally conservative state perhaps Truman was perceived as more likely than Dewey to conserve the sort of services its inhabitants had grown accustomed to.

On the other hand, though Truman proclaimed on November 3 that "labor did it," labor's strength in Michigan did not translate into electoral votes for the president. Truman's recognition of Israel did not win him New York. With some constituencies, such as Catholic voters of German, Italian, and Irish extraction, Truman may well have done better than Roosevelt had in the wartime election of 1944, but the states where such voters were most numerous split between Truman and Dewey. In only one instance related to ethnicity did Truman enjoy a clear advantage in 1948: black voters in the North supported him in greater numbers than even Franklin Roosevelt had received, around 70 percent overall. According to the political writer Theodore White, "The vital margin of Truman's victory in 1948 [came] from the black vote in three states—Ohio, Illinois, California." It was a trade-off McGrath had hardly sought when he had met so inconclusively with Thurmond and other Southern governors, but one he would have readily accepted: 78 electoral votes for 39 lost in the South. In Ohio the "Negro districts" of Youngstown were responsible for Truman's plurality of more than 14,000 votes; in Cleveland the black vote produced a plurality of about 11,000. In California, districts with heavy black registration in both Los Angeles and Oakland went for Truman by around 3½ to 1.

Results in many states, such as Illinois, reveal that Truman was swept along on the reverse coattails of Democratic statewide candidates. Some first-time aspirants for office polled as many as hundreds of thousands of votes more than the top of their ticket. In every dimension except the presidency, 1948 was a Democratic landslide, even more marked than the 1946 Republican sweep. State-by-state totals reveal that it was based more on the appeal of local candidates and issues than on Truman's impact. Democrats gained eight statehouses, bringing to power names that would later become familiar—Stevenson in Illinois, G. Mennen "Soapy" Williams in Michigan, Chester Bowles in Connecticut, and Paul Dever in Massachusetts. Nine Democrats replaced Republicans in the Senate, regaining the majority by 54 to 42 seats. New senators included Kerr, Humphrey, Douglas, Estes Kefauver from Tennessee, and Lyndon Johnson from Texas (dubbed "Landslide Lyndon" for his suspiciously narrow victory in the Democratic primary). Democrats elected 75 new House members. Their majority in the new House of Representatives would be 263 to 171. In Massachusetts, John F. Kennedy was easily elected to his second congressional term. In California, Republican Richard M. Nixon was reelected to the House without opposition. Democrats won 58 percent of the vote in senatorial elections, 8.5 percent more than Truman's share of the popular vote (over 4 percent more even with the Wallace and Thurmond votes added).

The greatest surprise to professional politicians and pollsters alike was how few people voted in 1948. Proportionately the vote was the lowest in twenty years. That was the *true* "upset." As Richard Kirkendall concludes, "Clearly, many people found Truman as well as Dewey uninspiring." The unexpectedly low turnout is an indictment of the campaigns of all four ostensibly major presidential candidates. Neither Wallace nor Thurmond successfully expanded their base of believers, marginalizing their messages and discouraging potential supporters from "wasting" their votes. Allowed to dominate the national discourse, Truman and Dewey, who beneath all the bluster differed little on major issues, debated even less. If the polls of voter interests are believable, the lack of any substantive discussion of foreign policy "turned off" as many voters as did Truman's strident partisanship and Dewey's banal generalities. Four years later, with only two major presidential candidates, Eisenhower and Stevenson, almost 13 million more Americans voted than in 1948, an increase without parallel in the history of the republic. Stevenson, the landslide loser, received over 3 million more votes than had the victorious Truman in 1948. Of those eligible to vote, 61.6 percent exercised their franchise in the presidential election of 1952, 10.5 percent more than in 1948.

The only scientific poll to get the results right was that of Department of Agriculture economist Louis H. Bean. His complex "Bean Poll," based on a long-term "political wave," is more akin to Einstein than to Gallup, Roper, and Crossley, but it worked. More mundane measurements also favored Truman, including a "Feed Bag Poll" conducted by a milling company in Kansas City. When farmers throughout the Midwest and Mountain states consistently bought more feed bags featuring donkeys than elephants, compiling the results was discontinued as "too improbable." Few observers on either side of the Atlantic were as prescient as Clementine Churchill. In a cable congratulating the president, her husband Winston noted that she had "predicted your success." Dwight Eisenhower reflected more than his own reaction when he wrote Truman that American political history could not "record a greater accomplishment than yours . . . traced so clearly to the stark courage and fighting heart of a single man." Admiration for the president, grudging or not, was exemplified by a "Prayer by a Whipped Republican," printed in the *Cleveland Plain Dealer:* "And in particular, O God, do Thou bless the little man who didn't have a chance—the president of the United States." At least on November 3, 1948, it spoke for the nation.

Truman, perhaps returning to his authentic persona, was as gracious in victory as Dewey was in defeat. At a jubilant victory celebration in Independence, the president's remarks were serious, thankful, and brief. Few moments on the train trip back to Washington were as gleeful as Truman's holding aloft the *Chicago Tribune*'s mistake, our enduring image of the 1948 campaign. Perhaps unable to break the habit, Truman whistle-stopped in several states—but with a much different message. In Vincennes, Indiana, he told the crowd, "I do not feel elated at the victory. I feel overwhelmed with the responsibility." His reception in Washington was truly overwhelming. The hastily prepared parade route from Union Station to the White House was lined by hundreds of thousands. Margaret Truman recalls, "Every band in the world seemed to be playing 'I'm Just Wild About Harry.'" A sign on the *Washington Post* building indicated their willingness to eat crow, a dish they would be obliged to share with every other publisher of prognostications.

Alben Barkley, finally reunited with his running mate, had fully recovered his verve. Quoting the trademark introductory line of the renowned comedienne of Nashville's Grand Old Opry, "Cousin Minnie Pearl," Barkley announced, "I am so glad to be here." Whatever its exhilaration, the campaign had been strenuous even by the standards of these two old Democratic warhorses. A week after it was over, Truman wrote his sister Mary Jane, "I didn't know I was so tired until I sat down." After a brief cabinet meeting and reorientation, the entire Democratic entourage went off to a two-week working vacation in Key West—with the emphasis on vacation.

On the Republican side, after the shock had receded, postmortems abounded in the gloom. Dewey, still only forty-six (*Time* had his age wrong), received almost as many messages of encouragement as Truman did of congratulations. He speculated that he might now enjoy life more and live longer. He told reporters he was as surprised as they were. Later, after he had studied the results, Dewey reasoned, "You can analyze figures from now to kingdom come, and all they will show is that we lost the farm vote which we had in 1944, and that lost the election." Later still he lamented the overconfidence of his supporters, citing this as the reason why "two to three million Republicans stayed home." Dewey declined suggestions that he ask for a recount in such states as Illinois, where questionable circumstances around Cook County were hardly a novelty, on the reasonable supposition that no accounting would yield him a majority. Dewey himself had won several states by narrow margins.

Years later, referring to 1948, the historian R. Alton Lee concluded, "There are as many interpretations of the results of this election as there are analysts studying it." At the time Brownell blamed the intransigence of conservative congressional Republicans for Dewey's defeat. Elliott Bell said, "The bear got us," stressing the spectre of the Soviet threat and the hesitancy of Americans to change their leadership in the midst of international crisis. John Foster Dulles suggested that foreign policy was too complex a matter to be debated in elections, ignoring its near-absence as an issue in 1948. James Roosevelt insisted that people simply liked Truman better than Dewey. John Burton complained that Dewey didn't permit voters to get to see him as he really was. Taft wrote Barkley, "I think we underestimated the effect of general prosperity . . . and I have to admit the fight put up by the president and yourself was the final determining factor." *Time* made the extraordinary discovery, after nearly a full term of Truman in office, that in 1948, despite all his earlier blunders, he had emerged as an "interesting" personality. Certainly he had been revealed to most of the electorate for the first time as a national campaigner, a role for which—unlike the presidency—he had a quarter-century of rehearsal. *Time* added that Truman "did it all himself."

After the dust cleared, political scientists at the University of Michigan tried to figure out what had happened. Their two main conclusions, elaborated on by others, still seem contradictory. On the one hand, Truman's vigorous campaigning mobilized just enough of the core of the New Deal electoral coalition to eke out his narrow victory, sustaining the Democrats as the majority party in the nation. That was the view Lippmann had also pronounced immediately after the election. On the other hand, an unusually large percentage of the electorate was undecided until late in the campaign. As Brownell wrote, "Dewey was ahead until the last two weeks."

After ascribing the low turnout to general dissatisfaction with the choice of alternatives, the Michigan researchers noted the extreme "partisanship" of those who did choose to vote for president. Their decisions were largely determined by their own "established party loyalties." Some 74 percent of those who voted for Truman were Democratic party "identifiers," and 71 percent of the Dewey vote came from Republican "identifiers." Only 6 percent of the vote for either candidate came from people normally identified with the opposing party. On this premise, whatever the size of the turnout, it is hard to imagine how Dewey could have won.

Yet the post-election studies of the major polling organizations, coordinated through the Social Science Research Council, somehow reached a different conclusion. They determined that one of every seven voters made up his or her mind during the last two weeks of the campaign and that three-quarters of these delayed decisions went for Truman. This not only demolished "Farley's Law" once and for all, it also appeared to destroy the conclusion about established party loyalties. Gallup blamed his own miscalculations for assuming that this unusually large group

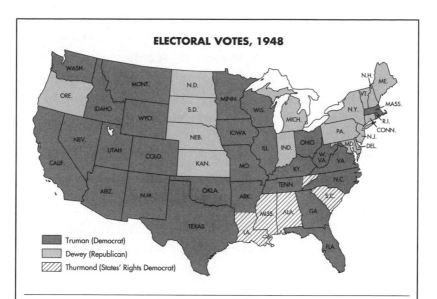

ELECTORAL VOTES, 1948

Truman (Democrat)
Dewey (Republican)
Thurmond (States' Rights Democrat)

States	Electoral Votes	Truman	Dewey	Thurmond	States	Electoral Votes	Truman	Dewey	Thurmond
Alabama	(11)	–	–	11	Nebraska	(6)	–	6	–
Arizona	(4)	4	–	–	Nevada	(3)	3	–	–
Arkansas	(9)	9	–	–	New Hampshire	(4)	–	4	–
California	(25)	25	–	–	New Jersey	(16)	–	16	–
Colorado	(6)	6	–	–	New Mexico	(4)	4	–	–
Connecticut	(8)	–	8	–	New York	(47)	–	47	–
Delaware	(3)	–	3	–	North Carolina	(14)	14	–	–
Florida	(8)	8	–	–	North Dakota	(4)	–	4	–
Georgia	(12)	12	–	–	Ohio	(25)	25	–	–
Idaho	(4)	4	–	–	Oklahoma	(10)	10	–	–
Illinois	(28)	28	–	–	Oregon	(6)	–	6	–
Indiana	(13)	–	13	–	Pennsylvania	(35)	–	35	–
Iowa	(10)	10	–	–	Rhode Island	(4)	4	–	–
Kansas	(8)	–	8	–	South Carolina	(8)	–	–	8
Kentucky	(11)	11	–	–	South Dakota	(4)	–	4	–
Louisiana	(10)	–	–	10	Tennessee	(12)	11	–	1
Maine	(5)	–	5	–	Texas	(23)	23	–	–
Maryland	(8)	–	8	–	Utah	(4)	4	–	–
Massachusetts	(16)	16	–	–	Vermont	(3)	–	3	–
Michigan	(19)	–	19	–	Virginia	(11)	11	–	–
Minnesota	(11)	11	–	–	Washington	(8)	8	–	–
Mississippi	(9)	–	–	9	West Virginia	(8)	8	–	–
Missouri	(15)	15	–	–	Wisconsin	(12)	12	–	–
Montana	(4)	4	–	–	Wyoming	(3)	3	–	–
					Totals	**(531)**	**303**	**189**	**39**

Source: *Congressional Quarterly*

of undecided voters would act in the same proportion as his earlier percentages of voter preference—that is, more to Dewey than to Truman. Smith cites the conclusion Brownell accepted: "Dewey was ahead until the last two weeks of the campaign, when millions of voters switched their allegiance. Some 14 percent of Dewey's own supporters changed their minds; another 13 percent didn't bother to vote. Nowhere did more votes change hands than in the farm belt. Wisconsin, Ohio, Illinois, and Iowa . . . all washed away in the Truman flood."

If established party loyalties were still so firm in 1948, would not a larger turnout have favored the Democrats? Dewey polled nearly the same numbers in 1948 as he had in 1944. How "soft" could his own core support have been? What did Truman change in the last two weeks of the campaign to bring about this shift? He only increased his stridency. The political analyst Samuel Lubell concluded that "the stay-at-homes . . . had not been primarily overconfident Republicans; instead they had been apathetic Democrats." According to Lubell, "If there had been a high turnout . . . Dewey would have received a drubbing akin to the one experienced by Landon in 1936." On balance this seems a reasonable assumption.

Thurmond and Wallace both recognized how close they had come, despite their low raw vote totals, to putting the election into the House of Representatives. Polling only a combined 2,326,191 votes, together they denied Truman 113 electoral votes. When asked later what influence the Progressive party had on his campaign in 1948, Truman predictably replied that it had none. Wallace required no acknowledgment. Little more than a week after the election he returned from his reveries to all but take credit for Truman's victory. In letters to the *New York Times* and the *New York Herald Tribune* on November 11, Wallace claimed to have "forced the Democrats to don the mantle of Roosevelt and to promise the American people a return to the New

Deal." He claimed to have "made peace an issue," on the basis of which Truman pulled through. Two days later Wallace issued a statement crediting the "all-out fight" he and his supporters had waged for convincing people to vote for Truman, "only after we forced him to compete with us on the peace program, on civil liberties, and on the revival of an expanded New Deal with emphasis on lower prices and housing."

There is little evidence that Truman "moved left" in 1948 because of Wallace. Truman's 1948 domestic agenda did not differ fundamentally from his earlier proposals. Each year, whatever the likelihood of congressional passage, Truman recommended measures that went beyond the New Deal. A more valid question is how thoroughly Truman believed in everything he proposed. In 1945 he needed to demonstrate his liberal credentials. In 1948, in his view, he needed to pull out all the stops simply to win the election. In terms of foreign policy, Wallace's presence in the race may well have motivated Truman to consider such possibilities as the Vinson mission to Moscow, but they did not materialize. The results of the 1948 election validated a cold war consensus shared by both Truman and Dewey. There was no Taft in the race to contest its implementation. With Wallace relegated to the sidelines by his performance, his only real impact on the 1948 election, like Thurmond's, was to make it closer.

From his opposing vantage point, Burton observed, "The president turned around his poor public image by his campaign." It may be so. The public saw a courageous, plain-talking man they could identify with, fighting for his political life. The 1948 presidential election, however, was no more an exposure of the real Harry Truman than of his Republican opponent, with his endless extolling of "home, mother, unity, and efficiency." It showed the president in only one dimension. Without compromising his assertive campaign, had Truman displayed more of the vision and idealism he was capable of—one sensible recommendation of his advisers—as he did in his Milwaukee atomic energy speech, he might have won by a much wider margin. Had Dewey followed up his forceful labor speech in Pittsburgh with similar efforts on issues of foreign policy, he might have pulled the election out, as he nearly managed to do. In either case, real issues would have been joined in spite of the relative similarity of views. Even a reasoned debate about American intentions in the Far East would have stimulated the electorate. But in the 1948 election neither Truman nor Dewey was at his best.

CHAPTER VII

The Legacy
of 1948

O N THE evening of October 25, 1995, a festive dinner in Washington, D.C., filled the great hall of what is now the National Building Museum. It celebrated, if a bit belatedly, Harry Truman's ascension to the presidency fifty years before. Under Peter Max's immense rendering of "Fifty Trumans" (a work its subject would have detested), an assemblage of notables did Truman honor. After praising his bipartisan foreign policy, former president Gerald Ford referred to his own bipartisan gesture of placing Truman's portrait between those of Lincoln and Eisenhower in the Cabinet Room of the White House. Former president Jimmy Carter remarked on how few of Truman's contemporaries could have predicted that he would turn out to be "the greatest president of the twentieth century." Vice-President Al Gore suggested that "every single American has a story or anecdote about Harry Truman." On film, Ronald Reagan revealed that his last Democratic vote had been for Truman, "today the politician most others would like to emulate." President Bill Clinton noted that his own family had supported Truman even "when he was alive." Finally the eloquent David McCullough, whose 1992 biography of Truman amounts, in the words of one reviewer, to a "1,000 page

Valentine," reaffirmed his affection for this quintessential American.

The real Harry Truman might have been induced to endure such an evening—rhetorical excess is, after all, a part of public life—but he would have viewed all this retrospective reverence with bemusement. Truman knew something about the unpredictability of public opinion. His peaks of popularity, shortly after he took office in 1945 and following his dramatic electoral victory of 1948, alternated with such periods as late 1951, when Truman's public approval rating of 23 percent was actually lower than Richard Nixon's when he was obliged to resign the presidency. Overall Gallup measured Truman's average approval rating throughout his years in office at only 41 percent, the lowest of any president between the first one they evaluated, Franklin Roosevelt, and Bill Clinton. Truman left office in 1953 diminished in reputation and succeeded by a national hero who vowed to restore honesty and dignity to the presidency, purpose and consistency to national policy.

Truman read history all his life, even if it was a "great man" sort of history. Although he emulated the Cincinnatus example of citizenship, he knew that an everyman called from his plow to serve the nation was not quite what most of the founders of the American republic had in mind for the presidency. Even the most egalitarian of them, Thomas Jefferson, envisioned an "aristocracy of achievement." Truman had been washed up at fifty. His career was resurrected by a venal political boss and elevated by an ailing, pragmatic president. Yet particularly in 1947 and 1948 Truman proved capable of making momentous decisions—most of them correctly. Perhaps these decisions did not loom large in the many reasons why Truman won what amounted to his reelection in 1948, but they form the foremost achievement of his presidency.

Scholars recognized this within a decade. The first president-ranking poll to include Truman, conducted by Arthur Schlesinger, Sr., in 1962, already measured the Missourian on the basis of his performance in office to be a "near-great" ninth in the list of most effective presidents. In the decades since, Truman has risen to an apparently secure resting place of seventh, a consistency of evaluation he never remotely enjoyed in office.

Even more remarkable has been the public's rising esteem for Truman, though most Americans today must rely on the recollections of others. This heightened appraisal of Truman, based more on perceptions of his personal qualities, has reached the affectionate level of "Trumania." Launched by such books as Merle Miller's oral biography of Truman, *Plain Speaking,* and sustained by James Whitmore's one-man stage production, "Give 'Em Hell, Harry," a simplistic reinvention of Truman emerged around the time of Watergate, not long after Truman's death on December 26, 1972. It said as much about the state of the nation as about Truman himself. As the historian Gar Alperovitz writes, Americans wanted Truman "to be something no man can possibly have been." A frequent reaction to even the critically balanced biographies of Truman by Robert Ferrell and Alonzo Hamby in the 1990s has continued to be, "Would that we had someone like that in public office today!" The twin myths of Trumania and the 1948 "upset," deeply embedded in the nation's collective memory, have a good deal of truth mixed in with their mythology, but Harry Truman was not at all a simple man. And, as noted by Herbert Parmet, his greatest electoral triumph "turned out to be ephemeral."

DEWEY, whose campaign strategy had been so firmly supported by the GOP's political operatives in 1948, did not escape their wrath the following January at a heated national committee meeting in Omaha. In Washington, Congressman Halleck, still smarting

from his rejection as Dewey's running mate, not only joined in
the belated chorus of criticism for Dewey's pallid "me, too" campaign but never forgave the New Yorker for his halfhearted defense of the 80th Congress. To Senator Vandenberg, Congress's
achievements of historic legislation in foreign policy infinitely
transcended any domestic deficiencies. Hugh Scott, who bore little blame for the 1948 debacle, barely survived as party chairman. Dewey didn't require the *Chicago Tribune* to announce the
obvious, that he would not again seek national office, and he accepted full responsibility for his failure to wage a fighting campaign.

Still, he was troubled by ideological divisions within the party
that had made it so difficult for him to be more aggressive in
championing the record of the 80th Congress—and said so.
Dewey was particularly (but more privately) concerned about the
heightened prestige of Taft, whose influence in party councils had
been enhanced by Dewey's defeat and whose views on foreign
policy Dewey considered dangerously obstructionist. Although
finished as a presidential contender, Dewey was still governor of
New York, and that base provided a platform for his views. He
decided to run again in 1950 for a third term. In an uninspired
campaign, marred by invective on both sides, Dewey was re-
elected by 572,000 votes. There was much left to do within the
Empire State, but Dewey inevitably began to think about 1952.
The more he contemplated the implications of a ticket led by Taft,
the more his mind turned to Eisenhower.

The differing views of Dewey and Truman toward their 1948
running mates is reflected in how each approached the election
of 1952. Both Warren and Barkley (even though he was near
seventy-five) made their most serious attempts at the presidency
that year. Both were long shots. Barkley would have required a
firm refusal from the uncertain Adlai Stevenson, and Warren a
deadlocked convention. In 1950, this time against real Demo-

cratic opposition in the person of James Roosevelt, Warren had won an unprecedented third term as governor of California by more than 1,100,000 votes. Perhaps Californians had already decided in 1948 that they preferred having Warren stay in Sacramento rather than losing him to Washington.

Dewey felt the same way in 1952. With Taft having lined up the most confirmed delegates for the national convention, Republican internationalists understood the need to unite behind a single candidate. From his North Atlantic Treaty Organization post in Paris, Eisenhower finally revealed—or decided—that he was in fact a Republican. It took a lengthy campaign to move the general from that admission to actual candidacy, finally secured by his concern with Taft's perceived isolationism. Dewey, immersed in the efforts to draft Ike, viewed Warren's presidential ambitions as a diversion. He dispatched an emissary to California to "soothe Earl Warren's bruised feelings" and get him on board the Eisenhower bandwagon. At the 1952 convention Warren was also passed over for the vice-presidential nomination in favor of a younger Californian, the ambitious congressman Richard Nixon.

Warren's subsequent sixteen-year career as a notably activist chief justice of the United States must have astonished Dewey, who during 1948 was prone to describe him to campaign aides as "that dumb Swede." It bewildered Eisenhower, the president who appointed Warren, but it made the Californian a worldwide symbol of America's affirmation of human and civil rights. Warren's lengthy record of public service abounded in irony. The governor who had approved the internment of Japanese-Americans in World War II came to be viewed as one of the great jurists of American history. The far right vilified him mercilessly, with bumper stickers calling for his impeachment. His reluctant agreement to chair a committee investigating the assassination of President Kennedy led to conclusions that are still controversial. Yet in 1948 he had personified national unity, the premise on which his whole electoral career had been based, far more authentically than the other governor who headed his ticket. His handsome family was an adornment of that campaign. They and their off-spring gathered in Washington as the old patriarch finally began to fade. Warren died in 1974, in his eighty-third year. Always a model of personal rectitude, he also represented the ability to grow in vision as his responsibilities increased. In his last public appearance, addressing the African-American students of More-house College in Atlanta, Warren reminded his audience, "We are only partway up the mountain."

In marked contrast to Dewey's indifference to Warren's ambi-tions, Truman did what he could in 1952 to gain the Democratic presidential nomination for Barkley. Although no Democrat ap-peared to stand much of a chance against Eisenhower, neither Truman nor Barkley could forget 1948's similarly dire predic-tions. Barkley failed to follow some of Truman's specific advice in 1952, such as the need to see labor leaders individually, but the president's counsel had been offered with evident generosity. Both men were irritated by Stevenson's apparent indecision, but when the Illinois governor finally acceded to "accept the cup," there was little for Barkley to do but withdraw his name, which he did with his customary grace. His political valedictory was the rhetorical highlight of the 1952 Democratic convention, just as his keynote addresses had brightened earlier conclaves. His per-sonal valedictory, delivered four years later, was an especially apt if abrupt conclusion to the life of a public man. Speaking to a col-lege audience in Virginia, Barkley ended his address with a typi-cal biblical injunction: "I would rather be a servant in the house of the Lord than to sit in the seat of the mighty." He then dropped over dead.

After the 1948 election Wallace returned to his farm in South Salem, New York, retiring from active politics to the less perplexing pursuit of his earlier vocation, scientific agriculture. The defiant Progressive manifesto of November 15, 1948, calling for such specifics as immediate termination of aid to the Chinese Nationalists, already bears the imprint of a committee. From time to time Wallace continued to express his views, moving gradually to the right. Although he opposed the establishment of NATO in 1949, he supported Truman's decision to intervene in Korea in 1950, declaring, "I hold no brief for the past actions of either the U.S. or Russia, but when my country is at war I am on the side of my country and the UN." Wallace also did what he could to purge known Communists from the leadership of what remained of "Gideon's Army." In 1952 Vincent Hallinan, the Progressive party's candidate for president, won 140,416 votes, about one-eighth of Wallace's 1948 total. In 1956 there was neither a candidate nor a party. Wallace died in 1965 at the age of seventy-seven. Earlier that year, in a letter to a friend, he had bitterly chronicled the genesis of the cold war coalition he had struggled to break: "We must remember that the Democrats inherited Vietnam from the Republicans who in turn had inherited their policy from Truman. Truman and Dulles took the steps which will make the USA bleed from every pore." Truman memorialized Wallace as an "asset" to the nation. His transcendent idealism, ill-suited to the realities of politics, might have been better harnessed to serve humanity.

Thurmond suffered politically in the short run, but unlike Wallace, he was wedded to politics. In 1950 he lost the Democratic primary for reelection as governor in the face of predictable accusations of disloyalty. He made a remarkable comeback, however, winning election to the United States Senate in 1954 as a write-in candidate. In 1964, reflecting a transition presaged by his own campaign of 1948, Thurmond became a Republican. His long-lived career in the Senate evolved with the times. When civil rights statutes passed into law, Thurmond accepted and implemented them, stressing constituent service to South Carolinians of both races. He always maintained that his 1948 campaign was not primarily about segregation and had been misrepresented by Truman. In political terms, Thurmond's unintended contribution in 1948 was the most lasting of any offered by the presidential candidates: he broke the traditionally solid Democratic South. Twenty years later a less respectable Southern governor named George Wallace, running for president on a similar platform and under the banner of another short-lived party (though without the word "Democrat" in its title), received nearly ten million votes. He won only five states because of the nature of the American electoral system, but 13.5 percent of the popular vote. Wallace's separatist campaign was opposed by Thurmond on the grounds that it could only help the Democratic ticket, headed by Hubert H. Humphrey.

Robert A. Taft had been a respected Republican spokesman since 1938 and his first election to the Senate from Ohio. The off-year congressional sweep of 1946 enhanced his leadership position with the congressional wing of the Republican party; Dewey's loss in 1948 seemed to secure it. In 1950 Taft was re-elected to his third Senate term by a resounding majority, rivaling Warren's margin in California. The two victories underscored Dewey's 1948 failure in these two key states. The cerebral Taft continued to examine suggested policies through the prism of national interest, never bound by doctrinaire certitudes. He was one of only thirteen senators to vote against the Atlantic Pact that established NATO, believing that modest ground forces in Western Europe were hardly an effective deterrent to potential Soviet aggression. On the other hand, he supported limited alliances with other nations and favored extending the American defense perimeter in Asia. When the Communist north attacked, Taft called upon all Americans to support American resistance to aggression in Korea. He criticized Truman's conduct of the war, however, and questioned the president's right to extend "dictatorial" control over the economy at home. In 1951 and 1952 Taft even called for Truman's impeachment.

In his later years Taft could seem inconsistent, stressing fiscal prudence and constitutional rights yet insisting that General Douglas MacArthur be unleashed to take the war beyond Korea itself, and offering no criticism of Senator McCarthy. His struggles with Dewey's "Eastern Establishment" brand of Republicanism continued. Its influence denied Taft his party's presidential nomination in 1952 for the third time. An embittered Taft loyally supported Eisenhower but vented his spleen by following Truman around the campaign trail, their heated exchanges stealing much of the thunder from the relatively tepid clash of the actual contenders. A Taft-Truman debate on real issues might have been more stimulating in 1948. Taft contracted cancer in 1953 and died short of his sixty-fourth birthday. Truman paid tribute to his longtime adversary as a "highly ethical, straightforward and honorable man . . . who spoke for his side vigorously and ably." Taft's side was rarely Dewey's. Although he vehemently denied it, Taft may well have felt that the ultimate interests of both his party and the nation were better served by Truman's winning in 1948, paving the way for Taft to claim the GOP mantle and lead legitimate Republicans to victory in 1952. Twelve years later a very different kind of conservative would finally carry the Republican banner, to a crushing defeat. Only four years beyond that, the entire American center would move to the right.

In 1954 Dewey returned to the practice of law, finally making the kind of money public service had denied him. He joined a venerable New York firm that promptly changed its name to place Dewey's first. He had relatively little to do with national politics after 1952, though he continued to attend conventions and speak for the ticket as well as for local candidates whose brand of "modern Republicanism" he favored. Presidents of both parties

asked him to head commissions, but he preferred the flexibility
and relative privacy of informal counsel. In 1970 his wife died
after a protracted struggle with breast cancer. Dewey's own death,
less than a year later, was more sudden—a massive heart attack
following a long round of golf. He was just short of sixty-nine.

Dewey's active political career ended in his fifties. It is tempt-
ing to speculate, as does Richard Norton Smith, on "the man who
might have been." Had the congressional results been the same,
but had an authentic upset put Dewey into the White House in
1948 (or Blair House, which the Trumans occupied while the Executive Mansion was being rebuilt internally), might he not have
had a more successful term than Truman? Many conservative Republicans, including Congressman Fred Hartley of Taft-Hartley
fame, were swept away in the Democratic tide of 1948. Dewey
shared the prudently progressive philosophy of most of the
Democrats who replaced them, and he opposed racial segregation
as staunchly as Truman did. Indeed, one of the many mysteries of
Dewey's misconceived 1948 campaign was why he did not make
greater use of his record as governor of New York. In civil rights
Dewey had succeeded in getting important legislation enacted;
Truman had to rely on executive orders.

Perhaps Dewey's very weaknesses as a candidate for president would have turned into strengths had he been elected. His
accomplishments in the Empire State were based on teamwork
and efficiency. The experienced people he relied on may have
misread the 1948 campaign, but many were skilled administra-
tors. As *Kiplinger* pointed out, Dewey's collaborative approach to
governing might well have smoothed "his path on Capitol Hill,
even with the conservative old guard of his party." Capable of
clearly enunciating national goals, Dewey might also have
emerged as a "great communicator."

What of foreign policy in a Dewey administration? Having
reaffirmed his belief in bipartisanship in policymaking toward

Europe, Dewey in the campaign tentatively expressed concern about Asia. He and his advisers believed that insufficient resources were being committed to support Nationalist China and defend a more clearly defined Asian perimeter of American interest. Anticipating a Dewey victory, respected Washington columnists recommended that Truman institute a sort of coalition government for the potentially dangerous seventy-nine days between the election and Inauguration Day. It was understood that Marshall was planning to leave as secretary of state, irrespective of who won the presidency. Marquis Childs suggested on November 2 that Truman name Dulles as Marshall's successor immediately, to ease the transition "at a time of turmoil and uncertainty." Childs believed that an administration "repudiated by the voters" should not control foreign policy for the following three months.

Based on what he said in the campaign, a Dewey presidency might have avoided the Korean conflict—and the United States' initial involvement in Vietnam. Had Dewey served two terms, to be succeeded by a Warren still in his mid-sixties, their sixteen years would have taken the United States through the 1964 election. It is reasonable to assume that the amiable Warren would have emerged as an activist version of Eisenhower, a father figure presiding over prosperous times but dealing with such issues as civil rights more in terms of morality than of legal necessity. Of course the nation would have been denied Warren's leadership on the Supreme Court, but problems that festered throughout the 1960s might have been dealt with sooner. It is difficult to imagine that Joseph McCarthy, who was first elected senator by a whisker in the Republican sweep in 1946, would have achieved such destructive impact with a Republican administration in office as early as 1949. Richard Nixon would surely not have been Warren's vice-presidential choice, and might never have risen to national prominence, despite his publicized pursuit in 1948 of

Alger Hiss. The success of consensus-building, containment-maintaining moderate Republicanism—buttressed by an expanded middle class—would also have denied impetus to the Goldwater brand of conservatism. The presidential campaign of 1948 may have confirmed Dewey—at least the version of Dewey who ran—as a less appealing candidate than Truman. It was not a referendum on Dewey's capacity to govern.

IT WAS Truman, however, whom the electorate chose. His margin may have been narrow, but post-election affection for the president made it seem like a mandate. Truman's initial desire to be viewed as a domestic president had been overtaken by events. More low-cost housing may have been desirable; a world strategy was essential. However little it had been discussed in the election campaign of 1948, the nature of America's relationship with its allies, the Communists, and the emerging nations in between would dominate Truman's administration to its end.

This emphasis was made clear in January 1949 by the way Truman approached his two major addresses: the annual State of the Union message, and fifteen days later his speech inaugurating a "new" administration. Each year since he had assumed office, Truman's State of the Union speech had stressed domestic concerns. In the president's view, an address even earlier than his first State of the Union, his twenty-one-point manifesto of September 6, 1945, actually "set the tone and direction for the rest of my administration." In 1949 Truman's fourth State of the Union address was again directed to the nation. His inaugural address, the only one he ever uttered, was directed to the world. This thematic separation was welcomed by his advisers. As Elsey put it, "The circumstances of the president's reelection thrilled the free world, and the dramatic occasion of his inauguration . . . will insure world-wide attention to whatever the president may say."

Worldwide attention merited worldwide issues, not whether to raise the minimum wage in the United States.

First the state of the union had to be conveyed. Truman endowed this fifth exposition of his domestic agenda with a new name, suggesting both continuity with the New Deal and a fresh departure. He started with this affirmation: "Every segment of our population and every individual has the right to expect a fair deal." It had been over a decade since the last New Deal measure had been enacted. A war of unprecedented ferocity and scale had followed. Truman's earlier proclamations of domestic goals were overshadowed by the aftermath of that war, the problems of reconversion, and the relative weakness of his own position. Rowe remarked, "Now domestically, until '48 Truman . . . didn't have a Congress. Not enough liberals." In January 1949 Truman finally had his Congress; how "liberal" remained to be seen.

Spelled out in a later budget message and detailed plans of specific proposals, Truman called again for national health insurance, real progress in civil rights (only the issue of women's rights was notably absent), an extensive public housing program, federal aid to education, and expansion of Social Security coverage. He urged an increase in the minimum wage from forty to seventy-five cents an hour, replacement of Taft-Hartley with a more equitable labor law, the development of natural resources and public power, an extensive farm program which became known as the Brannan Plan, a fairer tax structure, and a progrowth combination of flexible controls and government cooperation with business that would be guided by Leon Keyserling—all within the constraints of a balanced budget, hopefully even a surplus. This twenty-four-point "Fair Deal" evolved from but went beyond even Truman's earlier proposals. Dewey and Warren would have agreed with much of it, though with greater emphasis on state rather than federal powers. The 1949 version of Truman's agenda represented the most compre-

hensive program of domestic reform ever offered at one time to
an American Congress. Truman would never again have such an
opportunity.

Two weeks later, on January 20, 1949, the president stood up
on the east portico of the Capitol before a vast crowd to give his
inaugural address. The event was witnessed for the first time by
millions on television; many millions more listened on radio. Truman's remarks encompassed the entire world, including uncom-
mitted nations. He characterized democracy as the "vitalizing
force" that united people everywhere, and communism as a
"threat to the efforts of free nations to bring about . . . recovery
and lasting peace." The address was more than a general evoca-
tion, however. Truman made four specific points, two of them
new. Not only would the United States continue its support of the
United Nations and reinforce the Marshall Plan, Truman also proposed to help form a "defense arrangement" among the nations of
Western Europe "to make it sufficiently clear . . . that any armed
attack affecting our national security would be met with overwhelming force." He then turned to the peaceful side of the equation, calling for a "bold new program" to make the benefits of
American science and industrial progress available to "underde-
veloped" countries. Truman was announcing what became NATO
and the Point Four program. Point Four, the brainchild of an idealistic State Department staffer, ultimately became more symbolic than substantive. It was "shoved aside," as the historian
Thomas Paterson recounts, "by dramatic cold war events" and
bureaucratic discord, but it was the highlight of Truman's impressive address. NATO, on the other hand, took shape quickly.

Such "dramatic cold war events" as the detonation of an
atomic device by the Soviets in 1949 and the final withdrawal of
the Chinese Nationalists from the mainland to the island of Formosa, led to an influential National Security Council paper in
April 1950 called NSC-68. Recommending immense increases in

American military expenditures, its conclusions were forcefully supported by Secretary of State Dean Acheson, who had succeeded Marshall. Truman initially disagreed, persisting in his intention to fund both domestic and preparedness programs within a balanced budget. The attack of Communist North Korean troops on American-sponsored South Korea two months later changed everything. Its reverberations were felt around the world, from Seoul to Washington to Berlin. Since the next test of Western steadfastness by what was still viewed in Washington as Moscow-directed communism might come anywhere, steps were taken to defend West Germany from invasion. A coordinated NATO headquarters was set up in Paris, headed by Eisenhower. Through the United Nations, fifteen countries joined to resist Communist aggression in Korea, but the United States sent most of the troops and bore most of the cost. On July 4, 1950, young Americans were again fighting in Asia, less than five years after the end of World War II.

The historian John Lewis Gaddis computes that military spending in 1948 was only 5 percent of the gross national product. In 1952 it was 12.7 percent, and in 1953, 13.8 percent, based on programs forwarded while Truman was still president. The total for military investment in 1953 was over $50 billion, or 65.6 percent of total government spending, more than twice the 1950 percentage. Robert Pollard points out that by the end of the Truman administration, 80 percent of American assistance to Europe was military, and "U.S. military aid worldwide ($2.7 billion) exceeded economic aid ($2 billion). . . . Economic assistance had become an adjunct to military programs." Point Four never had a chance. Acheson wrote, "When the Soviet atomic explosion in 1949 and the attack on South Korea in 1950 called for a drastic revision of foreign and military policy," Truman was prepared to give fiscal considerations "second place if that was necessary in doing what had to be done in the interest of national security."

George Kennan did not prepare NSC-68. He left the policy planning staff of the State Department at the end of 1949, to be succeeded by Paul Nitze. In his initial conception of containment, Kennan already recognized Moscow's vulnerability to the potential of nationalistic Communist movements elsewhere. When "Titoism" in Yugoslavia confirmed this conclusion, Kennan anticipated its emulation more in Asia than in Europe. The emergence of the People's Republic of China represented a state sizable enough to contest with the Soviet Union for ideological leadership, an alternative power center. This by no means reduced the Communist threat throughout the world, but it greatly enhanced the possibilities for American initiative. NSC-68 dashed these hopes, continuing to view communism in a sweeping, worldwide context. Moreover, as Gaddis writes, "Kennan's strategy of defending selected strongpoints would no longer suffice; the emphasis rather would . . . be on a perimeter defense with all points along the perimeter considered of equal importance." After the Korean War broke out, Truman could only hope that continued economic growth in the United States would prevent military investments from excessively unbalancing the budget. The president uneasily increased his requests to Congress for defense appropriations for fiscal 1951 from $13.5 billion to more than $48 billion. Under the premise of NSC-68 the military budget could only rise.

Despite Truman's concerns about solvency and escalation, and the frustrating Korean situation that blighted his last months in office, Melvyn Leffler believes that "Truman accepted [his] legacy. In his view, it was the price that had to be paid for the pursuit of freedom and the containment of Communism. It was a small price, he thought, compared to his successful efforts to reconstruct Western Europe, co-opt German and Japanese power, and establish a position of preponderant strength for the free world."

The president had only eighteen months between his inauguration and the inception of the Korean conflict to secure his domestic legacy. Even before Korea, as Ferrell observes, "The proposals that Truman sent to Congress usually died in their pertinent committees. He tried to see them through, but Congress wouldn't respond." Some of the fault was Truman's. Normally a vigorous advocate for his programs, whatever their chance of passage, as soon as the 1948 campaign was over Truman executed an abrupt turnaround from confrontation to conciliation. This new approach was welcomed by the press but left liberal legislators adrift. They looked to the president for leadership, but when he readily took back in the fold those Southern senators and congressmen who had abandoned him in the election, Truman's constituency for domestic reform dissipated. Democratic House Speaker Sam Rayburn of Texas, for example, who supported the president in the election, had proclaimed earlier in 1948, "I am going to do everything I can for our state to protect our segregation laws. I think we can work out our local problems without any interference from the outside." Seniority remained sacrosanct. No one was purged. Leaderless, many of the newly elected congressmen and senators who might have supported the president were handicapped by the very lack of practical political experience that had made them attractive to the electorate.

Although results fell far short of liberal expectations, Truman's Fair Deal failure was not total. Some New Deal programs were extended in 1949 and 1950. The minimum wage was raised to seventy-five cents, public power was extended, and a loophole in the Clayton Anti-Trust Act was closed. The hopeful passage of the Housing Act of 1949, intended to construct 810,000 units of low-cost public housing, produced only a modicum. It soon bogged down in red tape, confused lending policies, inadequate financing, and local opposition. Instead the cities got "urban renewal" in the form of spectacular commercial developments.

They revitalized many downtown areas without doing much for the low-income residents who were removed to make way for such projects. In the following Eisenhower administration, thousands more of the poor, often in established communities, would be displaced by an extensive highway system, another form of "urban removal." Most of the 1.7 million housing starts in 1950 were the work of innovative private developers in the burgeoning suburbs. The largest, William Levitt, defended his firm's policy not to sell to African-Americans by saying, "We can solve a housing problem, or we can try to solve a racial problem, but we cannot combine the two." Truman's major contributions to civil rights remained his two executive orders of 1948.

The Fair Deal's most notable achievement was in extending mandatory Social Security coverage to 8 million people and voluntary coverage to 2.5 million more. As the historian Carolyn L. Weaver details, for the first time more Americans came under the federal program than received "old age" pensions based in the states. This 1950 legislation, incorporating thirty major changes in the original Social Security Act, was amended in 1952 to provide greatly increased benefits to recipients. The 1948 Republican platform, crafted by Dewey's lieutenants, had also called for expanding the program. Even in 1944, in Los Angeles, facing the largest audience of that campaign, Dewey had recited his support for Social Security. A degree of consensus on this issue developed in future administrations. Contrary to attempts of the 80th Congress to roll back much of the New Deal, candidate Dwight Eisenhower wrote in 1952 to his conservative brother Edgar, "Should any party attempt to abolish Social Security, and eliminate labor laws and farm programs, you would not hear of that party again in our political history." Later, in office, Ike told his budget director, Joseph Dodge, that within fiscal constraints the "extension of Social Security and old age benefits" was vital.

Truman boasted of having doubled Social Security benefits

during his administration, but he was disappointed by his failure
to overhaul the entire Social Security system, especially in adding
health-care provisions. As Donald McCoy writes, the legislation
enacted in 1950 and 1952, "important as it was in fine tuning Social Security benefits, was not the landmark that Truman called
it."

Although the presidential contest of 1948 had been defined as
a maintaining election, James MacGregor Burns points out that it
was "a different kind of maintaining election—an election that
sustained the Truman administration in its Fair Deal posture, but
most of all in its anti-communism." That the Fair Deal turned out
to be more posture than performance is not solely due to the lack
of leadership provided by the president. It also reflects the tenor
of the times. After so many years of turmoil, Alonzo Hamby
points out, "The Democratic coalition had ceased to be a 'have
not' coalition and had become chiefly interested in maintaining
earlier gains." Domestic reform, urgent in times of depression,
was a harder sell in an era of full employment. Passage of the Social Security Act of 1950 bespeaks overwhelming public support
not for the whole of the Fair Deal but only for this singular component of it, the goal of coverage for all working Americans. The
daunting comprehensiveness of many of Truman's other domestic
proposals made them difficult to absorb and harder to enact. Increasing the minimum wage was easier to understand than Keyserling's many-layered economic schemes.

That a president so experienced in legislative realities as Truman persisted each year in making things so difficult for himself
implies that he did not completely believe in what he was propos-
ing, or else that it represented a low priority in his thinking. Truman *did* believe in the essentials of his proposed legislation, but
in his rhetoric he often got carried away. As the historian Robert
Griffith observes, the president was capable of "self-deception"
as well as "plain speaking." Truman had supported the New Deal,

but it had been a selective and cautious support. By instinct and experience he became a "Vital Center liberal." Before 1949 he could proclaim any extensive domestic program, secure in the knowledge that it would not likely be enacted. He waged the 1948 campaign more on the premise of preserving than expanding the New Deal, but his words conveyed a commitment to go beyond it. In January 1949, as McCullough points out, "Unlike January 1948 . . . everyone now paid close attention." Truman was trapped by the weight of his own accumulated rhetoric to propose an even more comprehensive domestic agenda than he had before. Despite his protestations to the contrary, if all its components had been implemented, it would have taken fortuitous circumstances to keep the budget balanced. Truman was not yet aware that the political center both he and Dewey occupied would shift further to the right. The Fair Deal became moot after Korea, but even earlier the reality of residual congressional conservatism and public disinterest doomed most of it. At least in theory Truman never abandoned his pragmatic position that a country as fundamentally sound as the United States could afford butter as well as guns, but preparedness came first.

Four months before the North Korean army poured into South Korea, Senator Joseph McCarthy made his first list-waving speech in West Virginia, accusing the government of harboring spies and traitors. The House Un-American Activities Committee had been active throughout 1948, its dramatic charges—against Alger Hiss, Julian Wadleigh, William Remington, Harry Dexter White, and others—damaging to the administration. They would have been more damaging had Truman in 1947 not instituted his own security program. By 1951 the president was sufficiently influenced by the widened "red scare" to tighten the procedures of his loyalty review board, further compromising his reputation as a champion of civil liberties. There is little doubt that Truman was far more concerned with the threat of external rather than in-

ternal communism, but once again his political instincts overcame his equally grounded moderation. Distracting scandals continued to surface in his administration, the residue of cronyism,
but they never extended to the president personally.

Truman's domestic legacy was largely to preserve and extend
the most significant gains of the New Deal and to set an agenda
for future administrations, most notably the first two years of
Lyndon Johnson's. Setting an agenda was not exactly Truman's
conception of progress. In the end he could neither overcome his
own ambivalence about radical reform nor take the nation's representatives where they were less than willing to go.

In his book on presidential character, James David Barber
views Truman in the context of "active-positive combat." Barber
notes that "during a period of immense complexity, uncertainty,
and strife, Truman felt his way along. The outcome was far from
ideally satisfactory. It might have been tragic." Many historians
blame Truman for turning the United States into a crisis-driven
"national security state" and for institutionalizing the cold war
consensus that preoccupied national consciousness for the next
forty years. William Pemberton writes, "Beginning in 1947, as
the contours of the national security state emerged, the whole nation would have to be placed on permanent quasi-war status. . . .
These changes affected the United States politically, socially, and
intellectually and transformed its diplomatic, military, and economic structure. These results . . . were Truman's true legacy."

To what extent was Truman the author of this transformation?
Robert Dallek believes that had he lived, "Roosevelt would probably have moved more quickly than Truman to confront the Russians." By the time of the 1948 election, Republican leaders were
more "hawkish" than the president. When he requested fifty-five
air force groups, even the parsimonious 80th Congress authorized
eighty. Truman's appointments in foreign affairs reflected his pre-
dominant concern with finding the right international path. In the

State Department (and in the Department of Defense, after Marshall replaced Johnson and was later succeeded by Lovett), Truman felt the necessity to seek the counsel of seasoned professionals.

Early on, the president had asked such trusted generalists as Clifford and Elsey to compile a report on the state of the Soviet threat. By 1947 a more secure Truman relied almost exclusively on men with diplomatic credentials, starting with Harriman and including such former Wall Streeters as William Draper and John McCloy. The abortive Vinson mission was an election-driven exception. On Kennan's planning staff were economic specialists Will Clayton, Walt Rostow, and Charles Kindleberger. Other experts included Paul Nitze, "Chip" Bohlen, Loy Henderson, John Paton Davies, Robert Tufts, Robert Joyce, and Charles Bonesteel. When Marshall left the State Department after Truman's inauguration in 1949, he was replaced by Acheson, who was a devoted Democrat but had never been active in politics. The four-year relationship between Truman and Acheson, a most unlikely pair in every particular, developed into one of mutual trust and personal friendship. Harry Truman's whole administration is a testament to Aaron Wildavsky's "two presidents" theory that "since World War II, presidents have had greater success in controlling the nation's defense and foreign policies than in dominating its domestic policies."

To Truman, as to Dewey, American isolationism had been at the root of every international ill from the depression through World War II. Now, with Taft on the sidelines and Wallace rejected, the election of 1948 confirmed the triumph of internationalism. As Melvyn Leffler concludes, "There was no self-restraint here. . . . Truman saw himself struggling to safeguard the nation's security. . . . The rhetoric of anti-communism could rally the American people behind his initiatives." At issue was nothing less than a worldwide struggle between tyranny and freedom. The results of 1948 institutionalized not only the bipartisan policy of containment but American determination to sustain military and economic supremacy.

Whoever was most responsible for initiating Truman's foreign policy, early revelations from recently opened Soviet archives lend credence to the president's firm stand. Quoting Stalin himself on Soviet intentions, historian Vladislav Zubok writes, "On balance . . . a first peek into enemy archives vindicates the 'wise men' of the late 1940s more than it condemns them. Most of their concerns about Stalin's designs and ambitions at the end of the Second World War have been substantiated." Robert Tucker notes that even in his final years Stalin personally made his nation's key foreign policy decisions, including the Berlin blockade and, after repeated requests, approving North Korea's invasion of the South. Stalin's instinct was always to test Western will, pulling back only when forcefully challenged. The dictator's death in 1953, after Truman left office, "liberated Russia and the rest of humanity from this mortal danger" of immediate world war.

SINCE 1952 the United States has had nine presidents (one unelected): five Republicans and four Democrats. They have been, in no special order, both "liberal" and "conservative" in their approach to domestic policy, but largely "moderate"—and are becoming more difficult to categorize. Despite frequently divided governments, there seem to be fewer basic areas of disagreement between Republicans and Democrats, irrespective of which is in the White House or controls the Congress. Their issues of contention, as with Truman and Dewey in 1948, are more rhetorical than substantive. As of this writing, nine of the presidential elections since 1948 have been one-sided affairs, only three very close. The presidential landslides in 1964, 1972, 1984, and 1996 resulted in the election of both Republicans and Democrats.

By such measurements as have been made, the Democrats have continued to be the majority party of voter sentiment. In 1994 the Center for Political Studies of the University of Michigan estimated that 47 percent of the electorate (in "private housing units") identified themselves as Democrats, including 13 percent classifying themselves as "independent Democrats"; 43 percent were Republicans, including 12 percent who classified themselves as "independent Republicans"; 10 percent were independent. How frequently do these proportions follow in national elections? The Gallup poll, which takes more frequent measurements, agrees that during the first week of November 1994, voters identifying themselves as Democrats were 47 percent, and Republicans were 43 percent. But directly after their "Contract with America" congressional sweep in 1994, the Republican party enjoyed a 10 percent "bounce" in voter identification to a lead of 53 to 41 percent. Things soon returned to "normal" with modest Democratic majorities. On an annual polling basis, Democrats have been labeled the majority party in "identification" and "degree of attachment" in a virtually unbroken pattern since 1932. In 1972, for example, the year of the Nixon landslide, before the election 52 percent identified themselves as Democrats (15 percent "strong" Democrats), 34 percent as Republicans (10 percent "strong" Republicans), 13 percent as independent, and 1 percent as "apolitical." Put simply, public opinion polls of party preference, whether taken annually or weekly, mean little or nothing as opposed to polls (after 1948) on specific political races or issues.

The presidential election of 1948 bridged the past era of party-centered voting habits and the future pattern of greater independent voting, issue by issue, candidate by candidate. The circumstances that helped mold such disparate elements into the

New Deal electoral coalition—the continuing emergencies of depression and war, and the appearance of a charismatic leader—were temporary. No new electoral alliance of similar duration based on political parties has formed to take its place, except perhaps in the white South. "Racial" politics and "gender" politics, the ultimate separation of interest groups, are based more on perceptions of personalities and political positions than on parties, despite seeming to favor one over the other. In regional terms, consider what has happened in presidential elections to even those four deep South states claimed by Thurmond in 1948. In 1952 they returned to Democrat Stevenson, whose running mate was from Alabama. In 1956, despite an even more extensive Eisenhower landslide, all four states remained Democratic (one Alabama elector bolted to the Independent Democrat Walter Jones). This time Stevenson's vice-presidential candidate was from Tennessee. In 1960 they split between Democrat Kennedy and the symbolic candidacy of Senator Harry Byrd of Virginia. In 1964 all four states went to Republican Goldwater (joined only by Georgia and his home state of Arizona). In 1968 all were claimed by George Wallace and his American Independent party. In 1972 all were won by Republican Nixon; in 1976 by Democrat Carter of Georgia. Nevertheless Carter lost all four states in 1980 to Republican Reagan. Reagan and Bush claimed all four in 1984 and 1988, but Democrat Clinton of Arkansas reclaimed one of the four (Louisiana) in both 1992 and 1996, his vote in the others probably reduced by the Ross Perot candidacy.

There remains more Democratic party registration than Republican in major urban areas, but even in 1948 that did not translate to electoral votes. The growth of suburbia and the conservative trend extended from 1968 has seemed to favor Republicans, but two Democratic presidents have also been elected between 1968 and 1996 (and one was reelected overwhelmingly as a "new" Democrat). The often cited "critical elections" of

1800, 1828, 1860, 1896, and 1932 were all centered on the shifting status of political parties. The critical movement after 1948 was away from political parties and toward more independent voting. That, not the victory of Truman over Dewey, makes 1948 a watershed in American political history. The storage-bin controversy and black reaction to an unusual segregationist threat highlighted issue-based voting. Of all the reasons why Truman won, the extension of the Roosevelt coalition does not rank high. 1948 was not a "maintaining" election; it was transitional. By the way he campaigned, Truman failed to take advantage of the already significant numbers of independent voters. As a result, the bulk of his support was Democratic, and thus the total vote was limited— but the long-term trend had been initiated.

LIKE a commencement address, the 1948 election was both an end and a beginning. In legislative terms it ended the New Deal period (which in fact had been deadlocked since 1938), but it began the much longer period of consensus that its basic achievements would survive. In political terms it ended the New Deal electoral coalition. The 1948 election was the last, as Ferrell points out, for bloc voting by labor unions. It was "the farmers' last hurrah" as well as the end of the solid Democratic South and nationwide touring by train. It marked the decline of voting by inherited and group-oriented party loyalties, and an emphasis on personal campaigning of the sort Truman relished; these features were replaced with independent voting and an emphasis on the demands of the electronic media.

The decline of labor as a political force reflects changes in the American economy already under way in 1948. Truman's exploitation of his veto of Taft-Hartley and his "give 'em hell" campaign initiated on Labor Day encouraged both the AFL and CIO finally to support his candidacy. Not only Wallace's bid but its overwhelming rejection by the electorate steeled Philip Murray's resolve to seek a showdown within the CIO. Nelson Lichtenstein writes that with "the president's unexpected success . . . the Wallace supporters routed, and the Republicans at least temporarily subdued, the industrial union federation could clean house with the least possible institutional damage." Claiming that he had foiled a Communist "plot" to take over the CIO, by 1950 Murray had expelled eleven affiliated unions, encompassing more than a million members, because of their domination by Communists— and replaced the leadership of other unions. But Murray's triumph, like Truman's, turned out to be ephemeral. As the historian Robert H. Zieger recounts, Murray failed to follow up by aggressively recruiting new members and forming new unions. Only five years later, after the deaths of both Murray and William Green, the two great alliances of labor joined together under a single umbrella to form the AFL-CIO.

This merger could neither slow the gradual transformation of the United States from the world's industrial powerhouse to a service-based economy, nor sustain the strength of the union movement. In 1945 some 35.5 percent of American workers were union members; by 1950 the percentage was 31.5, and in 1996 only 14.5 percent of the work force, blue or white collar, belonged to unions. Despite strenuous efforts, the union movement never again mustered the political clout it showed in 1948. It could no more "deliver" the votes of its membership, particularly after the rightward swing of the electorate, than could the similarly diminished urban political machines.

In 1998 the ADA, still the leading multi-issue national liberal organization, boasted some 55,000 active members and its own political action committee. Its triumph over the PCA-spawned Progressive party in 1948, and the later purge of Communists by the CIO, should be viewed in the larger context of pervasive anti-communism throughout American society. The Taft-Hartley Act of 1947 already included anti-Communist provisions. In the summer of 1948, just about the time resentful Republicans were sabotaging President Truman's special congressional session, twelve leaders of the American Communist party were indicted under the Smith Act for advocating the violent overthrow of the government of the United States. Not only had the whole government gone "warlike," the entire nation was alerted to the red peril. Given this environment, ultimately the CIO would have purged itself of Communist influence and the PCA would have gone out of business even without the Wallace candidacy. "Popular-front liberalism," by the very nature of its slavish subservience to Moscow, would have found another cause over which to self-destruct.

IN ASSESSING the changes between 1948 and 1952, most of all Robert Ferrell notes the significance of the coaxial cable. "After it, nothing was the same." As Walter Cronkite adds, "Television and politics flirted in 1948. They wed in 1952." Dewey's use of public and media relations was quite advanced, but he turned down adman Rosser Reeves's suggestion for television "spot" commercials as undignified. Eisenhower would be convinced to use them in 1952, to great advantage, coinciding with the astonishing expansion in television sets and stations that was taking place. In 1952, at the cessation of the Federal Communications Commission "freeze" on television stations, 108 new stations were prepared to begin operating immediately. Within a year they were joined by 400 more. By 1960 over 85 percent of American homes had at least one TV set. Although the influence of television may have turned national conventions into "infomercials" and speeches into "photo ops," it has reduced neither the rigors nor the duration of political campaigning. With the growth in importance of presidential primaries and electronic polling (polls made a remarkable comeback after 1948 and merged with the development of computers), few candidates care to yield any possible advantage. The politics of exhaustion defies obsolescence.

A contemporary Richard Rovere would likely view such intensive touring as unnecessary—and, unlike in 1948, he would be right. Although the outcome should not have been so close, the vigorous personal campaigning of Truman and Barkley really was a determining factor in their election. Perhaps that is why whenever a presidential candidate indulges in a nostalgic train tour (as Bill Clinton did in 1996) or finds himself far behind in the polls (as Bob Dole was in 1996), the inspiring example of Harry Truman is invariably cited. As Barkley's hometown *Paducah Sun-Democrat* put it on November 4, 1948, "The people did their own thinking, and their own voting." The historian Harold Lew Wallace views Truman's and Barkley's triumph in 1948 as a demonstration that American voters are "capable of reflection as well as reflex." They have been reflecting ever since.

Most of all the election of 1948 solidified the cold war consensus that would last for the next forty years. The primary concern of government became national security. As Forrest McDonald observes, accepting an "innate antagonism between capitalism and socialism" resulted in viewing everything through "the prism of cold war ideology." In his memoirs Harry Truman allocated the whole of the Fair Deal all of thirteen pages. In his farewell address to the nation in January 1953, he recalled the most momentous decisions of his administration, citing only foreign and military policies. Most important, he contended, the United States, as in Korea, "established to the Kremlin the determination of free peoples to defend themselves." Then Truman spoke of his dreams for "a wonderful golden age," not only in the United States but throughout the world. Eight years later President Eisenhower's own farewell warned of the growth of a "military-industrial complex" in the nation. This followed a pres-

idential election in which the two youthful contestants were reduced to debating whether or not the United States should defend
tiny offshore islands between mainland China and Taiwan (the
"Formosa" the Nationalists had retreated to eleven years before),
and the reality of a "missile gap." The national discourse had nar-
rowed into one of methods and parameters, not ends.

In the context of both politics and policy, 1948 was a significant presidential election not so much because of which of the
similarly disposed major candidates won. Rather, trends in the
political culture—already in the making and abetted by technology—came to fruition, remaining dominant for decades to come.
The outcome of the election was no upset. It would have been if
Truman had lost, as he nearly managed to do. Merging fact and
folklore, the twin myths of upset and Trumania have endured,
however, dramatically dominating the deeper meaning of the contest. On the day he succeeded Roosevelt in 1945, Truman was already being described by the political writer Allen Drury as "one
of the squarest shooters who ever lived."

Even in 1948, an election keyed to the future, Truman campaigned in the past. The historian Michael Kammen writes: "Truman shrewdly ran against the Republican ghost of Herbert
Hoover than against the formidable dullness of Thomas E.
Dewey. . . . Memories and misconceptions of the past may have
played a crucial role in shaping both public opinion and government policies . . . the belief that a reading of history 'taught' that
thus-and-so seemed the prudent course of action to follow. Harry
Truman may be the most notable exemplar of that attitude." All
his life Truman cherished his history lessons, his simplistic mod-
els of rectitude. In the image of 1948, he has become one in the
collective memory of the nation.

A NOTE ON SOURCES

THE BEST brief account of the presidential election of 1948 is that by Richard S. Kirkendall, contained within the *History of American Presidential Elections 1789–1968,* vol. 4, edited by Arthur M. Schlesinger, Jr., and Fred L. Israel (New York, 1971). Kirkendall also edited two immensely helpful source books on the whole of Truman's life and legacy, *The Harry S. Truman Encyclopedia* (Boston, 1989) and *The Truman Period as a Research Field: A Reappraisal* (Columbia, Mo., 1974). Although a great deal has been written about the Truman presidency, and more recently about Truman himself, only two books are devoted entirely to the election of 1948, both by journalists: Irwin Ross, *The Loneliest Campaign: The Truman Victory of 1948* (New York, 1968), and Jules Abels, *Out of the Jaws of Victory* (New York, 1959). They express the customary view that Truman's victory was an upset and an extension of the Roosevelt electoral coalition.

In the succeeding thirty years many doctoral dissertations have been written on aspects of the 1948 election, particularly the rhetorical contest and the role of third parties. The most thorough chronological account of the entire election in this format is by Harold Lew Wallace, "The Campaign of 1948" (University of Indiana, 1970). Informative studies of Truman's pre-presidential career and campaigns are by Eugene F. Schmidtlein, "Truman the Senator" (University of Missouri, 1962), and Thomas J. Heed, "Prelude to Whistlestop: Harry S. Truman, The Apprentice Campaigner" (Columbia University, 1975). Although technically these dissertations are "unpublished," copies and complete Datrix lists of offerings on any subject can be obtained through University Microfilms International, Ann Arbor, Mich.

A helpful compilation of books and articles relating to Truman, including the 1948 campaign, is outlined in Richard Dean Burns, ed., *Harry S. Truman: A Bibliography of His Times and Presidency* (Wilmington, Del., 1984), see especially pp. 116–117. The Harry S. Truman

Library in Independence, Mo., publishes a comprehensive guide to its materials. Their holdings include not only Truman's papers but also those of many other Democrats prominent in the 1948 election, as well as a wealth of oral history interviews. The library and its related Institute publish an informative journal, *Whistle Stop,* and are generous in arranging interlibrary loans. All of Truman's speeches and many of his informal remarks during the 1948 campaign are included in *Public Papers of Harry S. Truman, 1948* (Washington, D.C., 1964). See also *Addresses and Messages by President Harry S. Truman* (Washington, D.C., 1949). A listing of videotapes of television programs devoted to Truman, many involving 1948, is available through the C-Span Public Affairs Video Archives at Purdue University, West Lafayette, Ind., as are the tapes themselves.

Three immensely readable major biographies of Truman were published in the 1990s: David McCullough, *Truman* (New York, 1992); Robert H. Ferrell, *Harry S. Truman: A Life* (Columbia, Mo., 1994); and Alonzo L. Hamby, *Man of the People: A Life of Harry S. Truman* (New York, 1995). Ferrell and Hamby have written most extensively about Truman. See particularly two earlier works, Ferrell's *Harry S. Truman and the Modern American Presidency* (New York, 1983) and Hamby's *Beyond the New Deal: Harry S. Truman and American Liberalism* (New York, 1973). Hamby also wrote *Liberalism and Its Challenges: FDR to Reagan* (New York, 1985). Ferrell edited a number of books incorporating Truman's own words: *Off the Record: The Private Papers of Harry S. Truman* (New York, 1980); *The Autobiography of Harry S. Truman* (Boulder, Colo., 1980); and *Dear Bess: The Letters from Harry to Bess Truman, 1910–1959* (New York, 1983).

The first biography of Truman, by one who knew him well, is still among the best written: Jonathan Daniels, *The Man of Independence* (Philadelphia, 1950). Truman's criticism of the book as inaccurate may have been due to his acute aversion to any intrusion into areas he deemed private. Other biographies of Truman while he was still in office, more difficult to find than Daniels's, include Henry A. Bundschu, *Harry S. Truman: The Missourian* (Kansas City, 1948); William Helm, *Harry Truman: A Political Biography* (New York, 1947); and Frank McNaughton and Walter Heymeyer, *Harry Truman: President* (New York, 1948).

A well-documented account of Truman before his presidency, portraying him more as a calculating opportunist than have other Truman biographers, is Richard Lawrence Miller's *Truman: The Rise to Power* (New York, 1986). A very different picture of Truman, based on informal interviews after he left office, is Merle Miller's *Plain Speaking: An Oral Biography of Harry S. Truman* (New York, 1973), which helped launch the "Trumania" phenomenon. The most thorough study of the Truman presidency is contained in the two volumes written by Robert J. Donovan, *Conflict and Crisis: The Presidency of Harry S. Truman, 1945–1948* (New York, 1977), and *Tumultuous Years: The Presidency of Harry S. Truman, 1949–1953* (New York, 1982). The best single-volume review of the Truman years, part of a notable series of presidential studies, is by Donald R. McCoy, *The Presidency of Harry S. Truman* (Lawrence, Kans., 1984). A good earlier account is Cabell Phillips's *The Truman Presidency: The History of a Triumphant Succession* (New York, 1966). Other biographies range from Alfred Steinberg's journalistic *The Man from Missouri: The Life and Times of Harry S. Truman* (New York, 1962) to Harold F. Gosnell's scholarly *Truman's Crises: A Political Biography of Harry S. Truman* (Westport, Conn., 1980). A less positive appraisal is Bert Cochran's *Harry Truman and the Crisis Presidency* (New York, 1973). From the British viewpoint is Roy Jenkins's *Truman* (New York, 1986). Excellent expositions of Truman's policies are William E. Pemberton's *Harry S. Truman, Fair Dealer and Cold Warrior* (Boston, 1989) and Robert Underhill's *The Truman Persuasions* (Ames, Iowa, 1981).

Truman frequently expressed his view that every scrap of presidential paper, public or personal, is the property of the American people, but he was reluctant to reveal much of his own unofficial documentation. The "facts" of his life, as presented in his heavily edited memoirs, Truman insisted should be devoid of any "introspective trimmings" and be laid out largely to correct misinformation provided by others. Truman's description of the 1948 campaign is also perfunctory, but vivid glimpses of the real Truman break through from time to time. In any case, perusing the two volumes of his memoirs is necessarily central to any consideration of the Truman presidency. The 1948 election is covered in *Memoirs of Harry S. Truman, 1946–52, vol. 2: Years of Trial and Hope* (Garden City, N.Y., 1956). The first volume is *Memoirs of Harry S. Truman: Year of Decision* (Garden City, N.Y., 1955). Later published under Truman's name were *Mr. Citizen* (New York, 1960) and *Truman Speaks* (New York, 1960).

More informative is the understandably affectionate biography of her father by Margaret Truman, *Harry S. Truman* (New York, 1972). Margaret also wrote a biography of her mother, *Bess W. Truman* (New York, 1986). Although President Truman was more forthright in expressing his views of others, he asked his daughter to delay until after his and his wife's death the publication of *Where the Buck Stops: The Personal and Private Writings of Harry S. Truman,* edited by Margaret Truman (New York, 1989). Margaret also edited *Letters from Father: The Truman Family's Personal Correspondence* (New York, 1981). Truman's candor is captured in Monte M. Poen, ed., *Strictly Personal and Confidential: The Letters Harry S. Truman Never Mailed* (Boston, 1982), and its companion, also edited by Poen, *Letters Home by Harry Truman* (New York, 1984). The flavor of the period is recorded in James N. Giglio and Greg G. Thielen, *Truman: In Cartoon and Caricature* (Ames, Iowa, 1984); Charles Robbins and Bradley Smith, *Last of His Kind: An Informal Portrait of Harry S. Truman* (New York, 1979); Robert S. Allen and William V. Shannon, *The Truman Merry-Go-Round* (New York, 1950); and R. Alton Lee, *Harry S. Truman: Where Did the Buck Stop?* (New York, 1991).

The definitive biography of Truman's major opponent in 1948 is by Richard Norton Smith, *Thomas E. Dewey and His Times* (New York, 1982). Dewey's papers are in the Department of Rare Books and Special Collections at the Rush Rhees Library of the University of Rochester. There are several thorough appraisals of the 1998 campaign of Henry A. Wallace, some encompassing his earlier career: Curtis D. MacDougal, *Gideon's Army,* 3 vols. (New York, 1965); Norman D. Markowitz, *The Rise and Fall of the People's Century: Henry A. Wallace and American Liberalism, 1941–1948* (New York, 1973); and Karl M. Schmidt, *Henry A. Wallace: Quixotic Crusade, 1948* (Syracuse, N.Y., 1960). A highly favorable view of Wallace is expressed by Richard J. Walton, *Henry Wallace, Harry Truman, and the Cold War* (New York, 1976); an acerbic explanation of Wallace's appeal is Dwight Macdonald's *Henry Wallace: The Man and the Myth* (New York, 1948). A rationalization of why he voted for Wallace is contained in the iconoclastic journalist I. F. Stone's *The Truman Era* (New York, 1953). Wallace wrote his own books publicizing his goals: *Sixty Million Jobs* (New York, 1945) and *Towards World Peace* (New York, 1948). Also see John Morton Blum, ed., *The Price of Vision: The Diary of Henry A. Wallace* (Boston, 1973). Wallace's personal papers are at the University of Iowa in Iowa City. His public papers are divided between the Library of Congress in Washington and the Franklin D. Roosevelt Presidential Library at Hyde Park, New York.

A comprehensive account of the States' Rights Democratic party is provided in Nadine Cohodas's *Strom Thurmond and the Politics of Southern Change* (New York, 1993). Documents relating to the Dixiecrats are centered in the State Department of Archives and History at Jackson, Mississippi. An interesting description of how States' Rights sentiments worked in one Southern state is William D. Barnard's *Dixiecrats and Democrats: Alabama Politics, 1942–1950* (Tuscaloosa, Ala., 1974).

Literature on the vice-presidential candidates is limited. Alben Barkley's autobiography, *That Reminds Me* (Garden City, N.Y., 1954), is predictably lighthearted and anecdotal. An informative account of Barkley's legislative career is provided in Polly Ann Davis's *Alben W. Barkley: Senate Majority Leader and Vice-President* (New York, 1979). An affectionate personal portrait is James K. Libbey's *Dear Alben: The Barkleys of Kentucky* (Lexington, Ky., 1979). The Ray Mofield Collection in Harlan, Kentucky, includes Barkley's speeches on tape and a newspaper file. Texts of his addresses in 1948 comprise part of the Alben Barkley Collection at the University of Kentucky in Lexington. A well-researched book on the whole of Earl Warren's career is Ed Cray's *Chief Justice: A Biography of Earl Warren* (New York, 1997). Warren's memoirs, though unfinished at the time of his death, were published in 1977 as *The Memoirs of Earl Warren* (Garden City, N.Y., 1977) and include a thorough account of his role in the 1948 race. Warren's addresses repose at the Library of Congress, and his papers are shared by the California State Museum in Sacramento and the University of California at Berkeley. The Progressive party's vice-presidential candidate is equated with Wallace's fate in F. Ross Peterson's *Prophet Without Honor: Glen Taylor and the Fight for American Liberalism* (Lexington, Ky., 1974).

The most stimulating collection of essays on many aspects of the Truman administration is Michael J. Lacey, ed., *The Truman Presidency* (Cambridge, England, 1989). Others worth reading include Barton J. Bernstein, ed., *Politics and Policies of the Truman Administration* (Chicago, 1970); Barton J. Bernstein and Allen J. Matusow, eds., *The Truman Administration: A Documentary History* (New York, 1966); Oscar Handlin, ed., *Harry S. Truman and the Modern American Presidency* (Boston, 1983); J. Joseph Huthmacher, ed., *The Truman Years*

(Hinsdale, Ill., 1972); William F. Levantrosser, ed., *Harry S. Truman: The Man from Independence* (Westport, Conn., 1986); and Eleanora W. Schoenebaum, ed., *Political Profiles: The Truman Years* (New York, 1978).

Biographies, memoirs, and reminiscences worth reading that involve the 1948 election or relate to the Truman administration include James T. Patterson's fine *Mr. Republican: A Biography of Robert A. Taft* (Boston, 1972); Robert A. Taft, *A Foreign Policy for Americans* (Garden City, N.Y., 1951); Dean Acheson, *Present at the Creation: My Years in the State Department* (New York, 1969); Forrest C. Pogue, *George C. Marshall, Statesman, 1945–1959* (New York, 1987); Clark Clifford, with Richard Holbrooke, *Counsel to the President* (New York, 1991); Herbert Brownell, with John P. Burke, *Advising Ike* (Lawrence, Kans., 1993), which also deals extensively with Dewey; Henry L. Stimson, with McGeorge Bundy, *On Active Service in Peace and War* (New York, 1948); James F. Byrnes, *Speaking Frankly* (New York, 1947); Lucius Clay, *Decision in Germany* (Garden City, N.Y., 1950); James A. Farley, *Jim Farley's Story* (New York, 1948); William O. Douglas, *The Autobiography of William O. Douglas* (New York, 1980); Chester Bowles, *Promises to Keep: My Years in Public Life, 1941–1969* (New York, 1971); Harold E. Stassen, *Where I Stand* (Garden City, N.Y., 1947); John Foster Dulles, *War or Peace* (New York, 1950); Ronald T. Farrar, *Reluctant Servant: The Story of Charles G. Ross* (Columbia, Mo., 1969); Hubert H. Humphrey, with Norman Sherman, *The Education of a Public Man: My Life in Politics* (New York, 1976); George F. Kennan, *Memoirs, 1925–1950* (Boston, 1967); William D. Leahy, *I Was There* (New York, 1950); J. Howard McGrath, *The Power of the People* (New York, 1948); Jack Redding, *Inside the Democratic Party* (New York, 1958); Gaddis Smith, *Dean Acheson* (New York, 1972); Rexford G. Tugwell, *A Chronicle of Jeopardy, 1945–1955* (Chicago, 1955); W. Averell Harriman and Elie Abel, *Special Envoy to Stalin and Churchill* (New York, 1975); Charles Sawyer, *Concerns of a Conservative Democrat* (Carbondale, Ill., 1968); Arthur H. Vandenberg, *The Private Papers of Senator Vandenberg*, ed. by Arthur H. Vandenberg, Jr., and Joe Alex Morris (Boston, 1952); Walter Millis, ed., *The Forrestal Diaries* (New York, 1951); David E. Lilienthal, *The Journals of David E. Lilienthal: The Atomic Energy Years, 1945–1950* (New York, 1964); Charles E. Bohlen, *Witness to History, 1929–1969* (New York, 1973); Claude D. Pepper, with Hays Gorey, *Pepper: Eyewitness to a Century*

(San Diego, 1987); and George E. Allen, *Presidents Who Have Known Me* (New York, 1950).

Of the many chronicles of American political parties and movements, those of particular relevance for 1948 include Malcolm Moos, *The Republicans: A History of Their Party* (New York, 1956); Hugh Scott, *Come to the Party* (Englewood Cliffs, N.J., 1968); Robert Blanchard, Richard Meyer, and Blaine Morley, *Presidential Elections, 1948–1960* (Salt Lake City, 1961); Herbert S. Parmet, *The Democrats: The Years After FDR* (New York, 1976); V. O. Key, Jr., *Southern Politics* (New York, 1949); Allen L. Yarnell, *Democrats and Progressives: The 1948 Presidential Election as a Test of Postwar Liberalism* (Berkeley, 1974); William B. Hesseltine, *The Rise and Fall of Third Parties: From Anti-Masonry to Wallace* (Washington, D.C., 1948); Clifton Bruck, *Americans for Democratic Action: Its Role in National Politics* (Washington, D.C., 1967); Dean Acheson, *A Democrat Looks at His Party* (New York, 1955); Samuel Lubell, *The Revolt of the Moderates* (New York, 1956); and David Plotke, *Building a Democratic Political Order* (New York, 1996).

A more general analysis of party structure and the nature of the American presidency may be found in William Crotty, *American Parties in Decline,* 2nd ed. (Boston, 1984); James David Barber, *The Pulse of Politics: Electing Presidents in the Media Age* (New York, 1980) and *The Presidential Character: Predicting Performance in the White House,* 2nd ed. (Englewood Cliffs, N.J., 1972); Herbert B. Asher, *Presidential Elections and American Politics,* 2nd ed. (Homewood, Ill., 1952); Richard C. Bain and Judith H. Parris, *Convention Decisions and Voting Reality* (Washington, D.C., 1973); Alan L. Clem, *American Electoral Politics: Strategies for Renewal* (New York, 1981); James MacGregor Burns, *The Deadlock of Democracy: Four-Party Politics in America* (Englewood Cliffs, N.J., 1963); William Nisbet Chambers and Walter Dean Burnham, eds., *The American Party Systems: Stages of Political Development,* 2nd ed. (New York, 1975); Fred I. Greenstein, ed., *Leadership in the Modern Presidency* (Cambridge, Mass., 1988); Donald G. Herzberg and Gerald M. Pomper, eds., *American Party Politics* (New York, 1966); William J. Keefe, *Politics, Parties, and Public Opinion in America,* 5th ed. (Washington, D.C., 1988); Paul Kleppner, *Who Voted? The Dynamics of Electoral Turnout, 1870–1980* (New York, 1982); Samuel Lubell, *The Future of American Politics,* 3rd ed. (New York, 1965); James I. Lengle and Byron E. Shafer, eds., *Presiden-*

tial Politics: Readings for Nominations and Elections (New York, 1980); Richard E. Neustadt, *Presidential Power and the Modern Presidents* (New York, 1990); Forrest McDonald, *The American Presidency: An Intellectual History* (Lawrence, Kans., 1994); Richard M. Scammon, ed., *America at the Polls* (Pittsburgh, 1965); Arthur M. Schlesinger, Jr., *The Imperial Presidency* (Boston, 1973); Nelson W. Polsby and Aaron Wildavsky, *Presidential Elections: Contemporary Strategies of American Electoral Politics,* 7th ed. (New York, 1988); Clinton Rossiter, *Parties and Politics in America* (Ithaca, N.Y., 1960); Larry J. Sabato, ed., *Campaigns and Elections: A Reader in Modern American Politics* (Glenview, Ill., 1989); and Earl Black and Merle Black, *The Vital South: How Presidents Are Elected* (Cambridge, Mass., 1992).

Results of the post-election analysis are detailed in Angus Campbell, ed., *A Study of the Presidential Vote, November 1948: A National Survey* (Ann Arbor, 1949). The 1948 polls are investigated in Frederick Mosteller, ed., *The Pre-Election Polls of 1948: Report to Committee on Analysis of Pre-Election Polls and Forecasts* (New York, 1949). In this regard, the Gallup Organization, Princeton, N.J., has extensive research facilities. Data from the other major polling organization active in 1948 is available through the Roper Center at the University of Connecticut in Storrs. Evaluation of 1948 as a "maintaining" election is derived from the work of Angus Campbell, Philip E. Converse, Warren F. Miller, and Donald E. Stokes, *Elections and Political Order,* 2nd ed. (New York, 1967). Also see Philip E. Converse, *The Dynamics of Party Support: Cohort-Analyzing Party Identification* (Beverly Hills, Calif., 1976). A related study by the same Michigan group of political scientists is Angus Campbell, Philip E. Converse, Warren F. Miller, and Donald E. Stokes, *The American Voter* (New York, 1960). Their findings are related to the conclusions of others: V. O. Key, Jr., *Politics, Parties, and Pressure Groups,* 5th ed. (New York, 1964); Walter Dean Burnham, *Critical Elections and the Mainsprings of American Politics* (New York, 1970); and Arthur M. Schlesinger, Jr., *The Cycles of American History* (Boston, 1986). The demography of the 1948 election is thoroughly documented in *Presidential Elections, 1789–1996* (Washington, D.C., 1997).

The foundations of Truman's early political career are explored in Lyle W. Dorsett, *The Pendergast Machine* (New York, 1968), and William M. Reddig, *Tom's Town: Kansas City and the Pendergast Legend* (Philadelphia, 1947). Truman's senatorial career is brought to life by the contemporary account of political writer Allen Drury in *A Senate Journal, 1943–1945* (New York, 1963). Truman's most prominent achievement in the Senate is evaluated in Donald H. Riddle, *The Truman Committee* (New Brunswick, N.J., 1964). Reflections of noted writers active throughout the Truman period are recounted in Clinton Rossiter and James Lare, eds., *The Essential Lippmann* (New York, 1963); Ronald Steel, *Walter Lippmann and the American Century* (New York, 1980); Murray Kempton, *Rebellions, Perversities, and Main Events* (New York, 1984); Marquis Childs, *Witness to Power* (New York, 1975); Arthur Krock, *Memoirs: Sixty Years on the Firing Line* (New York, 1968), James Reston, *Deadline: A Memoir* (New York, 1991); Joseph C. Goulden, ed., *Mencken's Last Campaign: H. L. Mencken on the 1948 Election* (Washington, D.C., 1976); Theodore H. White, *In Search of History* (New York, 1978); Herbert Lee Williams, *The Newspaperman's President: Harry S. Truman* (Chicago, 1984); and Drew Pearson, *Diaries, 1949–1959* (New York, 1974).

The structure and functioning of the Truman administration are recalled in Francis H. Heller, ed., *The Truman White House: The Administration of the Presidency, 1945–1953* (Lawrence, Kans., 1980); Ken Hechler, *Working with Truman: A Personal Memoir of the White House Years* (New York, 1982); Louis W. Koenig, *The Truman Administration: Its Principles and Practice* (New York, 1956); and William E. Pemberton, *Bureaucratic Politics: Executive Reorganization During the Truman Administration* (Columbia, Mo., 1979). The most thorough of the presidential-ranking surveys, representative of all the others from 1962 on, is summarized in Robert K. Murray and Tim H. Blessing, *Greatness in the White House: Rating the Presidents from George Washington to Ronald Reagan,* 2nd ed. (University Park, Pa., 1993). The complete text of all the 1948 party platforms is included in Kirk Porter and Donald Bruce Johnson, eds., *National Party Platforms* (Urbana, Ill., 1956). An interesting appraisal of the role of electronic media in 1948 is provided by Truman's radio adviser, J. Leonard Reinsch, in *Getting Elected: From Radio and Roosevelt to Television and Reagan* (New York, 1988).

Insightful overviews of the evolving American scene, encompassing the Truman years, are provided by a variety of books written over an extended period of time: Godfrey Hodgson, *America in Our Time: From World War II to Nixon: What Happened and Why* (New York, 1976); Richard Hofstadter, *The Age of Reform* (New York, 1955); John

Gunther, *Inside USA* (New York, 1951); David Halberstam, *The Fifties* (New York, 1993); T. E. Vadney, *The World Since 1945*, 2nd ed. (London, 1992; Robert D. Marcus and David Burner, eds., *America Since 1945*, 4th ed. (New York, 1985); Michael Barone, *Our Country: The Shaping of America from Roosevelt to Reagan* (New York, 1990); William H. Chafe, *The Unfinished Journey: America Since World War II* (New York, 1986); Robert A. Divine, *Since 1945: Politics and Diplomacy in Recent American History*, 2nd ed. (New York, 1979); James MacGregor Burns, *The Crosswinds of Freedom: From Roosevelt to Reagan—America in the Last Half Century* (New York, 1989); and Frederick Lewis Allen, *Since Yesterday* (New York, 1961). The primacy of Truman's foreign policy emphasis is explored in the context of Aaron Wildavsky's "two presidents" theory in Steven A. Shull, ed., *The Two Presidencies: A Quarter-Century Assessment* (Chicago, 1991). Related books include Robert Dahl, *Congress and American Foreign Policy* (New York, 1964); Samuel Huntington, *The Common Defense* (New York, 1961); and *Congress and the Nation, 1945–1964: A Review of Government and Politics in the Postwar Years* (Washington, D.C., 1965).

Domestic issues prominent in the 1948 presidential campaign and the Fair Deal proposals that followed are examined in Carolyn L. Weaver, *The Crisis in Social Security: Economic and Political Origins* (Durham, N.C., 1982); Earl Latham, *The Communist Controversy in Washington: From the New Deal to McCarthy* (Cambridge, Mass., 1966); Susan M. Hartmann, *Truman and the 80th Congress* (Columbia, Mo., 1971); Allen J. Matusow, *Farm Policies and Politics in the Truman Years* (Cambridge, Mass., 1973); William C. Berman, *The Politics of Civil Rights in the Truman Administration* (Columbus, Ohio, 1970); Robert H. Zieger, *The CIO, 1935–1955* (Chapel Hill, 1995); Harvey Klehr, John Earl Haynes, and Fridrikh Firsov, *The Secret World of American Communism* (New Haven, Conn., 1995); Paul Buhle, *Marxism in the United States: Remapping the History of the American Left* (London, 1987); Patricia Sullivan, *Days of Hope: Race and Democracy in the New Deal Era* (Chapel Hill, 1996); Richard M. Dalfiume, *Desegregation in the U.S. Armed Forces: Fighting on Two Fronts, 1939–1953* (Columbia, Mo., 1969); R. Alton Lee, *Truman and Taft-Hartley: A Question of Mandate* (Lexington, Ky., 1966); Donald R. McCoy and Richard T. Ruetten, *Quest and Response: Minority Rights and the Truman Administration* (Lawrence, Kans., 1973); Richard O. Davis, *Hous-*

ing Reform During the Truman Administration (Columbia, Mo., 1966); Andrew J. Dunar, *The Truman Scandals and the Politics of Morality* (Columbia, Mo., 1984); and Monte M. Poen, *Harry S. Truman Versus the Medical Lobby: The Genesis of Medicare* (Columbia, Mo., 1979).

By far the largest body of literature concerning the Truman administration involves consideration of foreign relations, particularly Truman's atomic policy, the cold war, and the derivation, conception, and implementation of containment. For half a century scholarly discourse has alternated between studies supportive of American policy and many variations of revisionism. A balanced overall appraisal is presented in Melvyn P. Leffler in *A Preponderance of Power: National Security, the Truman Administration, and the Cold War* (Stanford, Calif., 1992). A thoughtful study in a political context is Robert A. Divine, *Foreign Policy and U.S. Presidential Elections, 1940–1948* (New York, 1974). Dorothy Borg and Waldo Heinrichs edited and contributed to a perceptive examination of an issue that loomed large directly after the 1948 election in *Uncertain Years: Chinese-American Relations, 1947–1950* (New York, 1980). George F. Kennan, the father of containment, reprinted a notable series of his lectures, including the text of his 1947 article on "The Sources of Soviet Conduct" in *Foreign Affairs,* in *American Diplomacy, 1900–1950* (Chicago, 1951). The end of this period is examined by Herbert Feis in *From Trust to Terror: The Onset of the Cold War, 1945–1950* (New York, 1970), and Wilson D. Miscamble in *George F. Kennan and the Making of American Foreign Policy, 1947–1950* (Princeton, 1973). The clearest account of the development of containment is contained in John Lewis Gaddis, *Strategies of Containment* (New York, 1982).

Finally, here is a representative listing of books written over several decades, expressing widely divergent viewpoints in this ongoing debate over American cold war policy: Thomas G. Paterson, *On Every Front: The Making and Unmaking of the Cold War* (New York, 1992); John Lewis Gaddis, *The United States and the Origins of the Cold War, 1941–1947* (New York, 1972); Gabriel Kolko and Joyce Kolko, *The Limits of Power* (New York, 1972); Walter LaFeber, *America, Russia, and the Cold War, 1945–1966* (New York, 1967); Frank Kofsky, *Truman and the War Scare of 1948* (New York, 1993); Athan Theoharis, ed., *The Truman Presidency: The Origins of the Imperial Presidency and the National Security State* (Standfordville, N.Y., 1979); Marc Trachtenberg, *History and Strategy* (Princeton, 1991); Ronald Steel,

Pax Americana (New York, 1967); Lloyd C. Gardner, *Architects of Illusion: Men and Ideas in American Foreign Policy, 1941–1949* (Chicago, 1970); Fraser J. Harbutt, *The Iron Curtain: Churchill, America, and the Origins of the Cold War* (New York, 1986); Gar Alperovitz, *Atomic Diplomacy: Hiroshima and Potsdam* (New York, 1965) and *The Decision to Use the Atomic Bomb and the Architecture of an American Myth* (New York, 1995); Martin J. Sherwin, *A World Destroyed: Hiroshima and the Arms Race,* 2nd ed. (New York, 1987); David Holloway, *Stalin and the Bomb: The Soviet Union and Atomic Energy, 1939–1956* (New Haven, Conn., 1995); Ernest R. May, *Lessons of the Past: The Use and Misuse of History in American Foreign Policy* (New York, 1973); Thomas J. McCormick, *America's Half-Century: United States Foreign Policy and the Cold War* (Baltimore, 1989); Martin Walker, *The Cold War: A History* (New York, 1994); Stephen J. Whitfield, *The Culture of the Cold War* (Baltimore, 1991); William Appleman Williams, *The Tragedy of American Diplomacy* (New York, 1959); Daniel Yergin, *Shattered Peace: The Origins of the Cold War and the National Security State* (Boston, 1977); Paul Boyer, *By the Bomb's Early Light* (New York, 1985); H. W. Brand, *The Devil We Knew: Americans and the Cold War* (New York, 1994); and McGeorge Bundy, *Danger and Survival: Choices About the Bomb in the First Fifty Years* (New York, 1988).

This listing perhaps leans in the revisionist direction. The recent publication of materials from the archives of the former Soviet Union, tending to justify Truman's decision to take a firm anti-Communist stand, will likely result in a new wave of literature endorsing his foreign policy. George Kennan once suggested that histories of the Cold War might best be assembled after it had ended, echoing Harry Truman's assertion that an equitable account of his administration could be written only fifty years after he left office.

INDEX

A NOTE ON THE AUTHOR

Harold I. Gullan was born in Baltimore and studied at The Johns Hopkins University. He received an M.A. from St. Joseph's University and a Ph.D. from Temple University. Mr. Gullan's work on presidential politics has appeared in the *Presidential Studies Quarterly*. He is now an independent scholar and lives in Philadelphia with his wife, Elizabeth.